Mary Hallock Foote

The Oklahoma Western Biographies
Richard W. Etulain, General Editor

Mary Anna Hallock, ca. 1874. This item is reproduced by permission of The Huntington Library, San Marino, California.

Mary Hallock Foote

Author-Illustrator of the American West

Darlis A. Miller

UNIVERSITY OF OKLAHOMA PRESS : NORMAN

Also by Darlis A. Miller

The California Column in New Mexico (Albuquerque, 1982)
(ed., with Joan M. Jensen) *New Mexico Women: Intercultural Perspectives* (Albuquerque, 1986)
Soldiers and Settlers (Albuquerque, 1989)
Captain Jack Crawford, Buckskin Poet, Scout, and Showman (Albuquerque, 1993)
Above a Common Soldier, Frank and Mary Clarke in the American West and Civil War, 1847–1872, *from Their Letters* (Albuquerque, 1997)

Publicaton of this book is made possible through the generosity of Edith Kinney Gaylord.

Library of Congress Cataloging-in-Publication Data

Miller, Darlis A., 1939–
Mary Hallock Foote : author-illustrator of the American West / Darlis A. Miller.
p. cm.—(Oklahoma western biographies ; v. 19)
Includes bibliographical references and index.
ISBN 0-8061-3397-X (alk. paper)
1. Foote, Mary Hallock, 1847–1938. 2. Novelists, American—19th century—Biography. 3. Novelists, American—20th century—Biography. 4. Women and literature—West (U.S.)—History. 5. Women pioneers—West (U.S.)—Biography. 6. Illustrators—United States—Biography. 7. Frontier and pioneer life—West (U.S.) 8. West (U.S.)—In literature. 9. West (U.S.)—Biography. I. Title. II. Series.

PS1688 .M55 2002
813'.4—dc21
[B] 2001053000

Mary Hallock Foote: Author-Illustrator of the American West is Volume 19 in The Oklahoma Western Biographies.

The paper in this book meets the guidelines for permanence and durability of the Committee on Production Guidelines for Book Longevity of the Council on Library Resources, Inc. ∞

1 2 3 4 5 6 7 8 9 10

For Linda J. Lear,

who knows about friendship and the writing of biographies

Contents

Illustrations

Series Editor's Preface

STORIES of heroes and heroines have intrigued many generations of listeners and readers. Americans, like people everywhere, have been captivated by the lives of military, political, and religious figures and of intrepid explorers, pioneers, and rebels. The Oklahoma Western Biographies endeavor to build on this fascination with biography and to link it with two other abiding interests of Americans: the frontier and the American West. Although volumes in the series carry no notes, they are prepared by leading scholars, are soundly researched, and include a list of sources used. Each volume is a lively synthesis based on thorough examination of pertinent primary and secondary sources.

Above all, the Oklahoma Western Biographies aim at two goals: to provide readable life stories of significant westerners and to show how their lives illuminate a notable topic, an influential movement, or a series of important events in the history and culture of the American West.

In this clearly written biography, historian Darlis Miller demonstrates that Mary Hallock Foote is an illuminating figure in western history. An eastern woman who came west in the 1870s with her engineer husband, Arthur, Foote lived in several western areas in the next half-century. In California, Colorado, Idaho, and California again, she experienced mining, irrigation, and agricultural Wests. While in the West, Foote kept intact strong links with her family and with Helena de Kay Gilder, a cultured New Yorker and wife of *Century Magazine* editor Richard Watson Gilder. In her friendships as well as in her writings and artwork, Foote illuminates several sociocultural tensions between the American East and West from the 1870s to the 1920s.

Miller also thoroughly demonstrates Mary Hallock Foote's signal importance as an author and artist of the West. Foote was the most significant woman writer and illustrator in the Local Color school. Particularly noteworthy were her revealing treatments of a woman's West even as her contemporaries Owen Wister, Theodore Roosevelt, and Frederic Remington portrayed the region as the domain of heroic men.

Miller details all these important facets of Foote's life and career. She has used extensively every major archive of Foote letters and documents, she has read Foote's numerous stories, essays, and novels, and she has examined all pertinent sources on her subject's life and works.

Miller's biography of Foote is in every way a balanced examination. She notes Foote's human limitations even as she devotes most of her life story to Foote's important achievements as author and artist. Foote could be an overly protective mother, something of a social snob, and too tied to her eastern, elitist prejudices. To her credit, Miller admits these frailties without underplaying Foote's manifold accomplishments.

We also see Foote's place in divergent western contexts. Miller expertly describes Foote's reactions to her western homes, to frontier mining camps and towns, and to eastern and western conflicts. Gradually, as Miller demonstrates, Foote became a westerner, especially after her family relocated to California in the 1890s, where they remained for nearly three decades.

In short, Darlis Miller has produced an insightful biography of an important western woman. In all ways, her rewarding book is a valuable addition to the Oklahoma Western Biographies series.

RICHARD W. ETULAIN

University of New Mexico

Preface

MARY Hallock Foote (1847–1938) gained considerable fame during the late nineteenth and early twentieth centuries as a novelist and illustrator of the American West. Her career as an illustrator began first, soon after she graduated from the School of Design for Women at Cooper Union in New York City in the late 1860s. Thereafter she received important commissions to illustrate the works of such literary luminaries as Henry Wadsworth Longfellow, John Greenleaf Whittier, Nathaniel Hawthorne, and Alfred, Lord Tennyson. A talented and exceptional woman, Foote successfully pursued careers in two fields at a time when society expected women to devote themselves to families and household.

Mary Hallock Foote's story is fascinating and deserves to be better known. During her lifetime, she published twelve novels, four collections of short stories, more than a dozen and a half uncollected stories and essays, and innumerable illustrations—most dealing with the American West. Foote, in fact, was one of the first and most articulate women to write about the West and was the first to write about mining camps from first-hand knowledge. In both her illustrations and writings, she provided the nation with vivid images that differed sharply from those offered by male artists and writers. Her accomplishments have been heralded by several literary scholars and historians, but her name is largely unrecognized by today's public. It is my hope that this biography will introduce this remarkable woman to a new generation of readers.

I have built this biography on both primary and secondary sources, which are discussed in the bibliographical essay. But two important works deserve special mention because they pointed me in the right direction: Rodman W. Paul's edition of Foote's reminiscences, *A Victorian Gentlewoman in the Far West, The Reminiscences of Mary Hallock Foote* (San Marino, Calif.: The Huntington Library, 1972), and Lee Ann Johnson's *Mary Hallock Foote* (Boston: Twayne Publishers, 1980).

In writing about Mary Hallock Foote's life, I have attempted to address several issues that are important to many of today's readers and scholars. These include Foote's growth as an artist, writer, and businesswoman; her sense of self as an artist and writer; her views of wifehood and motherhood and the constraints these placed upon her career; east-west tensions in her life and work; and her portrayal of the West in fiction and drawings. This work also focuses on Foote's lifelong friendship with Helena de Kay Gilder and examines the importance of Helena and her husband, Richard W. Gilder, a key literary figure in the East and editor of *Century Magazine,* to her life and artistic development.

Mary Hallock Foote and her husband, Arthur D. Foote, a mining and irrigation engineer, created homes and raised their family in key western areas of development—New Almaden, California; Leadville, Colorado; Boise, Idaho; and Grass Valley, California. Consequently, they witnessed important developments in western mining and irrigation, but their combined stories also reflect many of the tensions that besiege modern-day couples—long separations, financial difficulties, alcohol abuse, and childhood illnesses and family tragedy. But Molly (as she was called) probably would have agreed that the rewards and successes outweighed the pain and failures in her life. This is the story, then, of a gifted and spirited woman, a devoted wife and mother, whose resilience, resourcefulness, and quiet resolve allowed her to surmount life's frustrations and adversities.

Some readers may have formed an impression of Mary Hallock Foote from Wallace Stegner's Pulitzer Prize–winning novel *Angle of Repose* (1971), in which the fictional character Susan Burling Ward is modeled on the real Mary Hallock Foote. Stegner changed the names of Foote and her family and close friends but kept those of professional acquaintances. He also borrowed wording and passages from Foote's letters and autobiography and followed closely events in her life prior to the move to Idaho. But he creates a more strident persona for Susan Ward than the Foote documents warrant and exaggerates the tensions that developed between Molly and her husband. Moreover, he departs radically from events in Molly's life during the Idaho years and totally neglects her long residence in Grass Valley. All pertinent published evaluations of Stegner's use or misuse of Foote's life can be found in the bibliographical essay.

Series editor Richard W. Etulain first introduced me to Mary Hallock Foote when he invited me to submit a book proposal to the Oklahoma Western Biographies series. He knew a lot about Mary Hallock Foote and shared with me his knowledge about sources. Since then, he has been a strong supporter of this project and offered many valuable suggestions for revision during the final stages of turning the manuscript into a book. Like Richard Gilder, editor for much of Foote's work, Dick has been a wise and gentle critic.

Mary Hallock Foote's granddaughter, Evelyn Foote Gardiner, has been a great inspiration through the course of writing this biography. At the start of this project, I visited her in Grass Valley, California, where her childhood was spent in the company of Mary Hallock Foote. After a lively discussion in her lovely home, she led my husband and me on a tour of the grounds surrounding the North Star House, where Molly and Arthur resided for more than twenty-five years. Since that first visit, she has shared memories of her grandmother in our correspondence and has generously granted me permission to quote from her grandmother's correspondence. This manuscript has also benefitted from the courtesies extended by Evelyn's daughters, Ann and Janet Gardiner, and from Helena Gilder's descendant, Helena Pappenheimer. I owe special thanks also to other Mary Hallock Foote scholars, who have offered ideas and copies of their own work on Foote, including Christine Hill Smith, Susan Armitage, Judy Austin, Benay Blend, and Mary Ellen Walsh.

Special thanks go to those who introduced me to Mary Hallock Foote territory, especially to Judy Austin, at the Idaho State Historical Society, who gave a memorable tour of Molly's Boise, Idaho, residences. My sister-in-law, Sylvia Walker, served as driver on my first trip to New Almaden and Grass Valley and then provided lodging while I worked at Green Library at Stanford. Her daughter and my niece, Ann Walker, served as tour guide of Santa Cruz, another of Foote's residencies. (And thanks to the entire Miller clan, both on my husband's side and mine, who have always expressed interest in the progress of this biography.) My colleague Jamie Bronstein graciously volunteered to track down Foote-Gilder letters in the New York Public Library, and long-time friend Pamela Herr introduced me to the Hawley Papers in the Library of Congress. I am indebted to two other long-time friends and colleagues who read the entire manuscript and suggested ways in which it could be improved, Joan M. Jensen and Jo Tice Bloom. Mary Hallock Foote scholar Christine Hill Smith also read the manuscript and offered valuable commentary. I wish to thank Shirley Leckie and Susan Armitage, the manuscript's readers for the University of Oklahoma Press. Their comments have helped make this a better biography.

I owe special thanks to the staffs of the libraries that hold Mary Hallock Foote correspondence, including the Department of Special Collections, Stanford University Libraries, the Huntington Library at San Marino, California (particularly to Peter Blodgett, who always answered my inquires with dispatch and enthusiasm), the Houghton Library at Harvard University, the Harriet Beecher Stowe Center in Hartford, Connecticut, and the Lilly Library at Indiana University, where Saundra Taylor permitted me to read the recently acquired (but unprocessed) Helena de Kay Gilder letters to Mary Hallock Foote. Staff members at the following also supplied copies of important correspondence: the Mary Lea Shane Archives of the Lick Observatory, University of California, Santa Cruz; the Harry Ransom Humanities Research Center, the University of Texas at Austin; and the Clifton Waller Barrett Library of American Literature, Special Collections Department, University of Virginia Library. I am greatly indebted to the above facilities for granting me permission to quote from letters by or about Mary Hallock Foote located in their collections. I also thank staff members at the Historical Society of Wisconsin, the Art Institute of Chicago, the Cooper Union Archives in New York City, the New York Public Library, and the Adriance Memorial Library in Poughkeepsie, New York, and Sid Huttner at the University of Iowa Libraries for their assistance in locating material. I would also like to thank the interlibrary loan staff and Cheryl Wilson, head of Special Collections, at the New Mexico State University Library for contributing to the researching of this biography. I have retained Foote's spelling in most cases when quoting from her correspondence to avoid the overuse of *sic*—for example, when she left out the apostrophe in *don't,* as was her usual practice.

As always, my thanks to August Miller, for his continuing support. He made the trips through Mary Hallock Foote country, especially to Leadville both before and after I was caught up in this project, most memorable. And finally to Linda J. Lear, my friend of more than twenty-five years, who has listened to stories about Mary Hallock Foote and shared her expertise in the writing of biographies, I dedicate this book.

DARLIS A. MILLER

Las Cruces, New Mexico

Mary Hallock Foote

CHAPTER I

A Quaker Upbringing

AS a child, Mary Hallock Foote demonstrated such a remarkable talent for drawing that her parents arranged for her to receive professional training. At this early stage, probably no one envisioned that she would become a successful writer as well as an artist. But brief residencies in the West following her marriage to Arthur De Wint Foote, a mining engineer, made her knowledgeable about a way of life unfamiliar to most eastern readers. By becoming an "exile" in the West, as she often thought of herself, Molly found a subject to write about.

Years later, at the end of her prestigious career as both artist and author, Molly started work on an autobiography, describing in detail the hardships and disappointments that accompanied the Footes' migratory existence in the West, as Arthur moved from one engineering job to another. Writing in her seventies, Molly looked back with nostalgia on her Quaker childhood in the East and described her Quaker ancestors with great admiration. Although she chose not to raise her own children within the faith, she never lost her appreciation for the old customs.

A Quaker upbringing on her parents' farm overlooking the Hudson River was, in fact, at the very core of Mary Hallock Foote's identity. She was emotionally tied to the countryside, and her deepest memories were attached to the Hallock farm. Here she was surrounded by Quaker relatives who cared for and sustained her. "I am anchored here by my girl life," she exclaimed after returning from her first trip to Leadville, Colorado, in 1879. And years later, after establishing homes in Idaho and California, she still felt "curious haunting longings" for the old places in the East. "Once you have it in your blood," wrote the seventy-five-year-old novelist, "you never get it out."

This deep emotional pull eastward colored the stories that Molly wrote and the pictures she drew after she married Arthur and left the Hallock homestead. Much of her early work centers on the experiences of eastern emigrants in the West and their confrontations with new cultural and natural landscapes. For many years this reluctant westerner yearned to return to the more sophisticated world she had known in the East. How this eastern-born and eastern-educated woman became "an authentic voice of the West" (as the literary press called her) will become clearer as her story unfolds.

Molly's birthplace was a side-hill farm in Ulster County on the west side of the Hudson River, four miles south of Poughkeepsie and only a half-mile from the village of Milton. As a child, Molly walked to Milton to pick up the mail. For much of the year, the Hallocks witnessed the busy river traffic of sloops and steamboats carrying passengers and supplies between Albany and New York City. When the river froze over and navigation stopped, pleasure-seekers could be seen sailing over the ice in wind-propelled iceboats. Although steamboats provided the loveliest view of the river, visitors to the Hallock farm had the option of taking the Hudson River Railroad to a station opposite the village and then crossing the river in a ferry—or in a horse-drawn sleigh in the winter. Some robust souls crossed the ice-covered river on foot.

During Molly's childhood, the family's two-story farmhouse, with a sitting room, dining room, and front and back parlors downstairs and bedrooms upstairs, sheltered the four Hallock children, their parents, and their maternal grandparents. A second-story stairway led to a large garret, where the Hallocks stored a miscellany of old garments, furniture, magazines, and other castoffs, which the children never tired of investigating. The "dooryard" or lawn was kept long enough to be cut with a scythe, with the grass then fed to the horses. Nearby a water fountain splashed and a garden displayed its colorful mixture of vegetables, roses, chrysanthemums, and other favorite flowers. In the distance a large barn had been built against a hill with one side of the roof extending nearly to the ground, which made a perfect slide for the children.

Beyond the barn stretched a number of stone-fenced apple orchards. In the fall, Molly's father stored apples for cider making in the barn-loft and apples for market in barrels in the cellar of the fruit-house until he could haul them to the steamboat landing. A path over a nearby hill led to Uncle Edward Hallock's house and the family burying ground, also enclosed by a stone fence and with locust trees and a chestnut tree shading the tombstones. At some distance from the main house an upper barn quartered the spring lambs. Years later Molly vividly remembered her childhood joy in trudging with her father along "the icy lanes in March" to watch him feed cut turnips to the hungry creatures.

Also on the family farm were a mill and millhouse, which was home for Molly's aged Uncle Townsend Hallock and his wife Rachel (until their deaths) and then for the miller, John Crosby, and his family. In the spring the young Hallocks hunted wildflowers near the three mill ponds, which stored the water that powered the mill, and in the winter they skated on the frozen ponds. Molly later recalled that in the "perfect woods" between Long Pond and Old Pond the sound of the mill fell silent. She fondly remembered also the fog hanging over the Hudson, the gurgling flow of the millponds, the stillness of the ice-bound river, and the happy songs of summer boating parties. All of these rural sights and sounds became deeply imprinted on Molly's memory and conditioned the young artist's sensitivity for landscape and seasons.

Molly's Quakerism was also deeply rooted in this Milton countryside. Foote writes in her reminiscences that the Hallock farm was first settled in 1762, when the Quaker Edward Hallock sailed up the Hudson with his wife, Phebe Clapp, and their eleven children to take up land that was still part of the frontier. The mill that he built ground flour for both armies during the American Revolution, and his stone house sheltered American

General Horatio Gates after his victory at Saratoga. The Hallocks' two sons and nine daughters soon "peopled the countryside" with a new generation of Quakers. In an unpublished essay, Molly writes: "It need not have been a jest when our father used to say he was related to half the New York [Quaker] Yearly Meeting, and he would add that when he married Ann Burling he was connected with the other half."

In 1833, thirty-two-year-old Nathaniel, the grandson of Edward Hallock, married eighteen-year-old Ann Burling of New York City and brought her to live on the Milton farm. Their son, Thomas Burling, was born in 1837, and three daughters followed: Elizabeth (Bessie), in 1841; Philadelphia (Phil), in 1843; and Mary Anna (Molly), on November 19, 1847. Within this close-knit and affectionate family, the children flourished.

Molly and her siblings started attending Quaker meetings with their parents most assuredly at an early age, since Quakers believed that boys and girls, like men and women, had the potential to hear God's word through an Inner Light. For the rest of her life, Molly recalled the charm of these meetings—men and boys seated on one side, women and girls on the other, and the elders sitting on a bench facing the main body. The silence of these gatherings, broken now and then by testimonials and selected readings, helped to shape Molly's gentle and unpretentious demeanor. Possibly the most lasting legacy of her Quaker childhood, however, was a strong sense of self-worth fostered by the Society of Friends' respect for male and female equality.

Molly's parents allowed the Hallock children a good deal of freedom growing up. They had shed the stricter rules of their faith that frowned upon music, dancing, art, novels, and idle conversation, but they retained the Quaker emphasis on reasoning and persuasion in their child-raising. In her reminiscences, Molly singles out her mother as being one of the dominant influences in her early life. Although a quiet and reserved "gentlewoman," Ann Hallock was also strong-minded and shared decision-making with her husband. Molly recalls that her mother never argued about her rights but "knew how to get her way" with Nathaniel. And she demanded obedience from the children, but then "left us to our own decisions and spared comments on some of their obvious results." Ann Hallock's legacy to her daughter included a devotion to truthfulness, simplicity in appearance, and a refined instinct for behavior proper to one's place in society. The relationship between mother and daughter was one of deep sympathy and affection, which is reflected in the tenderness with which Molly refers to her mother in her reminiscences and in her correspondence with her lifelong friend Helena de Kay Gilder.

From her father, Molly acquired a fondness for books and good conversation. An avid reader, Nathaniel Hallock liked to quote poetry and debate the great political issues of the day. He belonged, Molly writes, "to the last of his breed of thinking and reading American farmers, working their own lands which they inherited from their fathers." He often read aloud to the family in the evenings the congressional debates and editorials published in the *New York Tribune,* as well as selections from his favorite authors, Tennyson, Scott, Burns, Pope, and Cowper. As a schoolgirl, Molly seemingly devoured whatever reading materials entered the Hallock household, including the *Atlantic Monthly* and *Harper's Weekly*. But certain books and essays made such an impression that she later singled them out as being special: Charles Dickens's *A Tale of Two Cities,* Sir Walter Scott's *The Talisman*, Alfred Tennyson's *Idylls of the King*, Charles A. Dana's *The Household Book of Poetry*, and two "unforgettable" Quaker classics, Whittier's "Barclay of Ury" and Hawthorne's "The Gentle Boy." This enchantment with the written word continued undiminished for the rest of Foote's life.

In this Quaker house of reading and learning, no one was more important to Molly's intellectual awakening than her widowed Aunt Sarah Hallock. Like Nathaniel Hallock, Sarah was a passionate reader and conversationalist. She was also a member of the New York Anti-Slavery Society and wedded to the twin causes of anti-slavery and women's rights. At her invitation, well-known advocates for each reform, including Frederic Douglass, Susan B. Anthony, and Ernestine L. Rose, came to speak in Milton and often to spend their evenings in further discussion around Nathaniel's fireside. Molly was a devoted listener. By the time she was fourteen, she had acquired a unique understanding of some of the crucial issues facing the nation. As she later recalled, "I have always regarded this phantasmagoria of idealists and propagandists and militant cranks and dreamers as one of the great opportunities of our youth. . . . For they were brilliant talkers; all the villages in the valley of the Hudson and the Mohawk put together could not have furnished such conversation as we heard without stirring from our firesides."

This link with the larger world seems all the more remarkable (and significant) when juxtaposed with the Hallocks' isolation from other elements in society. Set apart by their Quakerism, they did not often participate in the affairs of Milton, where they were called the "Quaker Hallocks" and their neighborhood was labeled "Hallock Hollow." Still, the relationship with the villagers must have been congenial because some elected to send their children to the Quaker school held in the meeting house on Hallock property. Molly recalled that one of these little schoolmates sometimes came to the farm to play but that she (Molly) "was not allowed to go to her house." Nor did the Hallocks interact with the larger New York Quaker community because of a principled stand that her Uncle Nicholas Hallock had taken years earlier. Although the Society of Friends had long opposed slavery, they often disagreed on the proper means of ending it. When Nicholas refused to modify his strongly worded anti-slavery pronouncements, the New York General Conference "laid down" or terminated the meeting that supported him. Thereafter the Milton Hallocks turned inward for spiritual and social fellowship. As a child Molly grew accustomed to her family's isolation, which may help explain her tendency in later years to remain apart from her western neighbors.

Still, Molly had plenty of companions growing up. "Our little neighborhood," she later recalled, "was packed with Hallocks on the adjoining farms with boundaries in common and lanes and footpaths across lots shortening the way from farm to farm." With her Milton cousins, Molly went ice skating, played chess, and discussed stories in the *Atlantic Monthly*, and from her visiting New York City cousins she learned new songs and dances. She acquired the common household skills thought essential to every young girl's education: sewing, ironing, cleaning, baking, and butter-making. But she did not become a skilled cook, since the Hallocks generally employed one or two local girls to handle the kitchen chores.

Molly and her older sister Bessie developed deep emotional ties at this time and would become life-long confidantes. Bessie was the one who comforted Molly when she was too young to accompany the older children on evening buggy or horseback rides. Molly later avowed that Bessie "was half mother as well as sister, 'half angel' in my eyes." Molly also established firm bonds with her sister Phil, who remained single all of her long life, and the two kept up a steady correspondence after Molly went west. With her brother Tom, ten years her senior, Molly maintained cordial relations until their parents died and then visited him and his family only infrequently in later years.

Molly received her first formal education in the Quaker school that her father had helped establish on Hallock land. She then attended the Poughkeepsie Female Collegiate Institute, the same private secondary boarding institution where Bessie had studied. Because of the emphasis that Quakers placed on education, all four Hallock children probably received a year or more of secondary education, an expensive undertaking for the parents. The basic tuition at Poughkeepsie for the 1863–64 school year (when Molly is known to have been in attendance) was $200, with the school assessing an additional 5 percent because of the "present unusual expenses of living."

Although secondary education in the United States was not common for either sex until after the Civil War, Molly benefitted from the tremendous growth in female "seminaries" that occurred between 1830 and 1860. The founders of these schools strongly believed that education should prepare young women for their roles as wives and mothers. They typically offered a wide range of courses, following the advice of Catharine Beecher, a proponent of "Domestic Feminism," who believed that women needed to be educated adequately to impart virtue and right ways of thinking to their husbands and children. The paramount concern of the Poughkeepsie Female Collegiate Institute—to instill in its students "a high degree of moral feeling"—reflected Beecher's thinking. Like other mid-nineteenth-century educators, Dr. Charles H. P. McLellan, the school's founder, also stressed physical culture, advocating daily walks and exercise in the school's gymnasium.

By the time Molly entered the Institute, Reverend C. D. Rice, a Congregational minister, had succeeded McLellan as principal and supervised a staff of thirteen instructors, nine of whom were women. Courses included the basics in arithmetic, geography, history, English, and the sciences (botany, chemistry, physiology, astronomy, and geology), as well as mental philosophy, natural theology, and the capstone course taught by Reverend Rice, Evidences of Christianity. Like his predecessor, Rice encouraged Molly and her peers to take walks in the open air and to make use of the gymnasium. The school instructed boarding students, in fact, to bring good walking shoes and assured parents that the girls would be accompanied by a teacher on their walks.

The Institute was housed in an impressive three-story building on the corner of Mill and Catharine Streets. The rooms of boarding students (as described in the local press) were "large and airy, neatly furnished and well warmed and ventilated." Hot and cold water was supplied to each floor and heating came from a boiler in the basement. Boarding students like Molly and her cousin Anna Hallock, who also attended the

Institute, furnished their own towels, napkins, napkin-rings, teaspoons, and forks.

Going to a boarding school apparently was not the trying emotional experience for Molly that it was for some girls experiencing their first separation from home. Molly very likely returned to her family on weekends, as her sister Bessie had done when she attended the Institute. What few references are found about the school in Molly's correspondence are positive ones. With her strong drive to excel and love for books and learning, she must have been a diligent scholar.

It was at Poughkeepsie Institute that Hallock received her first formal instruction in drawing. She had started to draw in early childhood and was called the "artist of the family" by the age of twelve. Under the direction of Margaret Gordon, head of the school's Department of Painting and Drawing, Molly's talents blossomed, though the drawing lessons cost her parents an extra $10 per quarter. Still, the young student long remembered this "dear lady" for her "kindness" and "encouragement."

Important as Gordon was to Molly's artistic development, it was Sarah Walter Hallock's influence that was crucial. The eldest daughter of Ellwood Walter, a wealthy Quaker businessman, Sarah had married Molly's brother Tom about the time that Molly ended her studies in Poughkeepsie. Sarah's opinions commanded respect in both families. After examining Molly's drawings, she convinced the Hallocks (perhaps with Bessie's help) that their youngest daughter ought to continue her training at the School of Design for Women at Cooper Union in New York City. She then arranged for Molly to spend the 1864–65 school term in the Walters' house in Brooklyn Heights, where Sarah and Tom were then living.

With great anticipation, Molly left home a few weeks shy of her seventeenth birthday to begin studies as a professional art student. Boarding school had given her an opportunity to socialize with peers of different religious faiths and backgrounds. Now she was ready, both socially and intellectually, to embrace new experiences. High-spirited and optimistic in her teens, Molly found her first year in New York City exhilarating, even though the nation around her was convulsed in civil war. And although parental support was absolutely essential to her well-being, the Cooper art school and the Walters' household would dominate her thinking. At Cooper Union, one of the few institutions offering art education for women, she was free to study art for days on end and to discuss art with like-minded students. At the Walters' she had access to a vast library and was given her first taste of society. She later wrote of this year: "I remember only being absolutely well and gloriously happy all those months."

The twice-widowed Ellwood Walter lived with his children from both marriages in a luxurious three-story house on Columbia Street. The rear room on each floor, including Molly's on the third, offered a magnificent view of the Upper Bay out to Governor's Island and the New Jersey shore. The rich Brooklyn Quakers, known as the "gay Friends," danced, went to the theater, and wore fine clothes. Sarah's younger sister Annie, entering society for the first time since the death of the second Mrs. Walter, was whisked away in a carriage almost every evening. And Molly spent many delightful hours in the company of twenty-five-year-old Ellwood, Jr., who lived at home after having completed his law studies. Molly described him as eloquent and magnetic, though he was a "young man who drank." She later confided to her best friend Helena de Kay, a fellow art student at Cooper Union, that Ellwood had given her a first lesson in flirtation.

Despite living amidst wealth and its social distractions, Molly seemed determined to excel at her art studies. Her shy exterior belied an inner strength and a budding ambition. She may not yet have fully articulated her goals, but she hints at her aspirations in a letter to Helena a few years later:

> I read in the Bible last night that a "meek and quiet spirit" is the only thing for a woman. But how can one ever do or be anything if meekness and quietness are the best things in life. I know plenty of women who have meekness but they

have attained it only by giving up all hope or thought for themselves. I could not do that without giving up ambition too.

To reach Cooper Union, Molly crossed the East River on the Fulton Ferry and then walked about two miles north to the magnificent six-story edifice on Fourth Avenue and Eighth Street in the heart of New York City. Established in 1859 by philanthropist Peter Cooper, the school offered free education in the mechanical arts and sciences to the laboring classes of both sexes. In a city of approximately 800,000, evening classes were packed with young people hoping to better their positions.

The pride of city boosters, Cooper Union was a community center as well as an institution of learning. The first two floors were rented as stores and offices to provide revenue for its maintenance. The public could also rent the great lecture hall in the basement, which seated 2,500 people and where free general lectures were held at frequent intervals. In 1860 Abraham Lincoln delivered a crucial speech here that some historians have said gave him the presidency. On the third floor of Cooper Union was the large reading room, open from 8:00 A.M. to 10:00 P.M., free to all and stocked with foreign and domestic newspapers and quarterlies. The School of Design for Women was found on the fourth floor, and classrooms and architectural and mechanical drawing rooms on the fifth and sixth floors.

Several years before Cooper Union opened, Cooper's daughter Amelia had been associated with the fledgling New York School of Design for Women, modeled after the School of Design in Philadelphia, which Sarah King Peter had founded in 1848. The aim of design education in both schools was to train women to make a living as professional artists. Since the New York school suffered for lack of funds, Peter Cooper integrated it into his establishment, and Amelia and her friends thereafter served as an advisory council. Cooper was a visionary on the topic of paid employment for women. He believed that middle-class women should have the opportunity to train for occupations suitable to their status and not be forced into menial labor or unsuitable marriages because of adverse circumstances. Supporters of design schools likewise held that artistic pursuits fell within women's natural sphere and were fully compatible with domestic responsibilities.

Many of the students attending Cooper's School of Design were among the best educated young women in the country. They may have envisioned eventual roles as wives and mothers but at the Union they aspired to become successful artists first. Nearly two hundred students regularly enrolled in the school, with instruction free to those intending to support themselves and costing between $1.50 and $2.00 per week for amateurs enrolled in the drawing and painting classes. Professional students (like Molly) could attend the school for a maximum of four years and specialize in drawing, wood and copper engraving, or in pastel, water color, and oil painting. The school term began on October 1 and ended on May 30, with classes held on weekdays between 9:00 A.M. and 1:00 P.M. Classrooms remained open in the afternoons and on Saturdays for students wishing to practice on their own. Under Dr. William Rimmer, who reorganized the art school in 1866, lecture courses were given on such subjects as Comparative and Art Anatomy, and Systematic and Structural Botany.

While Molly was absorbed in her art studies, the nation endured its final year of civil war. Seemingly no one had escaped its tragedies. Helena de Kay's older brother George was killed in skirmishes on the Mississippi in 1862. And three of Molly's Quaker cousins, the Ketcham brothers, whose farm adjoined the Hallocks,' died in 1863, two on the battlefield and one in Libby prison. Although Quakers were pacifists, as many as two or three-hundred joined the Union army to fight for their anti-slavery convictions.

And even though Quakers were universally opposed to slavery, they did not all support President Lincoln's conduct of the war, as Molly was to learn while living in the Walter household. Ellwood Walter, a "Peace Democrat," loathed Lincoln's attempt to coerce the South by force. Plenty of New Yorkers shared Walter's beliefs. In the 1864 presidential campaign, they staged noisy demonstrations on behalf of George B. McClellan, the Democratic Party's nominee. Emotions ran so high during the electioneering that on election day troops were stationed on ships on both the Hudson and East Rivers to be used in case violence broke out.

Some of this tension must have seeped into the Walter household, intensified no doubt because "Uncle Ellwood" (as Molly called her benefactor) refused to discuss the war with his family. "The silence in that house on the subject of the war," Molly later recalled, "was formidable." Surely the young student looked forward to the war's end and rejoiced with other New Yorkers when she learned of Lee's surrender. But news of Lincoln's assassination soon stunned the city. Not even this horrific event, however, broke through Ellwood Walter's silence. On the day Lincoln was shot, Molly later wrote, "I wished myself for the first time at home."

Molly probably did go home the summer of 1865, but it is unclear when she next enrolled in Cooper Union. In a biographical profile prepared in 1906 for the Knickerbocker Publishing Company, Foote states that she studied drawing at the Women's School of Design at Cooper for three winters and then spent one term in the studio of Samuel Frost Johnson studying color. The three years she attended Cooper Union, however, may not have been consecutive.

We do know that Molly met Helena de Kay at Cooper Union during the winter of 1866–67 and that this was the beginning of their lifelong friendship. They came from different backgrounds, but their attraction for one another was instantaneous. Molly's memory of this encounter, expressed in lyrical prose years later, suggests its importance to the young artist: "And then Helena dawned on my nineteenth year like a rose pink winter sunrise, in the bare halls of Cooper, sweet and cold after her walk up from the ferry. Staten Island was her home; a subsidiary aunt had taken me in that winter who lived on Long Island and I crossed by an uptown ferry and walked down. Across the city we came together and across the world in some respects."

Ten months older than Molly, Helena was born into an old New York family on January 14, 1847. Her father, George Coleman de Kay (a former Argentine naval commander), died when she was only two years old, and in 1859 her widowed mother, Janet Drake de Kay, took the family to Europe, where they lived for a time in Dresden. There Helena learned French, German, and Italian and developed a passion for art. Later she attended a boarding school in Middleton, Connecticut, and then enrolled in painting classes at Cooper Union.

In the exhilarating atmosphere of the New York art world, Molly and Helena soon developed an intense relationship. Both then and years later, Molly called Helena the first great passion of her life. Their shared emotional intimacy was typical of many female friendships of the nineteenth century, as documented by historian Carroll Smith-Rosenberg in her groundbreaking article, "The Female World of Love and Ritual: Relations between Women in Nineteenth-Century America" (1975). "Such deeply felt same-sex friendships," Smith-Rosenberg contends, "were casually accepted in American society." Friends shared confidences, exchanged intimate gifts, and kissed and hugged one another. They wrote of their happiness when together and of their pain and loneliness when apart. And they openly avowed their love for one another, as when Molly wrote to Richard Gilder, Helena's fiancé: "Do you know sir, until you came, I believe [Helena] loved me almost as girls love their lovers. I know I loved her so."

This intimate relationship, which brought joy and solace into their lives for a half-century, was based in part on shared interests, mutual trust, and the ability to bring out the best in each other. They also had in common many of the same characteristics. Both were intelligent, talented, articulate, and ambitious. They each had inquiring minds, though Molly believed that Helena's was superior to her own. The more reserved of the two, Molly blushed easily and in stimulating company talked with more volubility than was her habit. Both were energized by nature's beauty and enjoyed long walks in the countryside. Though each was sympathetic and caring, Helena's magnetism in particular drew a host of devoted friends. The artist Cecilia Beaux later wrote that Helena's smile, voice, and wisdom inspired confidence: "One could follow her counsel unafraid." And another old friend, the essayist Ehrman S. Nadal, cried out to Molly seven years after Helena's death in 1916: "How often I want to say things to Helena!"

In physical appearance, each young woman had pleasant features, and each wore her hair in a fashionable chignon. Helena was of average height, Molly somewhat shorter. Years later Helena wrote of her first impressions of Molly: "very youthful in figure, delicate and yet full of vigor. She rode well. . . . She skated on her little feet like a swallow flying, and danced with the same grace and lightness. She could outskate and outdance us all."

The three years that Molly studied at Cooper Union were perhaps the happiest and most carefree of her life. The year that she met Helena, however, was the most memorable of all. Helena was in the painting class and Molly was in drawing, but they attended anatomy lectures and Friday composition classes together. And like modern students, they scribbled remarks and quotations to each other on the margins of their notebooks while ostensibly listening to their instructors. Molly still had in her possession years later a page on which Helena had copied a line from Shakespeare: "Let me not to the marriage of true minds admit impediments."

They spent afternoons at the School of Design, sometimes working on their sketches and paintings, oftentimes talking in vacant alcoves "comparing our past lives and dreams for the future." Helena introduced Molly to the writings of new authors and thinkers and to new ways of viewing life. The very first book that she gave to Molly (in a lifetime of sharing books) was a volume of Emerson's poems. She also introduced Molly to the works of Matthew Arnold and John Stuart Mill, and together they pondered women's role in art and society.

They shared one another's friends and came to know one another's homes and families. Milton charmed the New York City girl who had seen Europe, while the young Quaker never forgot the shared intimacy of Staten Island ferry rides. As a young wife and mother looking back on these stimulating days, Molly wrote to Helena: "We have had our May day—darling! I believe very few girls knew better the joy of youth." And much later, writing in her mid-sixties, Molly acknowledged her intellectual debt to Helena: "Your mind has led mine for a good many years," and she referred to Helena as "the strongest influence my life has known outside of its daily companions—of flesh and blood."

Molly thrived at Cooper Union. Early in her studies she decided to specialize in black and white commercial illustration. The two instructors she later credited as having the greatest influence on her work were Dr. William Rimmer, sculptor, painter, and physician, and William James Linton, poet, printer, wood engraver, and political activist. Both were English-born and both had inspiring personalities. Helena later claimed, however, that Rimmer's personality was better than his teaching, which, she said, "was unsystematic and desultory."

Under Rimmer and Linton's tutelage, Molly learned the difficult technique of woodcut illustration. Lee Ann Johnson succinctly describes the process:

> She was taught to draw directly on the wood block rather than to use the easier but less satisfactory procedure of drawing on thin paper and then tracing the reverse image on wood. . . . To make her drawing, she had to prepare the surface of the block, usually cut from 7/8-inch boxwood, with powdered bath-brick or chinese wash. Then, using the direct black-line method, she would pencil in her sketch, which would appear as a dark line against a white background. The block would be forwarded to an engraver, who would excise the white and engrave the black lines on each of their sides. The image Mary had drawn would thus appear in relief, and, when inked, would produce her drawing upon a white page.

Rimmer died soon after Molly left Cooper Union, but Linton's influence remained strong for many years. Linton engraved some of her early work, and he included two of her illustrations in his *History of Wood-Engraving in America* (1882), calling her "the best of our designers on the wood." A few years later, Linton's daughter Nelly joined Molly in Idaho to serve as governess and tutor for the Foote children. Molly and the senior Linton remained on fond terms until his death in 1897.

It may have been through Rimmer's influence as superintendent of the School of Design that Molly received her first professional commission to contribute four drawings for Albert Richardson's *Beyond the Mississippi* (1867). The woodcuts are crude, reflecting the inadequacies of the engraving process more than the artist's shortcomings. Still, the excellence of Molly's work was recognized at commencement exercises in May 1868 when school officials awarded her the Lane Prize of $60 in gold for being "the most meritorious pupil in drawing" in the School of Design. This award was presented annually to a third-year student so that she might have the finances to remain another year in the school. Molly apparently did not attend commencement, however, and consequently did not learn of the silver medal awarded that year to Helena until she read about it in the *New York Tribune*. Shortly afterward, Molly's illustration entitled "Thridding my fingers through my hair" appeared in the August issue of the *Galaxy*, its publication causing one critic to call Hallock "a young artist whose compositions contain promise of no ordinary kind."

In September of 1868, Molly made plans to return to Cooper for another term. She may, in fact, have lived that winter with her cousin Alice Sutton on Long Island, affording her the opportunity of either returning to Cooper or studying with the New York artist Samuel Frost Johnson. Sometime during her drawing apprenticeship, she also received advice and encouragement from two area engravers, John H. E. Whitney, an instructor at Cooper, and Charles H. Burt, an engraver of government bank notes. Burt's family, in fact, befriended Molly, and she would later refer to the senior Burt as "a warm friend and sincere critic of my early work."

During these student years in New York City, Molly combined serious study with light-hearted social activities. She may even have developed a crush on Helena's talented and charming younger brother, Charles de Kay. Shortly after her marriage, Molly confided to Helena: "I cannot see Charley [in my mind] without a pang which I must get cured somehow, for I cannot have it lasting." That she enjoyed life in the city is not to be doubted. What should be carefully examined, however, is an often-quoted statement she made about her student days as she was approaching fifty: "New York was the world to me. . . . I was too happy to be serious about anything, and too mixed up learning to know myself and so many other things. Art never was to me, nor ever could be, the whole of life." In later years, Molly consistently understated her artistic and literary ambitions, subordinating them to the "higher callings" of wifehood and motherhood. Still, she had been displeased when this statement about her student days first appeared in Alpheus S. Cody's profile of artist-authors published in an 1894 issue of the *Outlook*. Molly had responded in writing to Cody's questions about her career, but she had asked not to be quoted "on the subject of myself." Although in the profile Cody described Foote as the "best-known woman illustrator that we have," he also pictured her as having been an indifferent student who could not resist the social pleasures of the city. "Once one breaks the good rule of silence to all but one's friends," Molly later lamented, "there is no safety from looking like a fool." That Molly was judged the most meritorious drawing student in her class testifies to her talent and ambition.

The publishing world, in fact, quickly recognized Molly's superior talent. By the summer of 1871 she had received commissions from the *Galaxy*, *Scribner's Monthly Magazine*, *Hearth and Home*, and one or two other popular journals. Some requests were for large, front-page illustrations. A difficult kitchen scene for *Hearth and Home* featured girls making cakes and pastry, young men playing with a cat, a small boy peeling potatoes, and a "stout Irish woman kneading bread with an eye on the small boy." Molly was so busy one month with orders from Jack Howard, a junior partner in the publishing firm of Ford and Company, and from "Miss Cary," probably Phoebe Cary, a poet and assistant editor of the *Revolution*, that she delayed a visit to Helena, explaining: "Now you know and I know that if we were together for a few days . . . there would be no such thing as work, and just now I cannot spare even those few days."

Public recognition of her work as a professional illustrator continued to appear in print. The January 1872 issue of *Scribner's,* for example, carried a review of *Songs of the Heart,* a holiday book of poetry, in which Molly's illustration for Edmund C. Stedman's "The Doorstep" was described as "delicate and quiet and true in sentiment." And commissions continued to flow in as well. In October 1872, Molly's "The Last of Summer" appeared on the front page of *Appleton's Journal,* and in the November 30 issue of the same periodical one of her drawings accompanied Alfred Tennyson's "The Gardener's Daughter." Another of Molly's many-figured illustrations, "On the Ice," depicting the joys of ice-pond skating, graced the front page of *Hearth and Home* in January 1873.

Scribner's consistently provided Hallock with work over the next several months. She illustrated Josiah G. Holland's serial novel, *Arthur Bonnicastle,* which appeared in twelve consecutive issues, starting in November 1872. In the following year she illustrated Bret Harte's western poem, "After the Accident" (a glimpse of mining reality that Molly was to know first hand in later years), and began working on Adeline Trafton's serial novel, *Katherine Earle,* the first installment appearing in November. She also completed an illustration for the *Young Catholic,* a youth magazine, and three drawings for Sarah C. Woolsey's *What Katy Did at School,* a book for young girls.

Molly worked on these commissions while living at home, sometimes using her sister Bessie and the kitchen chore girls as models. But conditions had changed on the Milton farm. After the war, the price of farm labor rose, and the price of farm products fell. To maximize profits, Molly's father concentrated on the fruit crop and cider making, renting his upper farm on shares to one of his Irish laborers. But Nathaniel Hallock realized very little from this rental arrangement. To compound problems, Molly's brother Tom had asked for, and received, an advance on the estate to invest in a business venture in New York City. When this enterprise failed, the first in a series of Tom's failures, Nathaniel continued advancing funds to his son, to the detriment of the farm.

Molly's father bore a heavy financial burden for many years. Sometime after their marriage, Bessie and her husband, John Sherman, joined the Hallock household to help with the work. But Molly was not asked to make sacrifices. In her reminiscences, she writes: "As long as I lived at home my work was protected and my profits, after paying my board as a son would, if he could, were my own." Still, Molly probably contributed more to the farm's upkeep than this statement implies. Because of "the pressure at home," she accepted commissions for work that was sometimes uninspiring. "You cannot imagine anything more hopelessly dreary and commonplace," Molly wrote to Helena, "than the two little books [my drawings] illustrate. . . . But I am mercenary and these melancholy little books are a fortune to me in the Micawber plan."

Despite the household's financial worries, Molly's early successes were electrifying. She later remembered: "I was in high spirits all through my unwise teens, considerably puffed up after my drawings began to sell, with that pride of independence which was a new thing to daughters of that period." Her drawings financed trips to New York City, where she conferred with publishers and talked with artist friends, vacations with her Long Island cousins, and visits to the de Kays on Staten Island.

Even at Milton, however, Molly mixed work with "rural gaieties." She often went horseback riding, sailed on the river, or rowed on the pond at twilight. With friends and family she went on picnics to Peg's Beach and Black Pond, gathered and roasted chestnuts, and went ice skating and sleigh riding in the winter. Talented guests often enlivened the Hallock household with their stimulating conversation, chess games, piano playing, and singing. Fellow artists Mary Stone and Katie Bloede visited. And Helena's extended visits to Milton every summer were golden days for both young women. Molly always felt a sense of emptiness when her friend departed. After one glorious visit, she wrote to Helena: "I am realizing more and more every day that my dearest girl is gone. I am afraid it makes me a little cross to be lonely. . . . [It is useless] for me to begin to tell you how I love you, how I revel in your brightness when you are here, and what a blank you leave behind."

When together, the two aspiring artists must have talked endlessly about their art, and when apart, they wrote to each other of their progress and concerns. Molly often expressed the need for further study. "I feel the lack of technical knowledge, especially on the big blocks,"she wrote to Helena. "I don't know how to work effectively and my sketches are always better than my blocks." She also wanted to paint, and, although nothing came of it, she inquired about taking lessons from an art instructor at Vassar, the recently established women's college in Poughkeepsie.

Helena, too, seriously pursued her art. After leaving Cooper Union, she had continued her studies at the National Academy of Design in New York City, where in 1871–72 she and artist friend Maria Oakey were members of the first life drawing class for women. Helena also received private instruction from artist Winslow Homer, and both she and Maria were tutored informally by John La Farge. Writing in August 1872, Helena confided to Molly: "Mr. La Farge was very charming and gave us good lessons." Later that fall, Helena and Maria shared a studio together on Broadway several blocks north of Cooper Union.

Sometime the following year, Molly and Helena made plans to open a similar studio in New York City. This was to be "a quiet place to work" during the winter, "not a place to receive our friends," Molly assured her mother. She was to live with her brother and sister-in-law in Brooklyn and travel into the city to work at the studio. But as the year progressed, a bewildering mixture of emotions assailed the young artist. Joyful anticipation turned to anxiety. And in mid-September, having wept over the decision, Molly wrote to tell Helena that she would stay in Milton that winter and establish a studio on her own in the back parlor of the farmhouse.

It is difficult to know exactly how Helena had viewed the joint studio venture. Clearly, Molly wanted her approval and understanding but feared Helena's reaction to the change in plans. The major stumbling block had been Molly's family. Although her mother appeared willing to go along with the studio plan, Molly sensed her silent disapproval. And sister-in-law Sarah held reservations as well. "I never in my life persisted in anything that my Mother and the family didn't approve," Molly wrote.

Molly further sought to justify her decision by contrasting Helena's temperament with her own. Helena had genius, Molly believed, which required the stimulation of an "art atmosphere." Sharing life with Helena in the city had always been intoxicating, perhaps too intoxicating. Molly's own "small talent" required a more peaceful atmosphere. "I am strong and well but *people* wear upon me more than I can tell you," she wrote. "My own people are so restful that it is a great change to leave this peaceful atmosphere for a whirl of [conflicting] influences and impressions. I don't think I can work when I am perplexed and excited, as I should be all winter long in one way or another."

Molly failed to mention in this letter to Helena, however, that a recent visit from Arthur Foote had stirred within her powerful new emotions, a factor that must also have affected her decision about the studio. In fact, both young women by this time had met and were getting to know their future husbands. The appearance of these male suitors would change in subtle ways (but not seriously alter) the devotion that the two friends felt for one another.

Sometime in the winter of 1871–72, Helena met her future husband, Richard Gilder, the assistant editor of *Scribner's*, through a mutual friend, the poet and author Helen Hunt of Newport, Rhode Island. Their subsequent courtship flourished in the heady milieu of concerts, art exhibits, lectures, and literature. During this time, Molly came to know Richard as well, admiring his lofty idealism right from the start. His faith in truth and beauty, his lovable personality and "boyish good humor," proved irresistible to many he encountered. But meeting Helena forever changed Gilder's life; she was the inspiration for his six love sonnets that soon appeared in *Scribner's*. In one, later titled "Love's Jealousy," Gilder shows his acceptance of Helena and Molly's love for one another. Gilder's jealousy is not of other men, "nor of the maid who holds thee close, oh close!" but of the sky, the red rose, and the breeze that win Helena's soul.

In June 1873, Richard accompanied Helena on a visit to the Hallock farm, writing his monthly column for *Scribner's*, "The Old Cabinet," while lounging in an outdoor hammock. Other suitors had courted Helena before but none so persistently as Richard. For a woman as passionately devoted to art as Helena, the prospect of marriage posed a terrifying dilemma. On the one hand, she loved Richard, but on the other she feared the loss of independence that wifehood would bring. And she fervently believed, as did other young female artists, that there could be no art for a woman who married.

Well-educated and older than most young women approaching marriage, Helena and Molly examined carefully the constraints it would impose on their lives. Molly was twenty-five years old when she met Arthur Foote at the Moses Beach residence in Brooklyn, where they were guests during Christmas week of 1872. Their first memorable encounter happened on New Year's Day after Molly retired to the Beach library to complete an illustration for *Hearth and Home*. Arthur entered the room and asked if he might stay. Molly recalls in her reminiscences: "I didn't believe that I could draw a stroke with him there; but I did!"

Although younger than Molly, Arthur shared with her an "instinctively upper-class" world view. Born on May 24, 1849, to George and Eliza Foote, he spent his boyhood on the family farm of Nutplains near Guilford, Connecticut. Arthur's father was a country gentleman, managing his rural properties while serving in the state legislature and as senior warden in his Episcopal parish. George Foote's sister Roxanna married Lyman Beecher, one of the most famous clergymen of the day, which made Arthur and his nine siblings first cousins to the equally famous Beecher children, Henry Ward Beecher, Catharine Beecher, and Harriet Beecher Stowe, author of *Uncle Tom's Cabin*.

Arthur received a good education in the Guilford public schools. Although he dreamed of entering West Point, he enrolled instead in the Sheffield Scientific School at Yale University in 1866 to study engineering. For the year and some months that he studied at Yale, he stayed with his cousin Katherine Foote Rockwell and her husband, Alfred, a professor of mining at the Sheffield School. A mistaken diagnosis of an eye problem caused Arthur to cut short his studies and to join a rich cousin on his sailing ship in the Bahamas.

By the time he encountered Molly on New Year's Day 1873, Arthur apparently had decided to continue his engineering education by working in the field. The historian Clark C. Spence notes, in fact, that during much of the nineteenth century, most mining engineers were self-taught. Accordingly, in late September Arthur made plans to join an expedition to Palestine, where he expected to acquire practical experience.

Whether Arthur's growing infatuation with Molly caused him to alter his plans is not known for certain, but he did not set sail for Palestine. He had spent nearly a week at the Hallock farm earlier in September, joining Molly, Bessie, and some of their friends on an overnight camping trip to Big Pond. It was an enchanting place with a waterfall located at the end of an indistinct trail through some woods. To reach the fall, the campers had to scramble down the bank of a wild stream and then cross over on some huge boulders. Fascinated by her surroundings, Molly "lay flat over the edge of the rock" to look down and under the fall into a cave hollowed out by the water spray. Bessie's shout for Molly "to come away" was lost in the roar of the water. But there had been no danger, Molly later reported to Helena, for "Arthur Foote held on to my feet (*not* a joke)." To Richard Gilder, Molly confessed about a month after the Big Pond trip, "I never was so happy in my life as those two days and one mysterious night."

It was shortly after this camping trip that Molly wrote to Helena explaining her reasons for backing out of the studio venture. What went through Helena's mind as she read this letter can only be conjectured. But she obviously was hurt and disappointed by Molly's decision, fearing that it signified a chill in their relationship. In a stiff, almost formal, reply expressing this fear, Helena closed with a brusque "very truly your friend."

Stunned by Helena's frigid letter, Molly rushed to reassure her friend that whether she went to New York or stayed home her love for Helena was eternal. Backing out of the studio plan, she reiterated, meant only that she "must stick to the family and the homelife." "Father and mother have done everything in the world for me," she continued. "I am *not going* to live a life that will imply that while I love them, I must seek a more congenial and stimulating atmosphere than their society affords. If my art cannot exist in my father's house where I belong, it will have to cease to be a part of me."

Both young women believed that love had its tides, and Molly acknowledged a "strong ebb tide this summer" in her affection for Helena. Responding to her friend's obvious distress, however, Molly declared her love for Helena with an emotional intensity rarely surpassed in their correspondence:

> I wanted so to put my arms round my girl of all the girls in the world and tell her . . . I love her as wives do (not) love their husbands as *friends* who have taken each other for

> life—and believe in her as I believe in my God. . . . If I didn't love you do you suppose I'd care about anything or have ridiculous notions and panics and behave like an old fool who ought to know better. I'm going to hang on to your skirts, young woman. . . . You can't get away from the love of your own MAH.

A short time later, Molly received a "sweet reply" from Helena, the breach between them apparently mended. Molly's decision to remain at home that winter, in fact, may have nudged Helena into accepting Richard Gilder's proposal of marriage. In mid-November Helena wrote to tell her mother of the engagement, revealing at the same time how difficult it had been to accept Richard's proposal: "When I tried to say 'no' to other men, it was hard, but easy compared to saying yes to this one."

Molly was elated by the news. She assured Helena that marriage was an inevitable part of a woman's life; she felt "sure that the right way of living must in the end bring the surest peace and happiness." But the Quaker artist herself held conflicting views about art and marriage. She believed it was right to sacrifice personal ambition to the highest law of woman's nature. Yet she also attempted to convince Helena that her art was not over: "If you choose to believe yourself in bonds, you might as well be, but if you act as if nothing had happened, if you dont let your palette and brushes into the secret of your changed life, everything will go on the same, with the advantage of a new and deep experience added to those already given you to express."

Once Helena announced her engagement, Molly spoke more freely of her love for Arthur. She told Helena in mid-December that for three months she had been blest with "an unreal tremulous sort of happiness." This love for Arthur had come unexpectedly. "It came to me unsought while my mind was fixed upon other people and other interests. It took possession of me unawares." She tried to deny it, finding security in old relations, "until at last came a sudden light and happiness . . . it lasted only a day or two in the happening—but it has gone to the roots of my life."

At the time Molly made this declaration, Arthur was in California seeking work as an engineer. They were not officially engaged but had reached an understanding that Arthur would return east after accumulating experience and the means to marry. At the start of his western sojourn, Foote very likely spent a few weeks in San Francisco with his older sister Mary and her husband, James D. Hague, a successful mining engineer, trained at Harvard and in Germany, with several years experience in the field, including a stint with Clarence King's Geological Survey of the Fortieth Parallel. In 1871, a year before he married Arthur's sister, Hague had entered private employ in California as a consulting mining engineer. He was to become one of the nation's foremost mining consultants and to open a host of professional doors for his younger brother-in-law.

Through Hague's influence, in fact, Foote went to work early in 1874 as assistant engineer on the Sutro Tunnel, then being cut to drain and ventilate the Comstock mines near Virginia City, Nevada. The letters he wrote and the photographs he sent piqued Molly's interest. "The country is very wild," she later wrote Helena, and "the people like those in Bret Harte's stories. . . . The very names—Carson Canon, Carson Desert, Six Mile Canon, have a charm for me." Molly wrote weekly to "the Sutro Tunnel Exile" and sent him copies of *Littell's Living Age*, a popular magazine. Later that year or early in 1875, Arthur returned to California, where he helped to survey San Francisco's Golden Gate Park and to locate the "loop" at Tehachapi Pass for the Southern Pacific Railroad.

While Arthur toiled in Sutro Tunnel, Molly threw herself into her work as never before. She meant to live to the fullest during Arthur's anticipated two years' absence and to absorb herself in her art "to keep from becoming one of that dismal army of waiting women." Helena and Richard continued to be an integral part of her existence. Molly witnessed their wedding on June 3, 1874, at the de Kay residence on Staten Island. Later in the summer, Helena visited Molly at Milton, and Molly spent a day and a night with the Gilders at "the Studio," their modest new residence on East Fifteenth Street in New York City, where Helena and Richard were to preside over weekly Friday evening gatherings of young artists and writers. Molly called it an "enchanted place."

True to her word, Molly worked diligently during Arthur's absence, her illustrations appearing in *Scribner's*, *St. Nicholas Magazine* (the best-known nineteenth-century juvenile periodical), and several James R. Osgood and Company publications. By the time Arthur Foote reappeared in Milton, Mary A. Hallock was well on the road to becoming "the dean of women illustrators."

Molly's first widely acclaimed success came through A. V. S. Anthony, head of the art department at James R. Osgood and Company, who commissioned her to illustrate Henry Wadsworth Longfellow's *The Hanging of the Crane* (1874). The poem was published in two forms, a special holiday edition with gilded edges and finely tooled Moroccan leather cover, selling for $9.00, and a less expensive clothbound edition. Of the forty-two major illustrations appearing with the poem, Molly contributed twenty-eight, and Thomas Moran, the landscape artist, fourteen. Molly's drawings won praise from both Longfellow and Anthony, who, along with William J. Linton, engraved the book's illustrations.

Amused and delighted by Longfellow's response, Molly described her success with some humor in a letter to Helena: "Mr. A. says that Mr. Longfellow was as much pleased as he was *surprised* when he found they were made by a young lady! Complimentary to young women in general, dont you think so? What is the use of doing anything more than is expected of 'young ladies'! Mr. Longfellow asked Mr. Anthony if I was 'handsome and accomplished' and how old I was. These, you see, are the important questions."

Molly's illustrations received favorable reviews from William Dean Howells in the *Atlantic Monthly* and from an unnamed writer in *Scribner's.* But the strongest praise came from a *New York Times* reviewer, who observed that Mary Hallock's "drawings reveal the hand of a thorough artist and . . . are as full of poetry and feeling as Mr. Longfellow's lines." Anthony soon hosted a gathering in Molly's honor at his residence in Boston, where she apparently met Longfellow and other distinguished New England authors. In her reminiscences, she calls this event "the surprise of her life." Too modest to list the other luminaries present, Foote states simply: "Everyone knows how generous they were, those makers of American Literature, to all the young pilgrims who worshiped at their shrines. You went to Boston for the accolade and your shoulders tingled ever after."

While completing the *Crane* illustrations, Molly worked on a full-page drawing for Thomas Bailey Aldrich's *Prudence Palfry* (1874), a story that Molly liked about a girl in the East whose young man went west to seek his fortune. And later in the year, she finished three small drawings for John Greenleaf Whittier's *Hazel-Blossoms* (1875), using the Milton countryside for background. She then went to work on illustrations for Whittier's *Mabel Martin* (1876), her second large project for James R. Osgood and Company. Three male artists, including Thomas Moran, helped to illustrate this handsome gift book. Twenty-six of the drawings (roughly half) are Molly's. Using scenes from the Hallock farm and pathways, Molly helped readers to visualize Whittier's tale of love and honor in the days of the Salem witch trials.

Everyone was pleased with Molly's drawings, except perhaps the artist herself. Self-doubts had assailed her as she struggled to get subtlety into the characters' faces. Sharing her frustrations with Helena, she lamented: "I hate failure so that it makes every new picture I begin a dread to me." But A. V. S. Anthony praised her blocks, and William J. Linton judged a drawing of Mabel Martin the best she had ever made. A reviewer for the *Atlantic Monthly* paid tribute to Molly's "sympathetic skill." Several of her illustrations, he believed, "have great beauty of execution," although he was critical of the gallows-tree scene for failing to express the horror that awaited Goody Martin. Still, he concluded, Mary Hallock "has here presented us with a beautiful series of drawings." Whittier himself was overjoyed with the publication. "Never was there a prettier book than 'Mabel Martin!'" he wrote. "If it does not sell well it surely cannot be the fault of the publishers and artists."

Arrangements were soon made for Whittier to meet the young artist, an event later described by Anthony: "Mr. Whittier, for whose 'Mabel Martin' Mrs. Foote had made some drawings, came to my house, to see her. The little lady sat at his feet, on a 'cricket.' I distinctly recall the Quaker kerchief she had about her neck, and she talked just as Mrs. Hopper [a friend of Molly's] said she would. Howells, Aldrich and some others were there, but the little lady was the bright particular star."

The payments Molly received for the Osgood commissions are unknown. But illustrators often made good wages. During a visit to Milton, in fact, Anthony bought all of her sketches, believing that a demand existed for them in Boston. After one admirer there paid $50 for a sketch, Molly exclaimed: "Did you ever hear of anything so generous!" These drawings mostly depicted Milton life and scenes. And they did so, the *Atlantic Monthly* enthusiastically reported, "with an accuracy, a spiritedness, and a shaping skill which would be remarkable anywhere, and are especially rare in America." This reviewer believed that Molly had her greatest success with feminine figures, singling out for special praise a drawing she had made using a mulatta model posed beside a covered well in an apple orchard.

Molly's success led to two additional large commissions in the year preceding Arthur's return. The first was with Scribner, Armstrong and Company to illustrate a new gift book edition of Josiah G. Holland's *Mistress of the Manse* (1877). Early in the project, when Alexander W. Drake, the art director at *Scribner's*, requested a meeting to discuss the volume, Molly anticipated combining business with a visit to Helena. In a light-hearted mood, Molly wrote: "Suppose I came down next Saturday in the afternoon train bringing two Mistress of the Manse blocks for you to abuse—spend Sunday with you quietly—that means talking all the time until you are relieved of all your latest troubles and I of mine." The visit would also afford opportunity to discuss a joint venture to illustrate a new gift book for the Osgood firm.

On Anthony's recent trip to Milton, Molly had expressed a desire to collaborate with Helena on a book. He liked the idea and soon suggested that they illustrate Longfellow's Norse ballad *The Skeleton in Armor*—Helena "to decorate and do land and seascapes" and Molly to draw the character sketches. In high spirits, Molly announced this decision to Helena, adding: "We will show them what harmony of intention in two women, both thoroughly in earnest, can do! Will we not?"

Early in January 1876, with Arthur's arrival less than three weeks away, Molly worked diligently on the Longfellow poem. She used male cousins as models for the Vikings and a young local woman as a Norse maiden. Helena's work on the project had been delayed by the birth of her first child, daughter Marion, in December. Still, once Helena began drawing again, Anthony found something wrong with her work, most likely in the subject matter rather than in technique, or maybe it was a mixture of the two. Molly was crushed by Anthony's reaction. She apologized profusely to Helena for having involved her in a project that had brought only trouble and annoyance. "It takes away all the pleasure I at first felt in the book," Molly bewailed, "and the pride I hoped to feel."

The Skeleton in Armor (1876), which the publishers had promised would be "the most elaborate and beautiful gift book ever produced in this country," appeared without Helena's artwork. It included, however, eighteen full-page illustrations, one by Edwin Austin Abbey and the rest by Molly. The *Atlantic Monthly* lauded her work: "The latter merit, in the main, the highest compliments. Miss Hallock has not given us in her previous efforts the evidence of dramatic conception which these new illustrations disclose." But the same reviewer was less kind in his discussion of Holland's *The Mistress of the Manse*, a poem that he ridiculed. Five artists had contributed illustrations, including Molly, Thomas Moran, and Helena. Ironically, the reviewer singled out Helena's decorative flower vignettes as deserving "very high praise," but of Molly's work he wrote: "Mary Hallock hardly does herself justice; her drawings in this series seem to have suffered from haste."

Molly's prodigious accomplishments came amidst the daily noise and activities of the Hallock household, enlarged by the birth of Bessie's two children, Gerald in 1871 and Mary Birney in 1875, and by visiting relatives and an occasional boarder. Milton continued to attract Molly's artistic and literary friends: Helena and Richard, Charles de Kay, Ehrman S. Nadal, Elihu Vedder (author and artist), William J. Linton, and others.

In her reminiscences, Molly pays tribute to these companions, noting that they included "some of the most brilliant and fascinating young people of their time." She writes: "In those early days the young poets were still on trial, the essayists and artists (except Vedder) in the stage called promising. . . . Reading of them later in far places where my life bestowed itself after marriage, I saw them—famous and bald and some of them fat—always as they were then; they had an immortality of youth for me."

Molly's infatuation with books and journals provided further companionship and intellectual stimulation. She frequently exchanged ideas with Helena about authors and essays and participated in a Friday evening reading circle, composed mainly of family members but also including Dr. Myers, a local teacher. She took special delight in sending Richard's first volume of poetry, *The New Day* (1875), to Arthur and was pleased when the sometimes stoic engineer used the poet's words "to express his deepest feelings." But work kept Molly so busy during one winter month that she had to limit her outdoor excursions to early evening tramps along the woods.

In her seventies, Molly looked back with humor upon her long-distance courtship, recalling that she wrote to Arthur "everything I was doing and all that happened to show that my life in the East was not made up of waiting, that it was going forward by leaps and bounds in a direction which did not point to marriage." Even though they had spent little time together, Molly and Arthur came to know one another through their letters, revealing details about themselves that increased their mutual affection and admiration. Molly also interacted frequently with other young men, which gave her some understanding of masculine behavior.

Still, like many other nineteenth-century women approaching marriage, she tested the depth of her lover's devotion. She describes the nature of this test in her reminiscences: "Every one of these incidents that gave color to my life, every pleasure and every triumph, I bragged of to my strategist in the West. It was ungenerous and crude of me, yet it may have been some latent instinct of Quaker prudence. . . . He stood the test—he remained calm and showed no trace of the begrudger."

An intelligent and self-supporting woman, Molly would enter marriage expecting some degree of equality with Arthur. Yet, despite her strength of character and their love for one another, Molly's anxieties reached a high pitch in the days preceding his return. They had spent months negotiating a time and place for the wedding. Arthur's new position as resident engineer at the New Almaden quicksilver mine south of San Francisco, which he had obtained through the help of James D. Hague, allowed little time for a wedding trip. Molly balked, however, when Arthur asked her to come west to be married at his sister's house. "I should have needed far more nerve than I possessed for the adventure itself," she later recalled, "to have entered another family in that way."

Marriage held uncertainties for all women, especially for those with careers or ambition. Molly's ambivalence about matrimony probably was as deeply felt as anyone's. Like Helena, she feared a loss of freedom. "It is only the thing itself—the surrender—the awfulness of it all that comes so much harder than I thought," she confided to Helena. "When you were so rebellious, I used to scold you and think you hardly kind to Richard. But I understand it all now." Arthur continued to press Molly for a wedding date. At one point he offered to give up his position and return to find work in the East. But the best engineering jobs were in the West, Molly realized. Besides, she told Helena, "I confess to a longing to see this wonderful new world." Molly's immediate concerns—to complete illustrations for *The Skeleton in Armor* and to see Helena through her first pregnancy—influenced the scheme that Molly and Arthur finally settled upon. They would wed in Milton in the winter when Arthur could best leave his work. Then Arthur would return to New Almaden alone, Molly to follow later.

And so they were married on February 9, 1876, a wet and windy day, in a short and simple Quaker ceremony in the Milton farmhouse. The bride must have looked radiant in her white wedding dress "with a little gleam of silk edging the ruffles." Molly later described the occasion:

> The bride comes down the stairs unveiled and takes the arm of the man who is waiting for her and they walk up the rooms unattended to their places confronting the assembly, in a silence presumably given to prayer (I remember hearing the rain drip from the trees outside): then, taking each other by the hand, "In the presence of God, with these our friends as witnesses," they pronounce the awful words which in their case are considered irrevocable. It is not a moment one is likely to forget.

Richard Gilder was among the witnesses seated in the front parlor, but Helena remained at home to tend the baby. She had written a special letter the night before, which was given to the bride moments before the ceremony. But, fearing "it would make me cry," Molly set it aside to read later. Inside her wedding dress, however, she wore a red rose that Richard had brought from Helena. He also brought as a wedding present a special copy of *The New Day*, in which Helena had painted a rose spray across the flyleaf and daisies in the back.

On their wedding journey, the newly married couple stayed a few days at the Brevoort House in New York City and then decamped for Arthur's childhood home at Guilford, where they spent as much time as possible outdoors exploring the seashore. One day, when Molly wanted to sketch an outcropping of rocks, Arthur built a barricade to shield her from the wind and a fire to keep her hands and feet warm. Molly's happiness is reflected in her lyrical descriptions of their stay at Guilford. To Helena, she admitted: "I shall always love this place for the sake of the happy time we have spent here."

On their way back to Milton, they stopped in New York City so that Molly could introduce Arthur to her best friend, who, incredibly, had never met him. Molly was half-afraid that he would disappoint Helena. And even after this first encounter, which apparently went well, Molly urged Helena: "Don't feel *bound* to admire [Arthur] for my sake. . . . It will come all the easier to like him bye and bye when we are more together."

Arthur left Milton to return to New Almaden about three weeks after the wedding. Molly spent the day wandering "about the house trying to pick up what is left of my old life," she confided to Helena. "Tomorrow I shall try to go to work again. Now my work will be more than ever a blessing." During the next four months, Molly completed the *Skeleton* illustrations and agreed to illustrate a new holiday edition of Hawthorne's *The Scarlet Letter*. She paid brief visits to the Gilders at the Studio and to Arthur's parents in Guilford, and then she prepared for her journey west. As the departure date neared, however, Molly's anxieties returned. "I am sure all will be well with me," she wrote, "though I confess to feeling awfully scared as the time draws so near. That silly trembling feeling *inside* that I used to have for days before I was married has come back again, and takes my strength. I feel as if I were going to jump in the river trusting to the chance of my knowing how to swim."

Her departure was eased by an outpouring of love and gifts from family and friends. Cousin Hannah and sister Bessie gave her a silk quilt, which they had quilted themselves, Charles H. Burt (the engraver) sent two volumes of an art encyclopedia, and Richard and Helena bestowed so many gifts, including a traveling stove, that Molly begged Helena to desist, saying "You have gone clean daft on the subject."

Looking back on her leave-taking nearly fifty years later, Molly recalled: "No girl ever wanted less to 'go West' with any man, or paid a man a greater compliment by doing so." But this remembrance surely belies the complexity of Molly's mental state at the time she left Milton. She was, after all, anxious to rejoin Arthur. She anticipated staying in the West no longer than two years. She looked forward to seeing the land of Bret Harte and probably saw this western sojourn as an adventure, equivalent to Helena's trips abroad. And she may have welcomed a respite from the Milton household's financial struggles, for later she was to write from Idaho about the "Milton of latter days, when I wished to be away." Though saddened by the thought of leaving her dear mother and dearest friend Helena, Molly never regretted her decision to marry Arthur and to follow him west to New Almaden. She was, after all, a young woman of spirit who liked an adventure and who possibly sensed the new opportunities that awaited her in the West.

CHAPTER 2

A Western Interlude

ABOUT midnight, on a warm July night in Poughkeepsie (1876), the twenty-eight-year-old artist said good-bye to her parents and stepped aboard the Overland Limited, bound for San Francisco and a reunion with Arthur. Mindful of her contract to illustrate *The Scarlet Letter*, Molly had employed a pretty young Canadian, Lizzie Griffen, to accompany her west as servant and model. Her traveling companions also included Lizzie's infant son George and Mr. Murray and his son Johnny, apparently family friends en route to Omaha. Until they reached this Nebraska way station, Mr. Murray would take charge of all travel arrangements.

From the very beginning of her western travels, Mary Hallock Foote's experiences contrasted sharply with those of most other nineteenth-century women who settled in the West. A successful illustrator whose drawings appeared in the best journals, she traveled across the continent in relatively comfortable circumstances, with a servant and a male chaperone (part of the way) to shield her from many of the discomforts that accompanied a three-thousand-mile journey by railcar. She would take up residence at the New Almaden quicksilver mine, a region well beyond the frontier stage of development and only sixty miles from cosmopolitan San Francisco, a city more like those she had known in the East than the primitive settlements she encountered in crossing the plains.

The nation in 1876, in fact, was a land of enormous contrasts. While thousands of its citizens celebrated one hundred years of progress at the Centennial Exhibition in Philadelphia, the U.S. Army embarked upon a full-scale war against the

Sioux in Dakota Territory and maintained an uneasy peace with Apaches in Arizona and New Mexico. Yet the railroad route that Molly traversed was relatively free of Indian-white conflict, and the young artist seemingly was unconcerned about western Indian wars. But she carried with her preconceived ideas about the West, ideas shaped by Arthur's descriptions of the Nevada mines and by essays and stories she had read in the leading journals. Her notions about this "new country" were also skewed by an upper-class social bias that equated goodness and respectability with culture and education.

Molly was unable to sleep very much the first night on the train. But the next morning, she said, she "awoke in a new world and began to look ahead instead of back." From Omaha she wrote: "Now the excitement of the journey has taken possession of me. I feel as if I could go round the world and back again if necessary." By luck she and her companions had obtained in Chicago at half the usual price "a cozy little compartment" containing a sofa, two chairs, a table, two mirrors, and two double and two single berths. The only discomfort that Molly experienced was the midday heat, but early mornings and evening sunsets were "perfectly delicious." Often she sat with Johnny on the top step of the platform of the rear car "with a glorious breeze blowing in our faces, and towns, counties and states whirling past." Lizzie took control of the large lunch basket that Molly's mother had packed and made tea with the little traveling stove that the Gilders contributed.

Like many nineteenth-century travelers, Molly marveled at the western landscape but was critical of the towns and people she encountered. Her letters betray the commonly held belief that the West was more primitive than the East and in need of civilizing. She described the settlers who came to gawk at the train just outside of Omaha as "gaunt wild looking men. . . . [The oldest] did not talk much but stared like an animal at the crowd." The towns that she passed had disappointed her; they were all alike and "*all* dreadful." Omaha was no better. The streets approaching the train depot were appalling, and the Omaha Stock Market was the epitome of bad taste: "*plaided, my dear, in squares of red, white, and blue*—the whole front of the building! . . . I suppose this horror was perpetrated in honor of the Centennial year." But her heart ached for the women standing in their doorways as the train whirled by. Sounding a theme that she later explored in her western fiction, Molly mused: "I wonder if they feel the hopelessness of their exile."

Farther west, as the scenery became more spectacular, Molly found much to admire—the alkali desert, the Great Salt Lake, and Echo and Weber Canyons, where the reddish and yellow towering rocks stood out brilliantly against a blue sky dotted with white fleecy clouds. On the last day of the journey, she arose at 4:00 A.M. to witness the passage over the Sierra Nevada. "The mining towns with queer Bret Hartish names—'Gold Run,' 'Dutch Flat,' etc. were passed before breakfast." Much to Molly's surprise, Arthur unexpectedly boarded the train at San Leandro, California, explaining that when her telegrams failed to arrive he had become uneasy and vowed to go east "till he found" her.

James D. Hague met the Footes when they reached San Francisco. In contrast to her own crumpled appearance, Molly thought her new brother-in-law looked "appallingly well dressed and handsome." When he learned that Molly's trunks had been delayed, he dispatched Arthur to borrow a change of clothes from his wife, Arthur's sister Mary, and escorted Molly and her retinue to the Occidental, where Arthur had reserved rooms. Gifts of welcome awaited the tired traveler. Mary Hague had sent a basket of roses, and Arthur contributed two Mexican water jars, some Fijian household decorations, and three volumes of art work—the latter so that Molly would not "feel as if [she] were doomed to barbarians." Molly met her "lovely sister-in-law" for the first time that evening in the hotel parlor dressed in Mary Hague's own black silk dress and lace jacket. She spent the next day at the Hague residence on Bush Street in San Francisco, admiring the flowers in Mary's courtyard and luxuriating in the peaceful atmosphere. But she was too tired to accompany Arthur into town to buy household goods.

After a second night at the Occidental, the Footes set out for New Almaden—by railcar to San José and then by private carriage the last twelve miles to the mine. In her reminiscences, Molly recalls that "the prudent wife" had said the stage was good enough for her. But with typical candor, she adds: "I went on, all my life, rebuking extravagance and enjoying its results." She was charmed, in fact, by the drive to New Almaden and by the "great live oak trees [that appeared] in groves all thro the Santa Clara valley and in massive groups along the road."

For the next thirteen months, Molly and Arthur lived in a small company-owned cottage a mile or so up a winding road that led from company headquarters and the reduction works at the base of the hills to the laborers' camps and mining shafts above. Cinnabar ore had been discovered in these hills in 1845. Within five years, mining operations were yielding such significant amounts of quicksilver, an indispensable ingredient for recovering gold, that the mine was named New Almaden, after the famous Almaden quicksilver mine in Spain. The firm that Arthur worked for, the Quicksilver Mining Company, had acquired ownership in 1864 and greatly expanded the enterprise. By the time Molly arrived, New Almaden was one of the world's largest producers of quicksilver.

Approximately one thousand people lived in New Almaden when the Footes took up residence. It was a well-ordered and socially stratified company town, under the authoritarian regime of James B. Randol, the general manager. The upper stratum, including the justice of the peace, company doctor, and other company personnel, lived in vine-covered cottages along a main street running parallel to a tree-lined stream at the base of the hills. The manager's elegant two-story mansion, called the Casa Grande, with a formally landscaped lawn, flower gardens, and shrubs, dominated this elite little settlement, known as "the Hacienda." Molly likened it to "a pretty New England village" but chose not to live in this section of town.

About halfway up the hillside was the Cornish camp, where Cornishmen and other English-speaking miners lived with their families in white-painted cottages enclosed with picket fences. At the center of the camp was a general store (which served as a mail distribution center), schoolhouse, mine office, and other company buildings, including a boarding house leased to proprietors. The Cornish had been migrating to California since the gold rush of 1849, but their numbers rapidly increased in the 1860s after hard times hit the Cornwall mining districts. When Randol took control of New Almaden a few years later, he apparently recruited as many Cornish miners as possible because of their strong work ethic and experience in underground mining.

The Mexican camp was at the top of the hillside, with a Catholic church on the crest and company cottages and other buildings spilling down its steep slopes. Holding less-skilled jobs than the Cornish, Spanish-speaking laborers received less pay. A small Chinese camp added to the ethnic mixture. Some Chinese worked as cooks and servants for company personnel, but others performed backbreaking labor on the dumps and around the reduction works for meager wages.

A day or two after reaching New Almaden, Molly wrote a long, optimistic letter to Helena, describing the last stages of her trip and her new surroundings. Her first night in New Almaden, she had dined with Arthur at Mrs. Fall's boarding house in the Cornish camp, where Arthur had lived when he was single. "Mother Fall," a likable older woman, had helped Arthur select furnishings for the cottage. Molly met some of Arthur's other friends that same evening, including Frank Hernandez, a young "well-mannered" Spaniard who had agreed to teach Molly and Arthur to speak Spanish.

The Footes soon settled into their small but adequate dwelling, recently refurbished at Arthur's expense. The dark floors, redwood-lined walls, and dark ceiling offered a cool retreat from the outside glare. And a strong breeze often swept through the piazza that extended around three sides of the house. Inside, over an archway, Arthur hung a curious mixture of masculine symbols: flags from his cousin's yacht, a hunting knife, belt, spurs, and a Confederate pistol his brother had captured in the war. After putting up shades and curtains, Molly exclaimed: "[The cottage] suits me to perfection."

The dwelling's remote location, slightly off the main road that led to the Cornish and Mexican camps, agreed with Molly's inbred reserve. It pleased her to be living on the hill, she told Helena, "with no near neighbors to bother us," rather than at the Hacienda where the cottages were all in a row and "people can look into each other's back yards." On occasion she caught a glimpse of mule-drawn wagons on a distant curve of the winding road, but little of the mine's bustling traffic intruded on their solitude. "The place is as orderly as a military post," Molly concluded, "and as quiet from our remote perch as if every day were Sunday." Reflecting on this prized isolation, Molly demonstrated a talent for descriptive writing that would contribute to her success as a novelist:

> We are as much alone as if we were in a light-house. And it makes me think of that when we look out in front down the cliff where the valley lies below as level as the sea. And the mountains rising all around, some in shadow some in light. In the early morning the valley is like a great lake, filled with fog which rises in waves—rolling up—sometimes blown off in light drifts.

The grand vistas, the isolation, and her own enthusiasm led Molly to exclaim: "I never felt so *free* in my life."

As Molly wrote these words, she was unaware that Helena and Richard Gilder's infant daughter Marion had died a few days earlier. When Molly finally received word of this tragedy, she shared as much of Helena's pain as was humanly possible, trying to console her with words, but knowing that her efforts were inadequate. Molly's own happiness seemed a mockery. "Now I know what distance means," Molly wrote, "to think happy contented thoughts about you for days after your poor head was bowed so low—to mock you with my letters full of unconscious selfish joy—to ask you to sympathize in my happiness when if I had only known it the wave of your great trouble was coming, was almost here." She concluded: "I will not torture you with any more words—but darling if you knew the love and grief that is in my heart, I wouldn't need to speak."

As the weeks passed, Molly continued to grieve for her friend. She wrote sparingly (yet tenderly) of baby Marion but described in detail her life at New Almaden, hoping to distract Helena, if only momentarily, from her sorrow. Lizzie had assumed all the household chores, leaving Molly to spend her days as she wished. Most mornings she walked with Arthur to his office in the Cornish camp and then continued up the road to the Mexican settlement. They had lunch together at the cottage, and in the evenings after dinner they walked to the Cornish camp to collect their mail and then returned to watch the sunset on the piazza. Arthur sometimes relaxed in the evenings, stretched out on the lounge smoking his pipe and listening to Molly as she read aloud from some literary work. After years of bachelorhood, Arthur seemed to relish this new domesticity.

During the day, Molly often walked with her dog, Stranger, a gift from the widow of the former company physician, or worked in the dining room on the *Scarlet Letter* drawings. But as the long dry summer progressed, Molly grew increasingly homesick. She had found few congenial associates in New Almaden. By choosing to live on the hillside, she deliberately cut herself off from the Hacienda residents, especially the women, who might have shared her world view and provided companionship. Her position as wife of the resident engineer prevented any meaningful contact with either the Cornish or Mexican women. Her social outlets, therefore, were limited primarily to the handful of visiting engineers that Arthur brought to the cottage and to Mother Fall and Frank Hernandez, two new acquaintances she seemed to enjoy but rarely spent much time with. Within two months of reaching New Almaden, Molly expressed to Helena her sense of alienation: "I feel as if Arthur were the only human being here—all the rest of the world are beyond the valley."

And even though the landscape initially captured Molly's imagination, the vast distances, "brooding mountains," and unrelenting sunshine soon became oppressive. On September 14 she wrote: "Day after day there is the same unvarying brightness and calm. It is beautiful, for a long time it is wonderfully exhilarating but there comes a time when it makes one desperate. The sunshine seems like a thing one is doomed to instead of a blessing." Nor did she feel equal to sketching her surroundings. Her impressions were too new; the vast expanses discouraged her and seemed to require color rather than pencil to bring out their true dimensions. Still, by spring, when the *Scarlet Letter* drawings would be finished and the season "perfect for out door work," she hoped "to get something characteristic of this unique place."

To assuage her loneliness, Molly wrote long letters home and to Helena and other friends, including Charles de Kay. The letters she received in return reinforced her ties to the East and her self-perceived identity as an exile. With Helena, she exchanged opinions on stories and drawings published in *Scribner's* and on current literary works, such as George Eliot's recently published *Daniel Deronda*, which haunted Molly for days after she read it. She admired Eliot's writing, and confided to Helena, "I think I have never imagined such a triumph of words as the two scenes between Deronda and [Deronda's mother]. Genius can no further go!"

But it was to Arthur that Molly turned in her loneliness. Their love and affection for one another continued to grow. She never felt lonely in his presence; the few hours they spent together each day were like "the bread of life," but during the long hours apart, she confessed, "I know that I am lost." With keen insight into the human condition, she wrote: "Don't you know how we lose the sense of our own individuality when there is nothing to reflect it back upon us."

As often as possible, they spent Sundays together exploring the countryside, either on foot or on horseback. One Sunday they rode into the mountains behind the Mexican camp and had supper by the stream that trickled through the canyon. Molly carried with her a recent issue of *Scribner's*, and, with an artist's eye for striking contrasts, she later described for Helena how, in this "wild place," she and Arthur had pored over the artist Frank Lathrop's beautiful pictures and Richard Gilder's "Old Cabinet." On another occasion, Molly went with Arthur into the mine, finding her way through the corridors by torch light. "It was all so strange and weird—the voices of the miners and the sound of their hammers which came to us it seemed through the solid rock." Though she pined for the "dear ones" at home, Molly would make the most of her stay at New Almaden; she embraced new experiences, observed closely the life of the mine, and stored up incidents and impressions that would later be turned into published stories.

It is clear that the Footes had started a good marriage. They were tolerant and affectionate with one another. They had been raised in stimulating, intellectual environments and would respect the important work the other was doing. Arthur felt joy in Molly's presence. He accepted her friends, nurtured her artistic aspirations, and allowed her space in which to grow. Molly likewise encouraged Arthur's success. She entertained his associates, learned the technical aspects of his work, and provided emotional support and understanding. Strengthening the bond between them, Molly believed, was their shared belief that New Almaden was only a temporary stopping place. "We are always talking and planning about our home in the East," Molly wrote in October 1876.

But misunderstandings were inevitable. And in the years ahead Arthur's economic reversals would place severe strains on the marriage bonds. The historian Rodman Paul has observed that Arthur Foote had "many of the qualities that ordinarily made for success in a new country": imagination, drive, physical stamina, and skill with machines and subordinates. But for a variety of reasons—many of them beyond his control—Foote often was in financial difficulty. A misunderstanding of sorts, caused in part by Arthur's reluctance to make excuses for his actions, occurred right at the start of their marriage. And it might have remained a point of contention had the young couple been less generous and forgiving with one another.

The trouble started when Randol, the general manager, went back on his promise to refurbish the Footes' cottage at the company's expense. Left to complete the repairs on his own, Arthur fell short of money and asked his wife of four months to pay her own fare to California, neglecting to explain why his savings were depleted. Years later Molly observed: "It must have cut him to the quick—it cut her too." Young wives at this time, she recalled, "were humiliated by the necessity" of paying their own way. The incident, indeed, must have bruised Arthur's ego since masculine self-esteem had long been linked to economic success. To his credit, however, when later forced to rely on Molly's earnings as writer and illustrator, he did so seemingly without resentment.

Financial difficulties aside, Molly would always admire Arthur's drive and ambition, even when it meant long hours apart, as it did at New Almaden. As resident engineer, Arthur sometimes conducted long, tedious surveys in the mine's interior where the physical discomforts were severe: bad air, water up to his knees, and cramped spaces forcing him to work in a stooped position. He worked around the clock, up to twenty-four hours without rest, since the main business of the mine had to be halted (idling several hundred men) to assure that blasting and other vibrations would not jar his plumb lines. Arthur was puffed up with pride when the final survey was completed and the various parts of his year-long effort came together exactly right. In describing his success to Helena, Molly added: "He feels now equal to any emergency in underground engineering."

Molly's own spirits were improving as well. A week of blessed rain in late October 1876 heralded the end of the dry season. And more rain followed, "wild" storms, with sheets of rain pounding against the house and strong winds shaking the foundations. Molly called it a "delicious rainy time" and enjoyed it immensely. She also continued to work diligently on the *Scarlet Letter* drawings. About the time the rains came, she sent her first completed blocks to A.V. S. Anthony in Boston. Later she mailed off two more to Helena seeking her friend's advice since the subjects were the most difficult she had ever attempted. "As you love me," she pleaded, "you must try to judge honestly and tell me just what you think." Molly finished the last of the drawings for Hawthorne's masterpiece in the spring of 1877, prior to the birth of her first child.

In late November, she set aside her blocks for a Thanksgiving visit to the Hagues in San Francisco. The Footes traveled by stagecoach to San José, and Molly, seated on top of the stage, thoroughly enjoyed the ride through the morning fog. About dusk, the afternoon train brought them into the city, where James D. Hague met them at the depot with a carriage. A round of dinners and receptions followed, at which Molly and Arthur were introduced to Hague's professional friends—engineers and geologists and successful investors in mines. Eastern-born and eastern or European-trained, they formed an elite group of "professional exiles," as Molly called them: bright, talented, cultivated, and well-traveled. They had "lived everywhere" and felt no particular attachment to any one place. Their wives were also from the East, "very charming women, well-bred, gentle, and very adaptable. . . . They would go anywhere in the world where their husbands [*sic*] businesses made it necessary, and make a home." Molly felt a special bond with the women, for they easily shared their stories of homesickness. But she almost cried when they spoke of their inability to truly go home again. They told her: "*We* do not forget . . . but *they* have no place for us when we return. We must be reconciled[,] for what we left behind us can never be ours again. We have lost our life in the East. We must make a new life for ourselves here." Fearful that this fate also awaited her, Molly sought reassurance from Helena: "I do not feel that any links have loosened so far, do you?"

For Molly, the trip to the city was invigorating. A fast-paced morning carriage ride on the beach below the Cliff House thrilled her; and she enjoyed the shopping trips to Mexican and Japanese stores. The people she met were stimulating—the type, she believed, that made desirable friends. Most memorable, however, was Thanksgiving morning when, during a church service, she felt for the first time the throbbing pulse of her unborn child.

Molly had become pregnant soon after reaching New Almaden but delayed telling Helena for several months to allow time for her friend to heal. Helena had been three-months' pregnant with her second child Rodman when the first had died; the thought that this "new life" in some way contributed to Marion's death had deepened her sorrow. On December 7, in a long letter describing her trip to San Francisco, Molly gently broke the news. "I hardly dare tell you one thing which the future holds for us, lest I may trouble you," she wrote. "Dont let it—I pray you for it has long since ceased to be anything but a happy though tremulous hope with me. . . . A child is coming to us."

She was "dismayed at first," since she and Arthur had taken "precautions," probably adopting the rhythm method of birth control. "The Doctor says change of climate alters everything. This feeling reconciled me at first, because it was simply inevitable. There was nothing to regret or to wish undone and I began to feel awed at this mystery of Nature which quietly sets aside our futile plans and carries out her own laws in spite of resistance."

Pregnancy for Molly was both a mystery and a miracle, but like many other women she would approach childbirth with dread. Although she must have believed that giving birth was a natural experience, she also knew about the pain and risks involved. She later called the day she gave birth to Arthur, Jr., "Dies Irae," the Day of Judgment. Still, when she announced her pregnancy, she did so with optimism. Sister Bessie and sister-in-law Sarah were sending their surplus baby clothes so that Molly could forgo sewing and concentrate on her blocks. Dr. MacPherson, a friend of Arthur's from the Sutro Tunnel days and now resident physician at the nearby Guadeloupe mine, would oversee the delivery.

But Molly was not leaving future pregnancies to chance. While visiting the Hagues, her sister-in-law told her of a "sure way of limiting one's family," and Molly offered to share this information with Helena, should she have "any miserable uncertainty" about the matter. It was clear to Molly that nature's method of birth control was unreliable. Nineteenth-century women rarely discussed their pregnancies or methods of birth control in their correspondence. Even Molly was fastidious when she introduced the topic of birth control to her best friend: "It is a delicate thing to speak of in a letter," she began. But shortly after Helena gave birth to Rodman, on January 8, 1877, Molly conveyed Mary Hague's advice: the husband must purchase shields (or condoms) from a physician or a first-class druggist. These provided a perfectly safe and sure way to prevent pregnancies, Molly assured Helena, even though they sounded "perfectly revolting."

Molly resumed work on her *Scarlet Letter* blocks after she returned from the city. The brief respite had given her time to reconsider Richard Gilder's offer, which she earlier had declined, to write and illustrate an essay on New Almaden for publication in *Scribner's*. This was to be a turning point in Molly's life. Although she began the project with great diffidence, its successful completion gave her the confidence to continue writing. Before many years had elapsed, Mary Hallock Foote would be recognized as one of the best western author-illustrators in the nation.

Molly already had published a short story for children, "The Picture in the Fire-place Bedroom," in *St. Nicholas Magazine* (1875). But, as she told Richard and Helena, "it is a very different thing doing a child's story for St. Nick and solemnly appearing in the Scribner, where such men as Richard, Nadal, Charley [de Kay], not to speak of older reputations have written real substantial thoughts." She was eager to provide sketches of New Almaden but felt that her writing would disappoint Richard. In December, however, she began "to write out some of the things about Almaden which have impressed me most." About two months later, she sent this material to Richard with the admonition that he must read it as if it were a schoolgirl's composition. She trusted Richard's judgment and his candor; nothing he or Helena might say about her work, she assured him, could possibly hurt her. Besides, if not acceptable for *Scribner's*, she playfully noted, "I will send it to Mother and *she* will think it *perfect!*"

Molly was elated by Richard and Helena's response but begged them to read her essay again more critically before making a final decision. She would make the sketches of New Almaden whether or not they were published, beginning just as soon as she could "get around" after the baby came. It was midsummer, however, before Molly began drawing again, and she was to send the last Almaden block to Richard in October 1877, after the Footes had severed their connection with the mine.

"A California Mining Camp" appeared in the February 1878 issue of *Scribner's*, accompanied by fourteen of Molly's drawings. The engravings by Henry Marsh, one of the magazine's foremost engravers, pleased her, as did the generous payment of $300. But she felt all along that Helena deserved as much credit as she did, for in editing Molly's work, Helena had inserted long paragraphs from her letters, making the essay more vivid and personal. Before she left New Almaden, Molly acknowledged her debt in a letter to Richard: "If anything comes of all this smoke I hope Helena will consider that the article is mainly her work. I ought not to be paid certainly for more than half, and am not entitled to that since it could not have been used without Helena's editing."

The New Almaden essay is a first-person account of the author's year-long stay in a western mining camp, with the passage of the seasons forming a backdrop against which she portrays the mine's "curious mixture of races." The opening paragraphs, which depict the exotic underground world of the miners, draw the reader into the story. The author then deftly sketches the multi-tiered social structure of the mine. The ability to walk freely through the Mexican and Cornish camps had given Molly knowledge of both settlements, but the Spanish-speaking residents seemed to fascinate her the most. She had peppered her letters to Helena with descriptions of Mexican wood-packers, water carriers, and bread deliverers and with detailed accounts of a Mexican ball and her encounters with the camp's more colorful personalities. These were the very passages, often verbatim, that Helena wove into the published article. Molly wrote admiringly to Helena, for example, of the "graceful, dark-eyed" Sambroña sisters, to whom she had recently been introduced. "Their soft voices and movements and a kind of slow, gentle self-possession, made me feel my own manners crude and angular by comparison." These same words appear in the published essay, although "manners" has been changed to "manner."

Christmas week in New Almaden, which Molly described both in letters to Helena and in the essay, reinforced her sense of living in exile. The weather contrasted sharply with what she had grown accustomed to in Milton, the days so warm, she wrote, that "I am sitting on the piazza—with broad sun hat and a gown I wear in June." She was also introduced to the Cornish tradition of caroling, when schoolchildren stopped at the Foote cottage on Christmas night to sing Christmas hymns. Molly invited the youngsters in for refreshments, and then after a final song they went away, leaving her "in a sort of bewilderment as to whether it were not all imagination." It was, she told Helena, "unlike one's idea of a mining camp." An older group's singing of the Messiah chorus the next evening deeply moved the young artist. These singers were treated to the cake and other "Christmas goodies" that Mother Fall had sent to the Footes earlier in the day. Later, alone and seated by the fire, Molly and Arthur "grinned at each other" as they surveyed the remains of their Christmas "treat." "But I wouldn't have missed it for anything," Molly exclaimed. "It was part of the experience."

The following weeks found Molly in good health and good spirits as she prepared for the birth of her first child. "Everybody is kinder than ever," she wrote in January. Mrs. Randol, the general manager's wife, had sent bunches of violets, roses, and heliotrope; but the other ladies, Molly believed, "are sorry for me, not knowing that I am happy and not afraid." Mary Hague came for a brief visit in February to give advice and comfort. And shortly thereafter Molly learned with great relief that her Milton family had located a young woman of excellent background, Marian Coggeshall, who would join the Footes in New Almaden to nurse Molly during the delivery and to care for the baby afterward.

As the spring of 1877 progressed, Molly took long walks over the hills to gather wildflowers, but she stopped going into the Mexican camp, not wanting to be "conspicuous."About three weeks before her confinement, the Footes had an unexpected five-day visit from Georgiana Bruce Kirby, a friend of Molly's Aunt Sarah Hallock. In her youth, Kirby had lived at Brook Farm, the famous cooperative colony in Massachusetts, where she met Margaret Fuller and other transcendentalists. She went to California in 1850 to join her friend Eliza W. B. Farnham, and together they farmed and built a house at Santa Cruz. Both before and after her marriage, Kirby was "passionately devoted to *causes*": abolition, education, women's rights, and women's health. Residents in Santa Cruz and New Almaden now regarded her as an "institution." Mrs. Randol, in fact, called on Mrs. Kirby at the Footes' on the afternoon of her arrival, and Mr. Randol came to lunch two days later. The conversation on both occasions had been brilliant. Arthur and Mrs. Kirby "contradicted each other with great freshness and vigor," Molly reported. But the visit left the expectant mother "very tired," in part because it had been so long since she had "listened to such a torrent of earnest, brilliant, *queer* talk as Mrs. K. had poured out during these few days."

Marian Coggeshall arrived shortly after Mrs. Kirby departed. The anxiety that Molly had felt about a refined young woman performing a servant's role quickly dissipated in the presence of Marian's "cheerful good sense." Early Sunday morning, April 29, 1877, with Dr. MacPherson in attendance, Molly gave birth to an eleven-pound boy. It had not been an easy birth. To Helena, Molly later confided: "It was a long dreadful day and night . . . a kind of dim bewildering Hell of pain all day—growing worse and worse and then came Heaven at last." In letters to family and friends written on April 29,

Arthur captured Molly's mood once the ordeal was over: "Arthur Burling Foote . . . is sleeping quietly by the side of his mother who says that she is 'ridiculously well' and too happy to be comfortable."

Because of medical complications, however, Molly did not fully regain her strength until midsummer. During this "dismal time," a carriage ride with Mrs. Randol had left her feeling so miserable that "I could have cried," she told Helena. "And remembering how gayly [she and Arthur] rode together over the great bare hills—thinking of the Sundays when I tramped with Arthur following the steepest trails without flagging a step, I thought to myself I can never be a *comrade* any more."

But on July 4, in a letter filled with details about the baby, Molly assured Helena that she was perfectly well. "There is nothing left of all my miseries but a little lack of strength which I suppose comes of nursing a hearty boy." Both parents "doted" on Arthur, Jr., frequently called "Boykin" by his mother, following Helena's habit of addressing Molly as "Mollikins." Molly's mother-love is unmistakable. "I miss him while he takes his long naps," she wrote, "and am so glad to get him in my arms again and see his smile. He smiles all the time and looks at me in a way that makes me quite wild with delight." She soon resumed her morning outdoor sketching forays, accompanied by Marian wheeling the baby in a pram and a "little caddie" carrying her sketching stool and big white umbrella.

In August 1877 Arthur Foote submitted his resignation to the Quicksilver Mining Company, finally fed up with Randol's tyrannical style of management. Molly understood Arthur's frustrations and shared his views. Over the months, she had described for Helena and Richard the terrible conditions under which the miners worked. Discipline was rigid, and the company stores, which were leased to proprietors, charged such exorbitant prices that the poorest miners were kept in peonage. Randol had some agreeable qualities, Molly admitted, and Mrs. Randol "was one of the lovely women of the

West." But working at New Almaden was killing her husband's spirit: he either had to "toady" to the manager or be crushed. It was useless to make public their complaints, Molly believed, because Randol's eastern backers viewed him as a good manager and the miners feared to speak out. Because of these factors, some modern writers picture Randol more as a benevolent autocrat than as the petty tyrant who appears in Molly's letters.

In mid-September the Footes left New Almaden for Santa Cruz, a seaside resort situated on the north side of Monterey Bay, which appealed to Molly as a temporary residence while Arthur was in San Francisco looking for work. Lodging was cheaper here than in San Francisco, and the fresh sea breeze was exactly what she wanted for her baby. Aware also that friends in San Francisco, including Mary Hague, had thought Arthur's resignation was unwise, Molly preferred the anonymity of this tiny seaside hamlet to the solicitous inquiries she faced in the city.

Molly had consulted Mrs. Kirby about a place to stay in Santa Cruz and a new position for Lizzie Griffen. In an arrangement that gave satisfaction to all, Lizzie went to work for a bachelor "milk rancher" a few miles outside of town, and within a year or two they were married. Molly, baby Arthur, and Marian Coggeshall began boarding with Mr. and Mrs. J. M. Cutler in a house perched on the lofty terrace that overlooked the town and the surf.

Molly's six-month-stay in Santa Cruz was a time of waiting and uncertainty, when her emotions seemed to be on a roller coaster. "I am fearfully down or else soaring," she confided to Helena. Arthur was away much of the time so that she was more alone than she had ever been in New Almaden. She was often afraid and in low spirits when he stayed in the city, but she felt like a girl again when he reappeared in Santa Cruz and together they explored the local scenes. One day they went to the bathing beach and then walked hand in hand across a high trestle bridge. "It was scary for the wind wrapped my skirts round my ankles and tossed my hat about, but I liked it."

Shortly after moving the family to Santa Cruz, Arthur began experimenting with a means of manufacturing hydraulic cement from local materials. He had no gainful employment when he started, but after about six weeks he perfected a formula that worked. Only after she could announce Arthur's triumph, however, did Molly reveal how afraid she had been that he would fail. "It was hard—those six weeks while Arthur was away and we did not know what was before us in the future. He made about a hundred trials—different combinations, subjected to different treatment, before the right chemical equation resulted in cement."

Molly was thrilled by Arthur's success. Not only would it mean a steady income, but it now also seemed possible to establish a home again, remain stationary while Arthur developed his cement works without having to traipse from one engineering job to another. Years later she recalled: "I wanted a safe place to hide my offspring in, a hole or burrow of some sort where I could stay and watch it. The spirit of adventure was dead in me for the time."

A home in Santa Cruz *did* seem possible, even though in the end Molly's hopes were dashed. Capitalists in San Francisco showed a keen interest in Arthur's discovery, since the large quantities of hydraulic cement used in California had to be imported from England. Arthur planned to organize a company with the backing of these investors and then serve as superintendent of the cement works. The Footes now talked of a ten-year stay in the West before establishing a permanent home in the East. They consequently spent time, when Arthur could spare it, exploring the coastline near Santa Cruz, searching for a site on which to build, finally locating a lovely spot on a peninsula about three miles from town. Here they would have "noble company," Molly wrote enthusiastically, "the mountains and sky and sea and all the wild birds with their cries, and winds and the booming of the surf." Later, still optimistic, she told Helena: "If we are to give up all our friends and kindred, we may as well repay ourselves richly as far as beauty goes."

But the wait continued as capitalists were slow to commit themselves to Arthur's enterprise. He spent Thanksgiving and Christmas alone in San Francisco, where he had found temporary work to help refill the family coffers. Molly's own earnings from the *Scribner's* article and the *Scarlet Letter* drawings paid for her and Marian's room and board at the Cutlers. No longer the naive young bride embarrassed at paying her own way, she now confided to Helena: "I shall never grumble about *blocks* any more for they have . . . helped us through our 'tight place.' It makes me so proud—and to show you how completely we are one in our work in everything—Arthur has given up his pride of refusing me my privilege of being a '*helpmeet.*'"

But the prolonged uncertainty about the company's fate added to the strain Molly felt when Arthur was in San Francisco. Not even her mother-love for baby Arthur was sufficient to raise her spirits very much. Moreover, the baby was cutting teeth, which kept him fretful at nights, and Molly was feeling the "strain of nursing him much more than at first." Looking back on this time, Marian Coggeshall observed that Molly only really seemed to enjoy the baby when his father was around. And Molly thought this probably had been true because she had missed Arthur so much and was constantly under strain. She was also aware, however, that the strain might have been much worse had it not been for Marian Coggeshall. In Molly's eyes, Marian was a woman "as good as gold," for she washed and dressed the baby each morning, took him on outings, and attended to many of Molly's errands.

In mid-nineteenth century America, hiring servants to perform domestic chores was a sign of middle-class success. By 1870 as many as one in eight families may have employed domestic help. It is not surprising, therefore, that Molly and Arthur, who were both raised in genteel households, viewed servants as a necessity, even when financially hard pressed, as they were at Santa Cruz and later in Idaho. Mary Hague held similar views. She "has lots of help and believes in it," Molly reported after a visit to her sister-in-law's. "So do I," Molly continued, "I am not going to economize on servants." Domestic helpers not only reinforced the class rank of the Footes and the Hagues, but the tasks they performed allowed Molly time for her artistic pursuits. Acknowledging both her duty as a mother and her privileged status, Molly wrote to Helena from Santa Cruz: "A Mother is nothing but a slave for the first two years—that time belongs to baby—if there are a few chinks to be filled up lets be thankful we dont have to fill them with *sewing* and cooking!"

Even with hired help and a supportive spouse, however, it was exceedingly difficult for Molly to balance family and career, just as it was for other women artists. Moreover, the conflict that she experienced between her duties as wife and mother and her creative instincts contributed to a deep-seated ambivalence about her drawings. She often denied that her work was "art," preferring to call it "an industry," since she specialized in commercial illustrations; "true art" described Helena's work in oils and water colors. Molly consistently wrote of her own talent in a self-deprecating manner. At Santa Cruz, after accepting a commission to illustrate a serial for *Scribner's*, she wrote to Richard Gilder: "I am not an artist in the true sense, but there is much to enjoy and be grateful for in my work as it is. I am only sometimes tired of being always just on the border line of better things—near enough to look across and yet impossible to get over." A few weeks later, she wrote to Helena: "As for art, I haven't a dream left in that direction. I shall draw on wood as long as anybody wants my work and I shall do my very best in that way, but that isn't art." Molly wrestled with her artistic insecurities for the rest of her life. At the end of her career, she was to write: "My best work was mere approximation to anything like Art. If to begin was excitement and fresh hope, to finish was disappointment that often verged on despair. But one could always try again."

In her modesty and uncertainty about her talent, Foote was typical of many creative women of her era who entered the marketplace. Mary Kelley found in her 1984 study of early nineteenth-century women writers that best-selling novelists, such as Sara Parton, Catharine Maria Sedgwick, and E.D.E.N. Southworth, questioned their own legitimacy as writers because their public literary careers were at odds with traditional feminine roles.

Denying that she was an artist "in the true sense," however, did not make Mary Hallock Foote less of one. By the time she took up residence in Santa Cruz, Molly already had received much acclaim as an artist. In the three major publications that she helped illustrate before she moved west, *The Hanging of the Crane*, *Mabel Martin*, and *The Skeleton in Armor*, Mary A. Hallock was listed as "artist." And the contemporary reviewers who lauded her work also accorded her that title. Michele Bogart observes, in her study of commercial art (1995), that in the last third of the nineteenth century, when the "Golden Age" of American illustration was under way, artists like John La Farge and Winslow Homer "had notable success in elevating the reputation of illustration from the level of a craft to that of a fine art." Although Bogart does not mention Foote in her study, Molly's superior work must have helped to cement this status for commercial illustration.

Moreover, Molly's drawings, which regularly appeared in *Scribner's* during the 1870s, were among the woodcut illustrations that helped establish that journal's reputation as one of the "best general magazines in the world." A huge chunk of the journal's budget, in fact, went into the substantial commissions paid to illustrators. Gilder had recognized Molly's talent soon after he became assistant editor at *Scribner's* and often hired her to illustrate the work of noted authors. In his review of *Mabel Martin* appearing in the December 1875 issue of *Scribner's*, Gilder not only praised Molly's drawings but wrote of her as "an artist whose figure subjects drawn on the wood are, after Mr. La Farge's, the best that are now being made in this country."

What made Foote exceptional as an artist, practically from the beginning of her career? Most critics found it difficult to single out any one special quality, but her drawings repeatedly were praised for their sentiment, their delicate execution, their strength and vigor, and their fine attention to detail: in other words, she exhibited an "indefinable quality [that] is peculiarly hers." The story is told of the artist Edwin Austin Abbey (who greatly admired Foote's illustrations) that when asked why he continued to fuss with a drawing that appeared to be finished, he replied "I'm trying to get the feeling that Mary Hallock Foote puts into her work—and I can't!"

Later in life, Molly on occasion overcame her insecurities and accepted the artist's mantle. At age fifty-seven, for example, looking back on her days as a new mother, she recalled the difficulty of being a "mother faithfully" and doing "one's work as an artist also faithfully." And still later, in her reminiscences, she refers to herself at New Almaden as the "artist-wife." But whether or not she called herself a bona fide artist, Molly was always a diligent worker, as committed to achieving excellence as any other professional artist. Even in the stressful Santa Cruz period, when she felt isolated both as a woman and an artist, Molly's ambitions were evident. Although the money she received from her work was now more crucial than ever before, she accepted new commissions primarily because of the satisfaction she felt when creating visual images to accompany a story or poem.

Molly, in fact, worked on several projects while in Santa Cruz, both for *Scribner's* and for *St. Nicholas Magazine*, including a series of drawings for Louisa M. Alcott's "Under the Lilacs," which appeared in the latter magazine December 1877 through October 1878. She also wrote and illustrated her second children's story, "How Mandy Went Rowing with the 'Cap'n'" (*St. Nicholas*, May 1878).

Like most other artists, Molly was elated by her successes and dismayed by her failures. When the new edition of Hawthorne's *The Scarlet Letter* was released in late 1877, Foote's drawings received mixed reviews. Writing in the *Atlantic Monthly*, William Dean Howells singled out several for special praise, including one of Hester Prynne with baby in arms walking through the forest, the same drawing that William J. Linton later included in his history of wood engraving in the United States. Howells judged that another drawing was "as yet quite unapproached in power by anything in American illustrative art." But he also pointed to several drawings that were "not so good." And the reviewer for *Appleton's Journal* concluded that, although Foote's illustrations were excellent, they failed to convey the spirit of Hawthorne's story.

Molly was "bitterly disappointed" when she finally saw her drawings in the new publication. "The Scarlet Letter was a blow," she wrote to Richard from Santa Cruz. "It looks so poor and mean." Even Arthur, who had thought the *Scarlet Letter* illustrations the best Molly had ever done, called the engravings "cheap and wooden." Some critics blamed the engraver, A.V. S. Anthony, for the poor quality of the published drawings. But Molly refused to place the blame on the engraver, telling Helena that "I'd rather have no reputation as an artist, than get it by criticism of those by whom my work is interpreted." Still, she wished that she could ignore the public and its critical reviews. "It is lovely to work—one couldn't help doing that but the moment the public comes in question begins the miserable part." On a lighter note, she concluded: "When we get to be old women we will paint for those who care for what we do and for them only."

Even while lamenting the poor quality of her published drawings, however, Molly took pleasure in how well Henry Marsh had engraved her illustration for H. H. Boyesen's Christmas ballad, which appeared in the January 1878 issue of *Scribner's*. And she and Arthur both were delighted with the February issue, which contained her composition on New Almaden, as well as a poem by Richard Gilder (accompanied by Helena's decorative oak leaves) and pieces by Charles de Kay and the naturalist John Burroughs, whom Molly much admired. "Think what you do for us out here, " she wrote with enthusiasm to Richard, "sending all that beauty and *soul work* across the continent." Commenting on her own contribution, she wrote: "Arthur is so happy over the Almaden article that I almost believe it myself to have been worth while—apart from the money and the diary it will be to us personally of our first home."

By the time her article appeared in *Scribner's*, Molly had submitted to Richard several pages of a travel piece on Santa Cruz. She hoped to make it superior to the Almaden article, but she begged Richard not to "coach" her through the second essay. "If I can not make it satisfactory myself, let it go," she admonished her friend. "You have not time or strength to spare in making a [magazine] writer of me." With Gilder's encouragement, Molly revised portions of the manuscript and completed at least ten drawings to accompany it.

"A Sea-Port on the Pacific," by Mary Hallock Foote, appeared as the lead article in the August 1878 issue of *Scribner's*. The essay opens with a description of the sandstone cliffs rising high above the sea and of the lighthouse that Molly visited with Mrs. Kirby soon after moving to Santa Cruz. As tour guide, Molly accompanies the reader along the beaches, through the lower town, and up the wooden stairway leading to the upper terraces. She frequently compares the local scene and climate with what she has known in the East. She also investigates local history, which she virtually ignored in the Almaden article, writing about the early Spanish explorers who visited the coast and the old Catholic mission. As in the first essay, Foote focuses on the town's diverse population, calling it "a heterogenous mass of transplanted life growing and blooming together," a statement that applies equally well to both the people and the vegetation. The most effective passages describe her visit to the priests' garden adjacent to the ruins of the mission, where she often went to sketch while Marian Coggeshall watched over the baby in his carriage. In the final paragraph, Molly suggests that there is more to California than "the sensational side" that one finds "in the Yo Semite guidebooks and the literature of Bret Harte."

Molly read the final proofs for the Santa Cruz article in Milton, where she had returned in late March 1878 following the collapse of Arthur's cement venture. She and the baby had traveled across the continent with the Hagues and their two children, who were en route to Europe where James was to serve as commissioner of mines for the Paris Exposition. Marian Coggeshall, who chose to remain in California, later went to Hawaii and married a widower with a large family. Arthur Foote, in search of a steady income, traveled to the Black Hills in Dakota Territory, where quartz mining required the skills of trained engineers. Placer gold had caused miners to swarm to the region in 1875–76, but investors soon turned their attention to lode claims. Foote went to work for George Hearst, the great mining magnate, who was part owner of the Homestake mine, destined to become, in the words of Rodman Paul, "one of the greatest gold quartz mines in the world."

Thus began a thirteen-month separation for the Footes, a time of great productivity for the artist-writer, secure in the warmth of the Hallock household, although she was to miss Arthur "terribly." They wrote to each other regularly, sometimes twice a week. Molly's letters have not survived, but the handful of Arthur's extant missives indicate that he too was lonely. He wrote in a light vein about the harsh conditions he found in Deadwood, the chief mining camp in the northern Black Hills, but he often expressed a deep longing for his wife. In June he wrote: "It seems as if I would give up every thing in the world to lie with my head in your lap and your hands stroking me." He signed this letter: "Your big loving boy, Arthur."

Later in the fall, Molly wrote to Helena that Arthur "in a moment of weakness as he said" begged her to come to Deadwood. In fact, at the time the Footes left California, Molly had planned to join Arthur after a long visit to Milton, but "the wise ones" in her household convinced her that it was foolish to travel west so late in the year. So, despite her husband's plea, she stayed in Milton. Foote soon severed connections with George Hearst, however, refusing to give false testimony for the millionaire in a lawsuit. Before year's end Arthur was in Colorado where development of the Leadville silver mines was in full swing.

Molly found it "sweet and natural" to be home again, "listening to the home talk round the table, with Phil's practicing [on the piano] filling the pauses." She quickly arranged a visit with Helena (the first of several such visits), carrying her blocks and sketches to the Studio and leaving little Arthur with his grandmother. A short time later, Helena arrived in Milton with baby Rodman, and the two friends relived their girlhood with a moonlight row up the river. For part of the spring and summer, the women coped with childhood illnesses, which kept Helena away from Milton for fear that Rodman would fall ill again.

Despite these and other distractions, Molly turned out an amazing amount of work during her stay at Milton. Several factors no doubt contributed to her productivity, including a renewed sense of well-being and unlimited help in caring for the baby. Then, too, reentry into the Gilders' intellectual world must have been exhilarating. The three friends would have discussed the latest visitors to the Studio, recent activities of the Art Students' League and the Society of American Artists (both of which Helena had helped to found), and publication of Richard's second book of poetry, *The Poet and His Master* (1878). These discussions, coupled with intimate talks with Helena, must have boosted Molly's confidence.

During these thirteen months, Molly completed several commissions for *Scribner's*, including two illustrations for Josiah G. Holland's poem, "The Puritan's Guest" (1878), several for John Burroughs's essays, "Picturesque Aspects of Life in New York" (1878) and "The Pastoral Bees" (1879), and one for Charles de Kay's piece on the Polish actress, Helena Modjeska (1879). She also wrote a children's story based on the Almaden days, "A 'Muchacho' of the Mexican Camp," which was published in *St. Nicholas Magazine* in 1878, and a short descriptive account of the ball she attended there, "The Cascarone Ball," which appeared in *Scribner's* the following year.

Molly's first works of mature fiction also date from this period. Success with the Almaden and Santa Cruz travel pieces encouraged her to experiment with her writing. She probably started "In Exile," her first adult short story (although not the first to be published) about the time she finished the Santa Cruz article. Still uncertain of her creative talents, she submitted this story to William Dean Howells, editor of the *Atlantic Monthly*, for an honest appraisal, as she feared that Richard and Helena's opinion would be biased. Molly later recalled the story's fate:

> When Mr. Howells took my first story, he had complained in his charming way that it was "too wantonly sad" (one never forgets the words of a first "acceptance"). Keen to win his entire approval, I set to work and added a second part ending in happiness and the rains! As at first written it was a dry-season episode, breaking off on a minor key as such an episode would in a place like New Almaden. He took the second part, rather gloomily—he said it was "good, but not as good as the first part."

Although not published until 1881, "In Exile" contains many themes that are common in Foote's early stories: sacrifices an eastern woman faces when moving west, a romantic plot involving a young mining engineer, comparisons between eastern and western society, and easterners perceived as exiles in the West. Like much of her later fiction, "In Exile" is based on the author's personal experiences. She writes about places she knows and incorporates small details about real people and events, all of which give her stories a ring of authenticity.

It is Foote's accuracy in describing local scenes and characters, in fact, that places her squarely in the local color movement, which dominated American literature between the Civil War and the end of the century. Local color writers emphasized the colorful inhabitants and peculiarities of a particular American place. They paid attention to dialect speech and to local lore and incidents. In the West, Bret Harte and Mark Twain led the way, with their humorous and satirical tales about California and Nevada mining camps and other western locales. Unlike Harte and Twain, however, Mary Hallock Foote eschewed humor in her early work and injected more realism into her western scenes than is found in such celebrated tales as Harte's "The Luck of Roaring Camp" (1868) and "The Outcasts of Poker Flat" (1869) and Twain's *Roughing It* (1872).

"In Exile" takes place in a California mining camp, where a mining engineer by the name of Arnold has worked two years to accumulate the means to bring his fiancée to join him. During a chance encounter with the camp's attractive eastern schoolteacher, Frances Newell, he muses about the propriety of uprooting an eastern woman from her associations: "You know most women require a background of family and friends and congenial surroundings; the question is whether *any* woman can do without them." Can an eastern woman be happy in the West? he asks the schoolteacher. Her response might well have been Molly's: "It is the kind of place a happy woman might be very happy in; but if she were sad—or disappointed—she would die of it!" Arnold and Newell are attracted to each other. But their relationship is not resolved until Arnold's sweetheart refuses to join him. The story ends with the rains breaking a seven-month drought and Arnold and Newell happily married.

Molly's second short story, "Friend Barton's 'Concern'" (*Scribner's*, 1879), is situated in the Hudson River Valley, a locale she knew better than any other, and showcases her talent for descriptive writing. Quaker Thomas Barton's "concern" is whether or not in the year 1812 he must leave an invalid wife and children to preach God's word. The romantic plot involves Walter Evesham, a young neighbor who rents Barton's mill pond while the Quaker is away, and Barton's nineteen-year-old daughter Dorothy. A string of misfortunes—the flooding of the mill pond, the loss of sheep, and a ferocious rainstorm—throw the young people together. When Barton returns, he finds that Evesham and Dorothy are in love, and, although it is against his convictions, he consents to their marriage.

The story holds the reader's interest because of Foote's close attention to detail. She vividly describes the rural scene and creates a believable strong-willed young Quaker woman, who breaks with tradition by falling in love with a non-Quaker. Arthur Foote called this "a sweet healthy story," but it shocked Molly's two elderly cousins, the author later confessed, because of its "exploitation in print of the faith of our common ancestors."

Molly referred to her third piece of fiction, "A Story of the Dry Season" (*Scribner's*, 1879), as her "Santa Cruz" story because San Miguel, where the action takes place, is the exact replica of the seaside resort she stayed in. The dry season (Molly's metaphor for human longing and suffering) finds young Dr. Benedict and Gertrude Ellison nursing the Ellison baby through a deadly fever. Benedict becomes infatuated with the unsuspecting young mother, whose husband is away at the Nevada mines. Ellison returns, however, and correctly assesses the situation. Gertrude plans to accompany her husband on his return to Nevada but asks the doctor if it is now safe to travel with the baby. She is dismayed when he replies, only "at the risk of [the baby's] life." In anguish, Gertrude remains in California while her husband leaves without her. But when the rains come, the doctor's conscience gets the better of him—he confesses that the child can go "with perfect safety." Gertrude rejoins her husband, and Benedict professes his love for a young Spanish-speaking woman he had earlier befriended.

In this story, Molly writes convincingly of the California landscape, the baby's illness, and Gertrude Ellison's vigil at crib side—all directly related to her own experiences. About the time she wrote this tale, in fact, Molly was nursing little Arthur through a serious crisis and was pondering the risks of taking him to Colorado. But Foote's portrayal of Ellison's reaction to Benedict and the doctor's love for the Hispanic woman is less successful.

Molly's fears that readers would perceive this story as autobiographical may have limited her ability to fully develop the love triangle. She had considered publishing under a pseudonym, but Arthur argued against doing so. If she used a pseudonym, she concluded, "those who can guess at the authorship will think it *is* personal or I wouldn't conceal my name." Writing from Leadville, where she had joined Arthur before the story was published, Molly expressed her concerns to family members in Milton:

> I also have a confession to make. I read my "Story of the Dry Season" as I called it (the Santa Cruz story) to Arthur. He said he didn't think it was personal at all and that he should have no hesitation in publishing it. We were then rather low in our minds about money—and the temptation was too great. I was having chills and was as I said low about my own chances of working—so I packed it off to Scribby. The result was this note and a check for $150, which I enclose.

When Arthur Foote left Deadwood in December 1878, he joined the flood of humanity making its way to Leadville, a mining camp in the Rocky Mountains about 10,000 feet in elevation. The camp had been founded on the site of worked-over gold placer diggings and was nothing more than a collection of crude huts and about two hundred transients when the silver boom began in 1877. Within three years the population had soared to nearly fifteen thousand.

Foote's first job in Colorado was as expert witness in a well-publicized court case held in Denver. His well-prepared testimony, based on two months' work making maps, surveys, and a glass model of a Leadville mine, helped win the case. As work continued to flow in, Arthur made money "hand over fist." But both Molly and Arthur felt the strain of their long separation. As the spring of 1879 approached, Molly made plans to join Arthur and to leave their son in the care of the Hallock women, since everyone seemed to agree that a mining camp was no place for a baby.

In February or early March, Molly made a final visit to the Studio before Richard and Helena left on a year-long tour of Europe. But five days before her own scheduled departure for Leadville, little Arthur fell critically ill with malaria. For five days and nights his fever averaged 103 degrees. Bessie stood watch with Molly through the long ordeal and helped administer to the feverish boy a tablespoon of milk every two hours and quinine dissolved in water every four hours. Only after the danger was over did Molly write of her fears to Helena: "I have had in this last week the keenest suffering that life has brought me yet—for the truth is in spite of all the Doctor said and every one else, I thought I should lose him."

After the child's recovery, Molly boarded a train in late April and headed west a second time for a reunion with her husband. On this occasion, she left behind a two-year-old son whom she would not see again for approximately six months. But as on her first journey west, she carried with her a commission for illustrations. During her son's illness, she had been asked by Robert Underwood Johnson, an editor at *Scribner's*, to cooperate with Ernest Ingersoll, who was to write a travel piece on Leadville. Sick with worry at the time, Molly nonetheless acknowledged Johnson's request. "Your letter would have given me a great deal of pleasure," she wrote, " if my little boy's illness did not absorb me just now—too much to think whether I am glad about anything or not." Still, she would be "very glad" to provide drawings *if* she went to Colorado.

On April 30, Arthur met Molly's train in Denver, where he insisted they spend a night or two at the American House to allow her time to rest. The city itself was "not very impressive," Molly wrote to her mother, but the mountains made an impact: "The Snowy range rises out of the plains as if we looked across the sea to a range of mountains lying along the horizon."

In her first letter to Helena from Leadville, dated May 12, 1879, Molly gave a vivid account of their journey west from Denver. They traveled the first seventy miles by rail to Webster, with the tracks at times running beside a swift-flowing mountain stream and making "endless sharp curves round the spurs of the mountain." They covered the remaining one hundred miles in a rented two-horse carriage. The road from Webster, which wound upward through pine forests to South Park, had been so badly rutted by heavily loaded freighters that travel was difficult. Molly, in fact, had joined the silver rush to the

Rockies. During the spring and early summer of 1879, nearly fifty freight wagons a day rolled into Leadville, as well as one hundred new residents. "Everyone was going there!" Molly exclaimed.

The artist was awed by her surroundings. South Park was magnificent—"a glorious sweep of rolling hills" and in the distance "the Snowy Range—awful, beautiful, unreal!" At dark the Footes reached Fairplay, where they spent the night, and the next day they made the arduous trip over the Mosquito Range, by way of Weston Pass. Sometime before noon one horse fell ill with "lung fever." Then on a steep grade, with a precipice on their left, the Footes met the Leadville stage traveling downhill at full speed. For a terrifying minute or so, Molly feared that the two vehicles would collide—there simply was no room for the stage to pass. Arthur lashed his horses relentlessly and forced them up the side of the cliff, avoiding a serious accident by inches. The sick horse died soon after, but Arthur hired another at a way station called "English George's." From there, they traveled over the pass and reached Leadville "by lamplight."

For the next six months, Molly lived in a one-room log cabin built on a hill about a half mile from Leadville's central district and facing the "Snowy range." Although the cabin stood alone on the banks of the Stevens and Leiter Ditch when Molly arrived, other houses soon sprang up around it. By the end of the summer, their hillside—now called "Capitol Hill"—was considered the most fashionable district in Leadville.

Molly's letters to family and friends written from Leadville provide images of the camp that differ sharply from those found in most history books. She was writing from an upper-class woman's perspective, telling her loved ones how she occupied her days and revealing many details about the camp's domestic life. Most other writers, however, have focused on the sensational aspects of the silver boom. One scholar's succinct description is typical: "Leadville stands high in the list of rip-roaring camps where money and liquor flowed freely and sin was a twenty-four-hour-a-day proposition."

Another historian stresses the camp's lawlessness (which Molly also refers to but in more subdued tones): "It is no exaggeration to say that Leadville was very lawless in 1879. Daily there were quarrels and general turbulence, with whiskey often inciting the participants to drastic actions. Holdups were routine. . . . A wise man did not go out after dark if he could help it . . . those who had to walk late at night kept their pistols habitually drawn and often cocked."

In a letter to Helena, Molly described her new residence as the "jolliest little log cabin," its inside walls lined with a heavy, oak-grained building paper, which also covered spaces between the pine beams in the ceiling. To add color to the room, the Footes pinned up geological survey maps, which delighted the geologists who came to call. The cabin was furnished with a round table in its center, a kitchen table, five chairs, an iron fireplace, and a bed secluded behind drapery, which was called the bedroom.

Molly and Arthur soon fell into a comfortable routine. Most mornings, Arthur made the fire, boiled coffee water (which he scooped from the ditch that fronted their property), and broiled a steak for their breakfast. He spent the day surveying and inspecting claims, while Molly worked at her blocks. They lunched separately and dined together in the evening about 6:00 P.M. at the Clarendon Hotel, said to be "one of the most elegantly appointed hostelries west of St. Louis." In a letter to her mother, Molly described the hotel as "a surprisingly nice place . . . everything is very good and they put on as much style as possible." But years later she remembered that the "bedlam of male voices" and "the clatter of dishes" had made conversation almost impossible.

In the evenings the Footes invited to their cabin a host of young men, well-educated and from good families, who did not wish to frequent the saloons and had nowhere to spend their leisure hours. Married women, Molly discovered, were "expected to be hospitable." To a friend, she confided, "I have no evenings literally."

Still, she enjoyed the many visitors who frequented the little cabin. Among the most memorable was Helen Hunt Jackson, poet, writer, and friend of the Gilders, who later gained fame for championing Indian rights in such works as *A Century of Dishonor* (1881) and *Ramona* (1884). "H. H.," as she often signed her stories, was in Leadville with her husband, William S. Jackson, a Colorado financier and railroad man. Molly describes in her reminiscences her first encounter with the Jacksons. On a particularly fine day, H. H. walked out from town to the Foote cabin alone. Molly was in the midst of dressing when she heard a knock on the door. Not knowing her visitor, Molly set a chair on the porch and asked her to wait a few minutes while she finished inside, meanwhile keeping up a conversation through the partially opened door. Only after Molly emerged did H.H. introduce herself. "Fancy asking Helen Hunt to wait on one's porch!" Molly exclaimed years later. That same evening the Footes and the Jacksons dined together at the Clarendon, which was as crowded and noisy as ever. "By sinking our voices below the storm key of sound and speaking almost in each other's faces we managed to communicate," she recalled.

Other distinguished visitors included members of the U.S. Geological Survey, organized in 1879 with Clarence King as its director. In June Samuel F. Emmons, who headed the Rocky Mountain division, set up camp in the woods behind the Foote cabin and began a major study of the Leadville deposits. Molly enjoyed evenings spent at his campfire listening to the men tell stories of their past exploits. The geologists, in turn, made frequent visits to the Foote cabin. Molly later recalled that Emmons "was as fond of people as he was of rocks, which is saying much for an eminent geologist." But she saved her highest praise for Clarence King, already renowned for his work on the Fortieth Parallel Survey. He was in Leadville that summer as a member of the newly organized Public Lands Commission, charged with investigating public lands and land laws. James D. Hague, who was also in Leadville, brought

King to Molly's cabin one afternoon. "[King] is a delightful talker," she reported to her mother, "much gentler and more sensitive in manner than I had expected."

Thomas Donaldson, also a member of the Public Lands Commission, called on Molly shortly after King and Hague had left. In his memoir, *Idaho of Yesteryear* (1941), Donaldson gives a good description of Molly as she appeared that summer:

> She was dressed in white and she rounded out a pleasing picture in contrast to rugged nature all about her home. Mrs. Foote put us at ease with her sweet manners . . . . We went inside the house and saw every evidence of artistic taste and culture. The main room, which served for parlor, bedroom, and reception room, was skillfully decorated in brown and gray—as neat an arrangement as I had seen . . . . Mrs. Foote settled herself for a chat until her husband returned, and my, my, how she did talk! She was well read on everything and ripped out an intellectual go-as-you-please backed up by good looks and brightness. She told us of their hopes, hers and Arthur's, in Mr. Foote's engineering schemes. What was more interesting, she showed us some of her black-and-white illustrations for the work of other authors.

Shortly after Clarence King's arrival in Leadville, Arthur accepted an appointment to the Geological Survey as a "mining geologist." Molly called it an honorable position and "a handsome compliment from Mr. King," since several other men had applied for the job. Foote was to receive $200 per month plus expenses—not a great deal of money, Molly confided to her mother, but Arthur expected to benefit greatly by working with Arnold Hague, James's younger brother, who was chief of the California division. The job would entail much traveling and long separations. "My heart failed me at the prospect," Molly later admitted. But good fortune intervened. "While I was trying to imagine myself enduring that life of wandering and waiting which is one of the tragedies of women's lives in California," Arthur was offered, and accepted, an appointment as manager of the Adelaide mine.

Foote had been recommended for the position by their neighbor William S. Ward, manager of the Evening Star mine and former manager of the Adelaide. About midsummer, Ward (a bachelor) built a commodious two-story house next to the Footes and filled it with fine furniture. He also imported a housekeeper and invited Molly and Arthur to take meals with him, which delighted the oftentimes shy artist. No longer would she be subjected to the noise and stares of the Clarendon crowd. Moreover, Ward proved to be a generous host, frequently inviting eastern investors, mine owners, and other married couples to dine with them. In a letter to sister Phil, Molly described one of his dinners. The menu included soup, roast mutton, French peas, mashed potatoes, olives, sauce, strawberry pie, Swiss cheese with ice cream, cake, and fruit. Cigars with coffee followed, a "heathen custom," Molly said, but, she added, "I always sit through the smoking for there is no where else to go." She enjoyed these evenings, despite the cigar smoke. And since the conversation often focused on mines, she picked up a great deal of technical knowledge that she would later incorporate into her novels.

Molly did not lack for social encounters that summer. Shortly after reaching Leadville, the Footes attended the first in a series of select dances, called "the Assembly," held in the dining room of the Clarendon each fortnight. "The ball was quite nice," Molly told Helena, although she seemed somewhat surprised that she felt obliged to dance. "There was so small a proportion of ladies that good nature made it necessary for one to go through the form at least." Walking home after midnight, Arthur carried a pistol, just like other prudent residents.

As more wives arrived to join their engineer-husbands, Molly's social outlets increased. "There are some very pretty women here," she wrote to Charles de Kay in July, "very few of them are unmarried, and the marriages as a rule seem remarkably, even romantically happy." This was true, she said, because couples were coming together after a long separation and only wives who loved their husbands made the arduous trip. Several households exchanged evening socials, where the more talented harmonized on "jubilee" and church songs. "It is perfectly lovely!" Molly reported.

Some of these new friends joined Molly and Arthur on day-long excursions away from the mining camp. One Sunday they went by carriage to Twin Lakes, located at the foot of Colorado's highest peak, Mount Elbert, only a few miles south of Leadville. Like a modern tourist, Molly was awed by the landscape, which she described as "the loveliest place I ever saw! The most wonderful combination of beauty and wild grandeur!" On another trip they fished in the Arkansas River and drank "bumpers of the cold tingling water" from Soda Spring in Colorado Gulch. She especially enjoyed the "glorious" horseback rides, which on at least one occasion included an exhilarating gallop across Tennessee Park.

Molly spent most weekdays working on illustrations for Ernest Ingersoll's essay, but even on Sunday excursions she took along her sketching pad. Six of Molly's drawings, including one depicting the Footes in their cabin, accompanied Ingersoll's "Camp of the Carbonates," which appeared in the October 1879 issue of *Scribner's.* Helena wrote from England to praise the Leadville drawings. Dismayed to learn, however, that her best friend might stay on in Colorado, she added, half in jest: "How horrible if you should settle in Leadville and become a Westerner! I cannot believe it. It must never be and it shall not be."

Molly had no desire to become a westerner. But she missed her little boy so dreadfully that after Arthur accepted the Adelaide position she insisted that they live together in Leadville as a family. First, however, the cabin had to be enlarged. While the remodeling went forward, the Footes stayed with W. S. Ward, an uncomfortable arrangement since Molly had "no good place to work." Still, she was pleased with the results—two new bedrooms, kitchen, and stone fireplace and rooms filled with elegant furniture that the Adelaide company provided its manager. In writing of these additions, Molly assured her mother: "Thee would be contented about our comforts if thee could look in on us now."

When Molly left Leadville in late October to return to Milton, Arthur accompanied her as far as Denver, where he was to give testimony in another court case. For the rest of the journey, she enjoyed the companionship of James D. Hague, traveling east to rejoin his family now living in New Jersey. Molly still did not know if Arthur could get away that winter to join her in Milton, but if not, she told Arthur's mother, she would take little Arthur herself to Leadville before spring arrived. Long separations were too hard for the "poor young papa, who has worked so hard to make a home for the child!" Seeking to justify her decision to risk taking the boy to Leadville in the dead of winter, she added: "If Arthur were like some men, I w'd stay here with the child until mild weather—but he has nothing in the way of society that makes up to him for his home. I should not like a society man for a husband—one who is easily consoled for my absence—so I must take the disadvantages of the other kind and stay by him—lest he learn to no longer need me."

It was a joy to be home again with little Arthur and to take part in family meetings on Sundays. She wrote daily to Arthur, Sr., and worked hard on her blocks. Her good humor was evident in a letter she wrote to Helena, in which she disparaged her own work with some wit: "[My work] seems worthless to me, and I am sure it would to you if it were not mine but I dont care. . . . When I am as old as Mother and without pressing cares, I will pore over my work with spectacles on and be cheerful over it, for then I shall respect myself for working at all. My drawings will be shown perhaps at the agricultural fair as bed quilts made by eighty year old grandmothers are shown. 'Wonderful for such an old lady!'"

Several of Foote's drawings appeared in *Scribner's* in the months following her return from Leadville, including about a dozen superb illustrations for John Burroughs's article on the Hudson River, entitled "Our River" (August 1880). She contributed two illustrations for Tennyson's *A Dream of Fair Women* (1880), one of which, "Fair Rosamond," appears as the frontispiece. And she also wrote and illustrated a children's story for *St. Nicholas Magazine* based on her Leadville experience, "The Children's 'Claim'" (January 1880).

Toward the end of February 1880, Arthur returned to Milton, where he was reintroduced to a son he had not seen in nearly two years. In following weeks, the Footes made whirlwind visits to New York City, Boston, and Guilford, where they conferred with editors and mining directors and dined with family and friends. They called on Maria Oakey at her studio and visited a museum and an art exhibit, the very activities that Molly missed most when she was in the West.

On the trip to Guilford they persuaded Arthur's twenty-year-old niece, Lily Foote, to return with them to Leadville to help watch over little Arthur. In her reminiscences, Molly recalls that "on the strength of Lily Foote" she signed a book contract to illustrate a de luxe edition of Owen Meredith's narrative poem *Lucile*, a contract she would later be forced to break.

They left Milton in May when the fruit trees were in blossom and arrived at the end of the railroad tracks, which now extended to within thirty-five miles of Leadville, in a blizzard. With no place to wait out the storm, they went on, covering the remaining distance in a private carriage with their little boy wrapped in a down comforter. Arthur, Jr., weathered the blizzard in fine shape but soon came down again with malaria. What followed was a dreadful, two-week period of sleeplessness, for Molly watched by his bedside every night and was too anxious to sleep during the day. She had no confidence in the local doctor, who prescribed strange concoctions for the little boy to swallow. She later recalled: "I don't remember how many days the fear was acute—how long one carried about inside one a sickish lump which made food impossible to swallow." Molly's sleeplessness became chronic that summer.

Still, once the little boy recovered, Molly found much to enjoy. She often took walks with Arthur after dinner and watched spellbound as sunsets lit up the snow-topped mountains. Sometimes she played chess in the evenings and almost always the cabin was filled until a late hour with visitors. Her greatest joy, however, was riding horseback with Arthur or his young assistant, Ferdinand Van Zandt, sometimes riding to the valley below where there was space "for a long thrilling gallop."

But Molly also was troubled by physical ailments. It was in Leadville that summer, Molly recalls in her reminiscences, that she suffered a miscarriage. And on a three-week family vacation to Twin Lakes, now a tourist attraction with a hotel and cabins, she came down with dysentery. She could still appreciate the area's natural beauty, however, and allow her imagination free reign. While convalescing, she wrote to tell Richard Gilder: "I have a story I want to write when I get strength enough, but it will probably evaporate with a wider awake mood."

By mid-July Molly was back at work on her blocks. When she first arrived in Leadville, she had agreed to help illustrate a new edition of *Aucassin and Nicolette*, the twelfth-century French romance, which, when published later that year, featured three of Foote's drawings. But the *Lucile* illustrations were more than she could handle. Her little boy's illness, coupled with her own ailments and sleeplessness, led Molly to cancel the contract. Still, at least one (and possibly more) of Foote's drawings, which she completed in Leadville, appear in the 1881 edition.

Arthur's work placed additional strains on the family that summer. Foote was among the mine managers who rejected union demands for higher pay and shorter hours. This led to a bitter three-week strike, during which the mines closed down, the companies hired armed guards, and business in Leadville came to a standstill. Only after the governor declared martial law and called out the militia was the strike broken. As the summer wore on, a smoldering boundary dispute between the Adelaide and the Argentine, a rival mine, threatened to erupt in violence. When Arthur was called east to confer with company officials, he took Molly and little Arthur with him, "fearing trouble ahead."After reaching Milton, Molly wrote

Helena of the turmoil: "They have had actual war at the Adelaide. The Argentine had fifty men and forty stands of arms. The Adelaide has won the injunction suit and so I suppose quiet reigns again." The possibility of more violence and a lengthy lawsuit led the eastern owners to shut down the Adelaide, which left Arthur without a position but gave Molly the material for her first novel.

For most of the next three and a half years, Molly lived on the Hallock homestead where she wrote *The Led-Horse Claim*, the first of three Leadville novels that helped establish her reputation as a western writer. She wrote other essays and stories as well, including three travel pieces describing a memorable trip to Mexico. Arthur continued to look for work that suited him. On a journey to Idaho in 1882, he became involved in an irrigation scheme that would consume a decade and more of their lives and much of their income. And it was during these Idaho years that what Helena had feared would come to pass—Molly became a westerner.

CHAPTER 3

"Darkest Idaho"

AFTER their return from Leadville, Molly and little Arthur found a warm refuge in Milton while Arthur, Sr., was away looking for work. There were cousins for little Arthur to play with, family gatherings on Sundays, and long conversations with Bessie. Best of all, however, was a visit from Helena after a year and a half separation. "It was lovely of you to come," Molly later wrote to her friend. "I was unspeakably happy with you again."

Despite an illness which kept Molly from drawing that fall, she enjoyed reading books that Helena and Richard bestowed on her, including George Washington Cable's *The Grandissimes, A Story of Creole Life* (1880). Later, when she felt better, she visited them at their Studio and attended a matinee performance of the French actress Sarah Bernhardt, then making her American debut on the New York stage. But heartache soon replaced Molly's happiness, for around Christmastime she learned that the Gilders' new-born son had died. In a brief note asking if Helena felt strong enough for a visit, Molly expressed her own deep-felt sorrow: "I cannot even attempt to say how I grieve with you. It is too hard! My dear, dear Helena!"

Molly's immediate plans were uncertain, however, since Arthur talked about job possibilities both in Colorado and Mexico. In the end, he hired on to investigate mines in the province of Michoacán for a mining syndicate that Helena's brother Drake de Kay headed. Little Arthur was to stay with his Aunt Bessie while Molly went along to document their Mexican adventure for Gilder's magazine. Helena, in fact, thought the trip offered Molly "a splendid chance" to gain fresh recognition. "Mexico is so new and so wonderfully picturesque. I am already revelling [*sic*] in the thought of what you will do," Helena told Molly on the eve of her departure.

The Footes left for Mexico in January 1881, crossing the icebound river at Milton in a sleigh. They went by train to New York City, then by boat to Veracruz, stopping briefly in Havana harbor, and then by train to Mexico City. Once they entered the tropics, Molly's grand adventure truly began. She later recalled: "I knew [then] that we never had been anywhere before—we had merely romped about a bit in that 'historic vacuum' of the Far West." Despite her initial enthusiasm, however, Molly fell ill during their two-week stay in Mexico City, which left her wishing "with all my heart" that she had stayed in Milton. But the artist soon regained her health and good spirits and vowed to record on paper as much of this strange and picturesque country as possible.

The Footes covered the remaining 180 miles or so to Morelia, the capital of Michoacán, by stagecoach, stopping overnight at towns along the way. But a delay forced them to spend one night at a nearly deserted hacienda, where they bedded down on the stone floor. Ironically, Molly's sleeplessness, which had followed her from Leadville, now disappeared. "The stage journey was as good as medicine," she concluded.

In Morelia, the Footes were guests of the wealthy Prussian banker, Don Gustavo Gravenhorst, a widower who lived with his thirteen-year-old daughter in one of the town's most exclusive residences. While Arthur was away inspecting mines, Molly spent much of her time drawing. She sketched numerous scenes within the Casa Gravenhorst but made only a few sketching forays beyond its walls to avoid disrupting the household. To her dismay, custom required her to go forth in the family coach, chaperoned by the two ladies of the house (her host's daughter and sister-in-law), and assisted by a maidservant. As her stay neared its end, however, she gladly accepted an escort so she could stroll through the local marketplace in search of souvenirs. On the return journey, the

Footes rode horseback to Mexico City, accompanied by six mounted men and four pack animals. Bone-weary at times on the six-day ride, Molly sketched along the entire distance.

From the Mexico trip, Molly produced three illustrated travel pieces, the first appearing as the lead essay in the first issue of Richard Gilder's new journal, *The Century Illustrated Monthly Magazine*, which succeeded *Scribner's* in November 1881. With grace and vivid word-pictures, Molly conveys to readers her own enchantment with a land that some travelers considered as exotic as Egypt. She focuses on the beauty of the countryside, the strange clothes and customs of rural inhabitants, and the elaborate architecture of stately haciendas. She contrasts the poverty of Mexican peasants with the grandeur of their surroundings—the hills, the fields, and the village plazas with fountains and stone seats for the poorest to sit upon. The charm of Molly's essays is greatly enhanced by her superb drawings, among the best she ever produced. Well-placed in the text to achieve maximum visual impact, her black-and-white images capture both the wealth and poverty of Mexico's populace.

The Footes returned to Milton in mid-April and found little Arthur robust and happy, although both he and his cousin Birney had been sick with chickenpox in their absence. As summer approached, Molly looked forward to a visit from Helena and the opportunity to paint and sketch together in the "little north end room" of the Hallock household where Molly had her studio. "Your presence will inspire me," she wrote to Helena. In fact, Molly's isolation from the society of other artists made the Gilders' support of her work crucial. "I never feel that it is worth while to try to do anything," Molly confided to Helena, "except after a talk with you and Richard. . . . You and Richard make art a thing as holy as religion and help me to believe that even my niggardly little—honestly done may be a part of worthy living."

Sometime in June, Arthur went to Leadville to settle their affairs while Molly remained at Milton absorbed in her work. On July 8 she wrote to tell "Mother Foote" that her forthcoming trip to Guilford with little Arthur would be brief since she had not yet started the second essay on Mexico. At Milton the boy had other children to play with and required little supervision but at Guilford he would make more demands on her, leaving no time to work on the article. "Writing isn't like blocks," she explained, "I cannot write except I'm alone." Despite her misgivings, Molly soon took the little boy to visit his grandmother (Arthur's father had died in 1878)—and fell into a "fit of the blues," which lasted until Arthur joined her nearly three weeks later. Explaining her long silence to Helena during this state of listlessness, Molly admitted that she had not been sleeping well and always missed Arthur more at Guilford than anywhere else.

To escape the summer's heat at Milton and a recurrence of little Arthur's malaria, the Footes soon decamped to Deer Isle on Penobscot Bay in Maine for a lengthy vacation. They boarded in a little fishing village at the mouth of an inlet and spent their days sailing and exploring the beaches and nearby islands. Molly reveled in the cool, salty atmosphere and happily gathered blueberries with her son. She worked diligently on her second Mexico essay but confessed to Helena that "I ought to go out less in the boat and work more." Still, an early Sunday morning tramp along the shore with little Arthur provided the setting for one of the best stories she ever wrote, "The Story of the Alcázar" (*Century,* 1882). In a letter dated August 14, Molly described the scene:

> The boy and I got up early, 6 o'clock, had some bread and milk and wild red raspberries (provided over night) and took a long walk following the curving shore at low tide out to an abandoned vessel lying stuck in the mud near an old wharf—its rusty anchor chains and anchor buried in the mud, exposed. We went on board and Arthur played he was the capt. It was Sunday morning and the little fishy village was still asleep. Flocks of plover were flitting and calling along the wet beach.

Molly's story opens with Captain John recounting the strange history of the *Alcázar* to a schoolboy as they sit together at sunset near the hulk of the long-abandoned vessel.

Back in 1827 it had drifted into local waters, the narrator explains, and was towed into Penobscot harbor by an old veteran seaman, Captain Green, and his men. A search below deck revealed its grisly secret—the *Alcázar* was an old abandoned slaver with the skeletons of slaves still aboard. Despite misgivings, Green refitted the ship to carry lumber between Maine and New York. Its maiden voyage was a disaster—three men and the deck-load lost at sea. The surviving crew left the ship once it reached New York, calling it a "floatin' coffin." With new hands, Green started for his home port, drinking heavily en route, and was swept off deck and lost during a midnight storm. He shouted his last words to the mate who tried to save him: "Let me alone! I've got to go with her!" Captain John concluded long ago that Green had been the *Alcázar*'s original master and, running short of water, had abandoned the ship with its human cargo. In the end, says the narrator, "he knew that ship and him belonged together, same as a man's sins belongs to him. He knew she'd been a-huntin' him up and down the western ocean for twenty year, with them dead o' his'n in her hold,—and she'd hunted him down at last."

The success of this tale rests on Molly's wonderful mastery of detail. She evokes for the reader the sights and sounds of Penobscot harbor and uses nautical terms with authority, thanks in part to her husband's knowledge of sailing. She later told James D. Hague, who had written to say he liked the story, that "I couldn't have written it without Arthur's help."

Sometime after leaving Deer Isle, Arthur took a room at the Collonade Hotel in New York City to pursue engineering leads while Molly stayed at Milton with her son and began work on her first novel. Occasionally during the winter (1881–82) she joined Arthur in the city, where they dined and went to social gatherings with family and friends. Molly long remembered one gay evening when she and Arthur, together with the Gilders, the Hagues, and Edwin Godkin, Arthur's cousin-in-law and editor of the *Nation*, attended the first-night performance of *Patience*, a Gilbert and Sullivan satirical operetta, which left the audience shaking with laughter.

"Better fun and better company were not to be had in New York at that time," Molly recalls in her reminiscences.

Still, the winter's gaiety was tempered by the uncertainty of Arthur's job prospects. Molly knew that he longed to return to the field and felt some remorse that she was the reason he had remained that winter in the East. "If he were a single man," she told Helena, "he could have been off and away, long ago." In a burst of candor that revealed both her emotional dependence on Arthur and her acceptance of traditional gender roles in marriage, she wrote: "I used to say to myself with unspeakable pride and joy in earlier days that I could make my husband happy and make his lonely life a richer one—but dearest Helena—what a mill stone a woman is round a man's neck, and the more she loves him the heavier she hangs. Over and over again, I have lacked the timely courage to say to Arthur 'go, and dont mind me.'"

In the spring, Arthur went to the Wood River region in south-central Idaho where a mining boom had been underway for a year and a half. After a quick return trip to Milton in midsummer, he headed back to Idaho to manage the Wolftone mine, accompanied by his brother-in-law, John Sherman. Molly, on the other hand, still faced an uncertain future, not knowing when she would be reunited with Arthur or where her next permanent home would be. She told Helena shortly before Arthur went to Idaho: "I am born with roots which are always trying to grasp something and hold fast."

Meanwhile, she revised the final chapters of her first Leadville novel, incorporating Richard Gilder's editorial suggestions. He admired the story but disliked its unhappy ending in which the star-crossed lovers part forever, an ending that Molly believed gave the story credibility. As an editor, Gilder promoted a "genteel realism" that appealed to the *Century*'s upper-middle-class readers. "The more reality the better!" he avowed. "But let it be reality all the way through; reality of the spirit as well as of the flesh, not a grovelling reality which ignores the 'romantic spirit.'" Molly's story, he believed, called for a romantic conclusion.

As a first-time novel writer, Molly willingly rewrote the ending, although when she reflected on the revisions years later, long after Gilder had died, she wrote: "I think a literary artist would have refused to do it." Still, in 1882, the budding novelist relied completely on her friend's editorial advice, and she struggled with the new ending. At one point, she wrote to Helena: "I do hope Richard will let me condense the last part of my story. I do not in the least mind doing that sort of thing—as much as he likes. There are no *pet* parts. It was only having it *all to do* over that I dreaded—in case of his fundamental disapproval. With his encouragement—I can go on shortening and correcting as long as he likes."

Molly completed the revisions by the end of May but was unable to come up with a title that the *Century* people would accept. She rejected their proposal, "A Tragedy of the Silver Mine," asserting that it "isn't a tragedy in the first place and people who know how to write tragedies dont have to label them." When they asked her to find a title that suggested "locality," she turned to James D. Hague for technical advice. She told Hague that she could not "write a story without seeing the places" and so had situated her tale in that valley of the Rocky Mountains where Leadville was located. Yet she did not want the title to link her fictional mining camp with the real one. There was a lovely name of a canyon in western Colorado, however, that appealed to her. "Would it be an impropriety to steal the name of the Unaweep Cañon and transfer it to the other side of the Gunnison Valley? Has it a meaning which would contradict the nature of the locality I propose to apply it to?"

Molly eventually entitled her story *The Led-Horse Claim: A Romance of a Mining Camp.* The *Century* ran it as a serial, starting in November 1882, and James R. Osgood and Company published it as a book the following year. The story is illustrated by six of Molly's drawings; especially well-drawn is the introductory picture, "At the Foot of the Pass," which depicts the approach across South Park to the Mosquito Range and helps set the stage for the story that follows.

The Led-Horse Claim is a tale of romance and adventure. George Hilgard, superintendent of the Led-Horse mine, falls in love with Cecil Conrath, the beautiful sister of Harry Conrath, superintendent of the rival Shoshone mine. When the story opens, Hilgard suspects that Conrath's men have tunneled into the ore beds of the Led-Horse. As tension surrounding the two mines escalates, Hilgard falls deeper in love with Cecil. She returns his love but fears the violent nature of the mining dispute. She therefore exacts a promise from Hilgard to leave the camp to avoid a showdown with her brother and ruin their chances for happiness. Hilgard prepares to leave, but when he learns that Conrath and his ruffians plan to take the Led-Horse by force he feels duty-bound to protect the mine. Hilgard and his assistant descend into the mine and repel the invaders who have broken into the Led-Horse tunnels. Because Conrath is fatally wounded in the fight, Cecil believes that family honor demands she abandon her true love, and the couple separate. As fate would have it, Hilgard and Cecil accidently meet later in the East and eventually marry.

The first two-thirds of the novel, set in a fictional mining camp modeled after Leadville, captures the reader's interest because of its authentic detail. First-hand experience allows Foote to write convincingly of the camp's diverse population, social gatherings, and subtle changes it undergoes as more and more wives arrive. She uses mining terminology with confidence and educates her audience about the importance of eastern capital and the difficulties of managing a mine when its owners reside in the East. She also demonstrates a keen eye for seasonal changes, which reinforces the reader's sense of place. In describing a new snowfall in the mountains, she writes:

> Snow lay deep on the pass; its soft mantle covered the rugged cañons; it whitened the windward side of the pine-trunks and the gray canvas covers of the freight-wagons, bemired in the deeply rutted roads; it lay smooth on the roofs of the town, and deadened the tramping of feet on the board sidewalks.

Molly's skillful characterization of two minor figures, Dr. Godfrey, the camp's philosopher, and Mrs. Denny, Cecil's occasional chaperone, is also a strength of the novel. Foote uses both characters to demonstrate the deleterious effect of life in the West. The doctor, she writes, has slowly deteriorated over the twenty-six years he has spent on the frontier: "A pervading seediness had crept over his outward man. The moth of long isolation from gentle communications had corrupted his good manners." The change in Mrs. Denny after a six-month residence in the mining camp, however, is more subtle—"like a premature blight on a still full-veined flower."

The novel's denouement, set in the East, is less satisfying to the modern reader because of the contrived encounters between Hilgard and Cecil that lead to their marriage. Yet nineteenth-century readers were accustomed to happy endings, and they seemingly overlooked these implausible events and enjoyed Molly's tale. Several publications carried favorable reviews, including the *Atlantic Monthly*, the *Critic*, and the *New York Times*, whose reviewer called *The Led-Horse Claim* "a very charming story . . . and charmingly illustrated." The *Atlantic Monthly*'s critic thought Molly was at her best in the characterization of Cecil, who suffered because of her passion for Hilgard. Unperturbed by the implausible encounters that bring "the two young hearts" together, the reviewer went on to state: "it is a pleasure to find honest sentiment so victorious."

Molly must have been pleased when the first installment of *The Led-Horse Claim* appeared in the *Century* and when she later read the reviews. But with typical humility, she reassured Helena that she was "in no danger of being overwhelmed by my 'success' as a writer." Cousin Anna Haviland, the woman for whom Molly was named, had said that "it was the kind of story that some of my friends w'd probably be sorry I had written." And she told James D. Hague, after he had complimented her story, that she still wondered how she had the temerity to write about a mining camp when male writers of more genius than she and with wider experience dominated "the field." "Of course you can see how I have been helped by Arthur in the technical part and the masculine part," she added.

Years later Molly referred to *The Led-Horse Claim* as her daughter's twin, for the galley proofs of the first installment arrived shortly after the birth of Elizabeth (Betty) Townsend Foote on September 9, 1882. For about three years, Molly had yearned for another baby but feared after her miscarriage in Leadville that she was "fated to be an old hen with one chick." Still, she had been optimistic about this pregnancy. In good spirits, she worked steadily on her novel until midsummer, when the heat and her physical condition combined to slow her movements. After that she was content to sit outside under the apple trees, hemming diapers and watching little Arthur and his cousins play nearby. Her sleeplessness returned, however, and in a pensive mood she wrote to Helena: "I still prowl at night and sit at the window and wish I didn't look on the sky with so little comprehension." Helena, who had given birth to her daughter Dorothea in the spring, no doubt understood Molly's mood and discomfort.

Despite a difficult birth—and her own sleeplessness—Molly took delight in her newborn daughter: "I listen to all her noises at night—her puckerings and gruntings and her short soft breathing and am very happy but wide awake." Arthur, who was still in Idaho, soon jolted Molly's sense of well-being, however, by announcing plans to join Charles H. Tompkins, a New York civil engineer, in developing a large irrigation system in the Boise River Valley. As he explained it, apparently in a letter and then on a visit to Milton, the project would be of long duration and require the raising of vast sums to finance even the early stages of construction.

In her reminiscences, Molly writes of Arthur's decision with unusual emotion, for, as Rodman Paul points out, she "was not eager to go to Idaho." In the first place, Molly had lost faith in her husband's schemes. None of his earlier jobs had worked out, and he knew nothing about irrigation or the difficulties of raising investment capital. "I couldn't count this appalling undertaking as anything more than the stuff of wakeful nights for mothers of young babies." Then, too, she had reestablished her intimacy with Helena and grown accustomed again to life in the East. She enjoyed both the stimulating intellectual life of the city and the less-hurried pace at Milton, where she had help with the children and the leisure to draw and write. Going to "darkest Idaho," as she called it, "meant farewell music, art, gossip of the workshop, schools that we knew about, new friends just made who would forget us, old friends better loved than ever and harder to part from—all the old backgrounds receding hopelessly and forever."

Arthur's brief visit to Milton in mid-November helped to restore Molly's courage, but as soon as he left again for the Boise basin, her doubts returned. "When he is home I feel so young," she told Helena, "and then back I go a hundred years." She wrote daily to Arthur, sharing scraps of information from his letters with Helena and James D. Hague. In February 1883, Arthur traveled east again to confer with business partners—and to assuage Molly's fears. The doubting wife later recalled that "in one evening's talk upstairs by ourselves he convinced me that he was not mad. He was as quietly assured of the worth of what he was doing as I was of my own little scheme of a six months' baby asleep in her crib beside us."

And so they planned for their future home in Boise. To Molly's great satisfaction, John and Bessie Sherman would go with them, embracing the chance to break away from Milton and start life anew in the West. The two men left for Idaho that summer while Molly, Bessie, and the children were to follow in October. Meanwhile, to escape the heat and malaria season at Milton, Molly and her two children took a summer cottage, next to the one James and Mary Hague rented, at Point Lookout on the southern coast of Long Island. She continued to draw and write, but to her great disappointment she suffered a second miscarriage, which left her in such a weakened condition that, at the urging of the Hagues, she postponed her trip to Idaho. Bessie, who departed without her, was soon sending cheerful messages from Boise describing her new surroundings. Arthur no doubt harbored his own disappointment when his wife and children failed to arrive, although Molly later told Helena, he "takes his *cheat* as he takes everything else"—stoically.

Although Molly never fully recovered her strength that winter, she worked sporadically on her second Leadville story. In mid-December 1883, she reported to Richard: "The 'novel,' as you are gracious enough to call it, comes on slowly. But I shall dig away at it, until it is fit to show you. It seems a superfluous thing to be doing in these days when every other person one has ever heard of, is writing the novel of the period. In fact it is ludicrously uncalled for on *my* part. Yet, I know that I shall keep on till the story is finished." She continued illustrating the work of other authors as well, but the results did not please her, as she explained to Helena: "I am too restless not to work, and too low, physically to do good work."

When Arthur made an extended trip east in January 1884, the Footes took up lodgings on Lexington Avenue in New York City. The furnished rooms were spacious but cold, causing Molly to warn Arthur's mother to bring extra blankets when she came for a visit since most of their own household goods had been sent to Boise. Physically run-down and anxious about Arthur's business affairs, Molly did not enjoy much of this stay in the city.

Still, even during this "dismal" time, as she called it, the hours she spent with Helena must have been pleasurable. Their presence at a Sunday literary tea in March was noted by a New York diarist, who wrote admiringly of the thirty-six-year-old celebrity: "Mrs. Foote, for one whose name is so well known as writer and illustrator, retains her ladylike, bashful ways and prettiness wonderfully well." Later Molly spent two memorable days with her best friend before returning to Milton to pack for the trip west. Relatives came in waves to bid the Footes farewell. Hardest of all was saying goodbye to her mother and father, for Molly knew that Arthur's irrigation scheme would require a lengthy stay in Idaho.

The Boise project, in fact, fixed the direction of Molly's life for the next decade and more. As historian Richard W. Etulain has observed, these were years "filled with disappointment, failure, and family conflict. They were also [Foote's] most fruitful period as a writer." By the time she left the Boise basin for good, Molly had become the best-known woman writer and illustrator of the American West.

Ever the optimist, Molly must have absorbed some of Arthur's enthusiasm for the Idaho venture as they traveled across the continent. Then, too, having a beloved sister awaiting her at the end of the journey did much to allay her fears. So on that beautiful morning in May when they reached the Kuna railroad station near Boise, Molly was in fine spirits. She marveled at the spectacular scenery on the fifteen-mile buggy ride into town—the Sawtooth Range looming up ahead and the Owyhee Mountains behind. On the last bench above Boise Valley, she caught her first glimpse of the town, and a day or two later wrote approvingly to Helena: "The tallest spires are the court house and the school house, while if typical of the town, seems well for its behavior. I fancy it is a very proper, decent little town quite unlike the wild camps where my married morals have been cultivated."

Arriving at the Father Mesplie house, which Arthur had rented from a local resident, Molly received a joyous welcome from the Shermans. "Birney ran out to the gate to meet us under the young apple tree boughs," Molly reported to Helena, and "Bessie was not far behind Birney, looking so glad it quite thrilled me." For the next twelve months, the Footes and the Shermans shared this commodious house on the outskirts of town, built by Father Toussaint Mesplie, a Catholic priest. The dwelling was ideal for two families, with a sitting room, dining room, kitchen, and large parlor downstairs and several bedrooms upstairs. On the spacious grounds surrounding the house were fruit trees, flower beds, and kitchen garden. "But our joy and pride," Molly wrote in a letter to Mary Hague, "are the poplars. Lombardy poplars, well grown and tall, making a screen between us and the road on two sides."

In letters to family and friends written during the following five months, Molly displayed an irrepressible optimism. Almost all aspects of her new surroundings pleased her—the perfect weather, divine mornings and cool nights, just right for sleeping; the large, comfortable house without any close neighbors, except for the small military post on the other side of a "wild sort of common" where cavalry maneuvers never failed to amuse the children. In the evenings Molly or Bessie accompanied little Arthur and Birney into the hills behind the post to listen to the buglers sound retreat. Bessie, in fact, was the key to much of Molly's happiness that summer. They were constantly in each other's rooms and, as Molly put it, talked and talked "like girls." Bessie looked after Molly's children as if they were her own, which allowed the younger sister the time to work on her artistic projects. The pleasure Molly felt in her sister's company is evident in the letters she wrote to Helena, as when she exclaimed: "It is such a comfort to have Bessie! We enjoy so much talking about our children to each other and about their clothes and their manners. There is no one but a woman who can listen properly to this kind of talk."

The two families employed a Chinese cook, but the remaining household chores fell to Bessie, who no doubt received compensation for her labor. At first Bessie also gave Birney and little Arthur lessons each morning, but in the fall the two younger children joined thirteen-year-old Gerald Sherman in attending the public school in Boise, a "remarkably good" school, according to Molly. The children were "perfectly delighted" by this new experience, although Arthur, now seven, soon encountered the school bullies. On the day he wore his dark blue jersey and scarlet tam-o'-shanter to school (seemingly strange attire to these western boys), they followed him around making rude remarks, which sent little Arthur home in tears. At this point, we catch a glimpse of Molly's efforts to build her son's character, as she described the incident in a letter to the boy's grandmother. "After a little talk, the boy concluded that he would not be laughed out of his clothes, and went back and faced it out." To Molly's satisfaction, one of the older boys later complimented Arthur's cap and wanted to know where he got it. But two other boys soon started a fight with little Arthur. "He didn't run away," Molly reported, and the fight ended when the teacher intervened. "So on the whole the 'first fight' was perhaps as satisfactory as such things ever are."

During that first summer in Idaho, Arthur, Sr., rode ten miles to Boise Canyon each morning to supervise preliminary work on the irrigation project. The first primitive efforts to irrigate the Boise Valley had started in 1863. But settlement remained sparse for many years, with the town of Boise claiming fewer than two thousand residents in 1880. The large-scale system that Foote helped devise, as chief engineer of the Idaho Mining and Irrigation Company, was expected to attract thousands more to the valley when the storage reservoirs, dams, and canals were completed. Charles H. Tompkins, as president of the company, spearheaded efforts in the East to raise funds for construction while Arthur worked at solving practical problems in the field, assisted by a trio of engineers—Tompkins's son, C. H. (Harry) Tompkins, Jr.; Andrew J. Wiley; and a Mr. Kinney.

For most of the summer Arthur's assistants lived in a small, two-story cabin in Boise Canyon, which Molly visited as often as possible. The exhilarating ten-mile ride across the plains, the refreshing canyon breezes, and the always fascinating river made it a favorite destination. Molly's description to Helena of her first trip to the canyon is lyrical:

> We rode up there one sultry Sunday afternoon. The showers overtook us as we were crossing the hills towards the opening of the cañon. The trail winds steeply down, turning among the hills and crossing from one to another on the natural divides. The darkening sky was grand above the long ragged wall of basalt bluffs, precipitous and ending in a sloping slide of broken rock wildly tumbled together as if suddenly arrested in its headlong rush down into the river. I never saw the expression of *motion* in rock as in these masses of debris at the foot of the cliffs. Perhaps it was as good a way

> as any other to see the cañon for the first time, but by the time we were in sight of the house where the engineers are quartered, the rain was pelting down in sheets, making a gray veil before our eyes and confusing the sight itself. I dont know when I have been so soaked and pelted.

They spent a pleasant evening in the cabin's big upper room, filled with beds, books, and camp chairs, listening to the rain pounding down on the roof and the fire crackling in the stove. At bedtime, the young engineers turned the room over to Molly and Arthur and carried mattresses downstairs to sleep on the floor. After a second rainy day, the Footes started for home on a different and scarier trail, which ran high above the river and provided a spectacular view of the gate of the canyon.

On later trips, Molly used the upper room of the engineers' cabin as a studio while the men were at work, Arthur usually somewhere on the canal line and Tompkins downstairs updating the large map that documented the canal's progress. They took their meals together in a "jolly" cook-tent, presided over by a Chinese cook and situated in some willows near a stream that flowed into the river. Evenings often were spent lying on blankets on the river's little beach gazing at the stars or sitting around a blazing fire made of driftwood. On one occasion, when Molly's new friends Sarah Onderdonk and her brother James accompanied her to the canyon, Arthur proposed going down the river by moonlight in the engineers' boat. No one ever went out on that capricious river for pleasure. But, as Molly wrote Helena, "Eastern men have the same contempt for a Western man's rowing as a Western man has for an Eastern man's horsemanship. And we set off gaily without much thought of consequences." It was a wild ride of two and a half hours, the swift current and roaring rapids in some places threatening to capsize them. Molly found it a delightful experience and was eager to do it again, though Arthur vowed never to take another boat down the river with his wife aboard.

Molly had almost as much fun later that summer on a fishing expedition upriver to Moore's Creek. While Arthur and the young engineers fished, Molly sat in the shade of a big pine tree and sketched. A nearby ranching family provided supper and places for them to sleep—the young men in the barn and Molly and Arthur in the open air on borrowed sheets and bedding. Molly later confessed that she did not sleep much that night because of the multitude of stars overhead and the night-noises of the barnyard animals.

All through life, Molly enjoyed strange places and new adventures, but she was always somewhat shy and consequently not particularly gregarious, though to family and a small circle of friends she was charming, generous, and caring. In Boise she became fast-friends with Sarah Onderdonk, a former acquaintance from her Cooper student days, who now lived in Idaho with her mother and brother James Onderdonk, the comptroller of the territory. Sarah was the type of woman Molly most admired: cultured, artistically talented, and physically attractive. Molly also came to know and to admire the new governor's wife, Mrs. William Bunn. Before the year ended, the Footes, the Bunns, and the Onderdonks were exchanging pleasant little dinner parties.

But Molly was not inclined to make friends with the many other Boise women who formally called upon her at the Mesplie house—no fewer than seventy-two different ladies came calling in less than a year. To avoid being conspicuously rude, she returned many of their calls but found the obligation to do so "the most tiresome feature of the place." In her correspondence Molly described the women as being decent and kind-hearted but "fearfully poky and provincial" and totally uninterested in the things that mattered the most to her. Still, despite her annoyance with much of Boise society, Molly admired the accomplishments of its pioneers, many of whom came calling on New Year's Day. Afterwards Molly wrote to Helena:

> It took strong men to succeed and build up the town. We can make light of it—coming here after things are comfortable—but one has only to look from the pretty bowery streets in summers—the little lawns and fruit trees, out on the deserts beyond, to see what these men have done in

> about thirty years. Like all self-made men, they are prone to worship the work of their own hands.

The social expectations of Boise matrons simply were incompatible with Molly's literary aspirations. She enjoyed writing, took pride in her work, and regretted the time expended on formal calls. She had resumed work on her second Leadville novel, *John Bodewin's Testimony*, soon after reaching Boise. She wrote "a little" every day but failed to make significant progress until after she hired a full-time nurse for little Betty, approaching her second birthday. In mid-June she reported to Richard Gilder that the story was nearly finished, although she planned to keep the last part for final revision until it became "strange" to her, a technique she used throughout her writing career. But she requested that he return the manuscript in proof sheets—if he accepted the story. "I only know how much more quickly I could see the faults of the Led Horse in the proofs than in manuscript," she added.

When Gilder sent word of the story's acceptance, Molly went to work addressing his editorial comments, every one deemed beneficial by the author. She continued to rely absolutely on Gilder's judgment and, as she put it, would "not *dream* of questioning" his criticism. She told Richard: "I will try to have you see that like good seed sown through the pages of my MS they will bring forth good fruit." She accepted with good humor a comment he had penciled on one page and which was to become a byword in the family: "Hardly worth chronicling." Molly later commented on Richard's editorial style in a letter to Helena: "He never lets one be careless. No, I dont mean careless, exactly, for I fuss over my things quite all they are worth—but I get stupid about them and dont hear my own words. His 'point of view' is invaluable to me. It is so candid, so deeply appreciative and sympathetic and so unflinchingly just."

While Molly revised *John Bodewin's Testimony*, Richard Gilder was nearing the pinnacle of his success as editor of the

Century, considered by many literary critics to be "the best general periodical in the world." Aware of the interests of his upper-middle-class readers, Gilder published essays and editorials on important issues of the day, such as labor, marriage, divorce, and political corruption, as well as travel pieces, art reviews, and short stories and serialized novels by the best American authors—Henry James, Mark Twain, and William Dean Howells, to name a few. The *Century* also published much regional fiction, contributing to the popularity of such local color writers as Bret Harte, George Washington Cable, Edward Eggleston, and Mary Hallock Foote. By the mid-1880s, the magazine received more than 5,000 manuscripts a year, of which it published about 400, and had a monthly circulation of 222,000.

Gilder's own ideals shaped the magazine's publishing policy. He believed that truth and beauty were one and that by promoting good taste in literature and the arts he could raise the moral standards of American society. He rejected morally offensive material, excised slang and other crude language, and published nothing that would offend mothers or corrupt their daughters. He asked Molly to revise a passage in *John Bodewin's Testimony* that referred to a mother singing "Safe in the arms of Jesus" to her baby "in a monotonous nasal tone." Gilder believed that "the juxtaposition of these tender lines with the words that follow is unpleasant."

Like other gentlemanly editors of the day, Gilder developed a warm, supportive relationship with his authors. He was generous with his praise, gentle in his criticism, and always respectful of their work. He paid his contributors well. Henry James received $1,500 for the serialization of his novel, *Confidence*, the same amount that Mary Hallock Foote received for *John Bodewin's Testimony.* Gilder was a helpful and meticulous editor, demanding that dates, names, and quotations be verified. And he frequently requested changes in style and content of a manuscript. Many authors, in addition to Molly, were grateful for his guidance. John Luther Long, author of "Madame Butterfly," told Gilder: "If you are as kind to all scribblers as you are to me you certainly cannot escape canonization . . . at their hands."

John Bodewin's Testimony first appeared as a serial in the *Century*, starting in November 1885, and was published in book form by Ticknor and Company in 1886. Like the *Led-Horse Claim*, this story centers on a boundary dispute between two rival mines, the Eagle Bird, owned by Mr. Newbold, and the Uinta, owned by the unscrupulous Colonel Billy Harkins. John Bodewin, a mining engineer from Connecticut, has surveyed both claims and knows that Harkins is in the wrong. Because the Colonel once befriended Bodewin's sister, however, the engineer refuses to testify in court against him, without revealing the reason to the Leadville community. He reconsiders only after he falls in love with Newbold's beautiful daughter, Josephine.

Before the trial begins, Harkins hires Jim Keesner and his son Tony to kidnap Bodewin and confine him in their mountain cabin to prevent him from testifying. Keesner's daughter, Babe, develops a crush on Bodewin and helps him escape, on the condition that he deny ever having known her family. When Bodewin fails to describe his captors, he loses the support of the townspeople, who now suspect that he willfully stayed away from the trial. His credibility is further damaged when he refuses to identify the body of Babe Keesner, killed in a mining accident after following Bodewin to the Eagle Bird. Because he must honor his promise to Babe, Bodewin makes a poor showing in court. The jury rules in favor of Harkins, and Bodewin leaves town in disgrace. Eventually, after Josephine learns the truth, the two lovers are reunited and start life anew in the Far West.

The modern reader will find much to admire in Molly's second novel. The story of the downfall of Bodewin's sister is poignantly told, and the account of Bodewin's disappearance en route to testify in court generates suspense. The author's descriptions of the Colorado Rockies are superb and her depiction of Leadville scenes first-rate. Her characterization of the female protagonists, Josephine Newbold and Mrs. Craig, wife of Newbold's lawyer, deserves special mention. These are active women who enjoy life in the West—the beauty around them, gallops in the mountain valleys, descents into the interior of mines. They are also strong-minded and display at times more wisdom than their male counterparts. Sprinkled throughout the story are other women, their composite stories giving readers a domestic image of the West not found in the fiction of nineteenth-century male writers.

John Bodewin's Testimony received mixed reviews in the press. A writer for the *Nation* criticized Molly's "imperfect" construction and "feeble" characterization but praised her "graceful descriptions" and "easy, pleasant style." A reviewer for the *Overland Monthly*, on the other hand, called Foote's novel "an especially graceful and artistically constructed story" and applauded her characterization of Josephine, a genuinely nice American girl. This novel, he concluded, "contains many merits, and all but no faults, and is more likely to be underrated than overrated."

With publication of *John Bodewin's Testimony*, Molly's reputation as a "western" writer was firmly established. Not only did she gain recognition in the press, but miners and engineers wrote fan letters praising the authenticity of her novel. These western men, Molly reported to Helena, "treat me as a compatriot and an old campaigner and they send me newspaper accounts of murders and conspiracies connected with mining and land-grabbing and want me to do justice to these happy themes."

The Footes prospered during their first summer in Idaho. Arthur was happy in his work, and the children were thriving. Molly also was in good spirits as she sketched her new surroundings, completed drawings for *St. Nicholas Magazine,* and wrote her first Idaho short story, "A Cloud on the Mountain," which she sent to Gilder in September. She called it "the result of the first vivid but sketchy impressions of a new kind of life."

Published in the same issue of the *Century* in which *John Bodewin's Testimony* made its debut, "A Cloud on the Mountain" takes place along the banks of the fictional Bear River and tells the story of Ruth Mary Tully and her unrequited love for a man of higher rank. At the time of their first and only encounter at the Tully ranch house, Ruth Mary is betrothed to her father's young partner, Joe Enselman. This arrangement is more satisfying to the elder Tully than it is to Ruth Mary. During the long winter, with Enselman away in Montana proving up a claim, Ruth Mary's infatuation with the young railroad engineer named Kirkwood becomes stronger, and she resolves to break her engagement. But when her fiancé returns in the spring following a mishap in which he lost an eye, she forswears her deepest emotions and intends to wed Enselman, although in silent despair "she wished that she were dead. There seemed to be no other way out of her trouble." Indeed, her torment ends when she drowns while rushing downstream to warn Kirkwood of an approaching flood.

Despite its melodramatic plot, the story gave eastern readers a realistic glimpse of family life in the West. The Tullys—father, mother, and four children—cope with real problems. The geographic details, which are excellent, derive from Molly's several visits to Boise Canyon. The Tullys, in fact, must have been modeled on the ranch family that Molly encountered on the fishing trip to Moore's Creek. Her keen appreciation for the natural environment results in an accurate portrayal of the Idaho landscape as she experienced it.

Molly's summer happiness gave way to pain and anguish when she suffered her third and final miscarriage in October 1884. Two and a half months into the pregnancy, she experienced all the pains of childbirth. "You know how sad it was to lie there and suffer," she wrote to Helena, "and know it was all for nothing . . . . I was an awful baby about it, and cried like one." She was sorry to "lose this little hope" and vowed to get strong and "take good care" of the two she already had. But her convalescence was prolonged, and it was not until December that she began to feel like her old self again.

Christmas that year was a happy occasion, with Molly's health restored and gifts flooding the household. Mr. Kinney presented the Footes with a "lovely great white mountain goat skin," and all three of Arthur's assistants lavished presents on the children. The Chinese cook in the engineers' camp sent white silk handkerchiefs to Arthur and John Sherman and "a lovely pale blue crepe shawl" to Molly. A total of twenty-one new books arrived, many of them from the Gilders, including a volume of Edith Thomas's poetry, Albert Stickney's *A True Republic*, and John Burroughs's *Fresh Fields*. In surveying these treasures, Molly wrote: "I dont know anything that looks more Christmassy than a lot of new books lying around waiting for the leisure that should follow the Holidays."

Books and literature continued to link Molly and her best friend. They often exchanged opinions on the stories they read and quoted from favorite passages. Molly wrote of her disappointment in Edgar W. Howe's *The Story of a Country Town* (1883), an exposé of the sordid side of small-town America. She told Helena that she had felt ill after reading of Thea Meeks' children with their "weak eyes and scald head . . . living in a house like a packing box with saucers and bottles of medicine standing round apparently for promiscuous application to the diseases specified." This was a type of realism that Molly came to despise. "I wonder if this is the sort of realism we are coming to—if these are the novels our Dorotheas and Bettys must feed their love of romance and poetry on."

But the writings of George Eliot continued to uplift her. She asked Helena to refer to volume two of Eliot's journals and read "for my sake the words beginning—'There is always an aftersadness belonging to brief and interrupted intercourse between friends.'" Still, Eliot's work could be discouraging to a struggling novelist. "It is not that we expect to be George Eliots," Molly explained, "but we must all strive to deliver our small message clearly and without affectation." Eliot's life, she concluded, was "a thing to make one realize one's pygmy capacities."

In the spring, about a year after her arrival in Idaho, the unforeseeable jolted Molly's world. The eastern firm that financed Arthur's irrigation scheme failed, bringing construction to a halt. Most of the crew was laid off and salaries stopped, except for Arthur's, which Molly called "a waiting not a working salary." A few men were paid to perform the minimum work required by law to protect the water rights, but John Sherman and Arthur's three assistants all lost their jobs.

To save on expenses, the Footes and the Shermans moved to Boise Canyon where they would live rent-free in the now-enlarged engineers' cabin. Wiley, Tompkins, and Kinney pitched tents on the adjacent hill and joined the two families for meals in the cook-tent. Since Arthur and his backers considered this only a temporary setback, the men were not inclined to seek jobs elsewhere, expecting work on the canal to resume at any time.

During the 1870s and 1880s, visionaries like Arthur Foote whipped up enthusiasm for the construction of large irrigation networks, which would allow arid lands like those in Idaho to bloom. But most private canal companies experienced financial problems, and many ultimately failed. Arthur's enterprise was handicapped from the start by a downward spiral of the nation's economy, which began in 1883 and left investors unusually cautious. The Baltimore firm that inherited Arthur's scheme sent two representatives to assess the canal's prospects; the second advised against heavy investments. So the work did not start up again, although Arthur believed it was but "a question of time." No one foresaw the long delays and crushed hopes that lay ahead.

In the meantime, the little camp of seven adults and four children made the most of their summer in the canyon. Molly appreciated the beauty of her surroundings. She especially enjoyed moonlit evenings on the beach and sketching forays to the top of the bluffs overlooking the river. Arthur, Sr., had more time to spend with his son. And the two younger engineers, A. J. Wiley and Harry Tompkins, shot grouse, fished for trout, and helped entertain the children. They celebrated the Fourth of July on the beach, lighting up the night with rockets and pine torches. Later that summer, James D. Hague arrived on his way to California, bringing news of the outside world and enlivening their evenings with lectures on the constellations.

In the fall, the little canyon community underwent several changes. The most momentous was the arrival of Nelly Linton, the daughter of Molly's mentor at Cooper Union, to serve as tutor and governess in the Foote household. She had been en route to Idaho from France when the canal work shut down, allowing no opportunity for Molly to warn her of their changed circumstances. But Nelly, a quiet, practical woman, made a quick adjustment to her new surroundings. She was to remain a valued member of the family for nearly thirteen years.

About the time Nelly arrived, Bessie and John Sherman returned to Boise to place Gerald in school. They rented one of the best-furnished houses in town and soon took in boarders, which Bessie vowed was "better than getting into debt or going home." But the Footes chose to remain in the canyon. In September, with money Molly received for serial rights to *John Bodewin's Testimony*, they started construction of a stone house on the hill where the engineers had their tents. Designed by Arthur and built of local materials, the dwelling offered a splendid view of the canyon.

By mid-December the family had settled into their new home. Wiley and Tompkins had helped with the move—they carried trunks, put up beds, hung pictures, and performed a multitude of other tasks. "I did nothing but walk around and say where I wanted things to go," Molly reported to Helena. But it was she who had made decisions about the location of closets, the finish of the mantels, and the design of a stair rail. "All of this sort of thing," she confessed, "interfered with my desk occupations."

The house was comfortable right from the start. Three large fireplaces kept it warm in the winter, and two-foot thick walls would help keep it cool in the summer. On long winter evenings the family and young Tompkins often gathered beside the fireplace in the Juniors' room, a combination office and smoking room. Later, after Molly put little Betty to bed, she read to her son until his bedtime and then rejoined the men to listen to Tompkins read aloud from some literary work. Although Wiley had left the canyon soon after the Stone House was finished to find another job, Tompkins had orders from his father to stay on, becoming virtually a member of the family.

In her Christmas letter to Helena, describing the move to the new house, Molly announced she was pregnant. She told her friend, who only a few weeks earlier had given birth to another son: "I am, as usual following your example, though not so closely as usual." Now began a prolonged test of Molly's endurance, for the precautions she took to prevent another miscarriage greatly restricted her movements. This forced inactivity, coupled with anxiety about the canal's future, weighed heavily on her spirits. And her worries escalated after the baby's birth in June. Uncharacteristically, she kept her anxieties from Helena since Arthur feared that writing of the canal's problems, even in family letters, might harm his New York partners. Not until March 6, 1887, did Molly tell Helena of the project's failure and of the tensions this created in the household.

Meanwhile, five months before the baby was expected, Molly abandoned many of her favorite pastimes—horseback rides, trips to see Bessie, hikes to the top of the bluffs. Further into the pregnancy she gave up walking alone because of the hilly terrain. "But I *had* to walk," she later told Helena, inserting a whimsical note into an otherwise somber account of this time of waiting, "so I was led out every day, like a sick elephant." And she vowed: "This *must* be the *last* one! Three are not too many, but they are quite enough."

The strain of waiting for the baby and for orders to resume the canal work was felt by the entire household. In trying to keep busy, the men turned the old engineers' cabin into a workshop, where they invented an automatic waste weir and other irrigating devices. Nelly Linton also taught them bookbinding, having learned the craft from her father. Harry Tompkins read a great deal from his library of fine literature, while Arthur pored over his collection of irrigation reports and pamphlets, which Molly also read to understand better her husband's work.

The children's routine may have shielded them from their parents' anxieties. Arthur, Jr., took lessons with Nelly Linton during the morning, part of which time little Betty was also in her care. They walked with their tutor after lunch and later had an early supper under her supervision. But they joined their parents in the Juniors' room before bedtime. "Isolated as we are," Molly explained to Helena, "we find it necessary to keep up the little forms of civilization, as discipline is kept up on ship-board."

Despite domestic worries, Molly persevered with her art. Early in her pregnancy, she illustrated "two fine stories," one by Ellen Mackubin, titled "A Coward" (*Century,* 1886), a story of army life on the frontier, and the other by Lieutenant A. W. Greeley, "Our Kivigtok," (*Century,* 1887), based on his expedition to Lady Franklin Bay. Still later, before the baby arrived, she wrote "The Fate of a Voice" (*Century,* 1886), one of her most provocative Idaho stories.

"The Fate of a Voice" opens with an accurate description of Boise Canyon, the fictional Wallula River Cañon. In the third paragraph, Foote uses the phrase "angle of repose" to describe the fragmented rocks that had fallen to the base of the lava bluffs. Later, in her reminiscences, she applies this term to the family in Idaho, when "each one of us in the Cañon was slipping and crawling and grinding along seeking what to us was that angle." Wallace Stegner appropriated this term for his prize-winning novel, *Angle of Repose* (1971), based on the life of Mary Hallock Foote, although the novel's ending, as stated elsewhere, departs radically from Foote's actual experiences. But Molly's vivid description written while in her seventies accurately depicts her emotional state when she wrote "The Fate of a Voice." "[It] was written when I was sick and disgusted with myself and everything," she once confessed to Helena. Molly called it a "potboiler," a term she applied to her work with increasing frequency as Arthur's financial affairs continued to worsen. But income from her "potboilers" permitted the Footes to employ a domestic staff of surprising size—a governess-tutor for the children, a Chinese cook-laundryman, and a local girl as nurse after the baby came. Even though strapped for money, neither Molly nor Arthur with their upper-class sensibilities could conceive of running a household without domestic help.

"The Fate of a Voice" centers on the choice between art and marriage that faces eighteen-year-old Madeline Hendrie, a talented singer with a promising career. She meets a young engineer, Hugh Aldis, on a summer's trip west to visit her sister. He falls in love and proposes marriage. Although she is attracted to him, she spurns his offer, pledging loyalty to her voice. The night before she is to leave for three years' study abroad, they discuss their future while perched on a ledge just below the top of the lava bluffs. She tells Aldis, "I did not choose my fate. It has chosen me. . . . My life is pledged to a purpose as serious as marriage itself . . . . Love is not the only inspiration a woman's life can know." He argues that she is "blind to a career so much finer, so much broader, so much sweeter, and more womanly." At the end of their impassioned discussion, Madeline trips and almost falls over the precipice. In pushing her to safety, Aldis falls into the canyon when the rock crumbles under his foot. Thinking he has died in the fall, the singer loses her voice. But shrubbery cushions his descent and he emerges undamaged.

Madeline is guilt-ridden, convinced that her voice was taken because of her pride, but she refuses to burden Aldis with "the wreck she now thought herself to be." But she does agree to marry him if her voice returns. She then travels to New York, where she recovers her voice and stages a final concert, planning to join Aldis afterwards for the return trip west. But he arrives prematurely, witnesses her triumph in the concert hall, and believes he has lost her to her art. He leaves a letter at her hotel, in which he releases her from her promise. But in the end, the two lovers are reconciled and take up married life in the West. Years later those who had heard Madeline sing in New York said she had thrown away "a promising career, just at its outset, and went West with a husband—not anybody in particular. It was altogether a great pity." But the voice was not lost, Molly writes, for it was heard in engineers' camps, at Sunday services, and on mountain trails. In the final passage she suggests that an artist can find satisfaction in the West.

> The soul of music, wherever it is purely uttered, will find its listeners, though it be a voice singing in the wilderness, in the dawn of the day of art and beauty which is coming to a new country and a new people.

Foote projects many of her own fears and frustrations onto Madeline Hendrie. Like Madeline, Molly feared the effect of isolation on her art; like her, she believed that creativity was spurred by interaction with other artists. For Molly, as for her character Madeline, the demands of marriage ultimately took precedence over those of art. Yet Molly struggled all of her life to overcome the constraints that marriage imposed on her art. Days before the birth of her second daughter, she wrote to Helena: "Nothing *pays* so well as loving and caring for our own husband, children, family, friends—*doings* of any kind are no real, permanent satisfaction. Yet we have to keep doing, or love itself would stifle."

A second story from this period, which Foote may have written before her confinement, "The Lamb That Couldn't 'Keep Up'" (*St. Nicholas Magazine,* 1889), was based on an episode in Boise Canyon involving the children. Sheepmen driving a large flock up into the hills gave Arthur and his cousin Gerald a lamb that had fallen behind its mother and was trampled. The boys placed it in the shade and tried to force it to drink warm milk and brandy. But the lamb died in the night. Molly used Betty and Arthur as models in the illustration and sold the story to *St. Nicholas* "for a good round sum."

Tensions in the household became excruciating as Molly neared the time of delivery. "You cannot imagine," she later wrote to Helena, "what it was to have the whole household waiting for the event. . . . [There were] no visitors, no events[,] nothing to remove the thoughts of them all, or my own thoughts, from the one thing I didnt want to think about." A nurse came to stay at the Stone House a week or so before the baby was due. But when she fell ill, Arthur rushed to Boise and returned with Bessie to handle the delivery. After a "stifling hot" day, baby Agnes was born at sunset on June 23, 1886. Years later Molly recalled: "I had thought that in our uncertain way of life we needed another boy rather than another girl—queer how even in our family, where all the women were self-supporting, that old tradition still held; that boys are sure to be an asset and girls a liability."

After the baby came, "everything went wrong." Molly developed internal complications, which left her "awfully weak and restless and nervous." She worried about the baby, whose navel had not healed properly, and about the canal's future and the cost of running her household—$45 per month for the cook-laundryman, $25 per month for Nelly Linton, and $20 for the baby's nurse. Unable to travel comfortably, she did not venture beyond the canyon until late in the year, which meant she had spent a total of ten months within the confines of Boise Canyon. Later, she wrote poignantly of this time of waiting:

> Ten months imprisoned by these bluffs, with the ceaseless roar of the river, with the red sunsets night after night—the new moons month after month—the Canon wind, or the wind from the plains always blowing—the mail-bag coming day after day—and never the letter we were all looking for, but only letters telling of deaths, and trouble among friends at home.

Although Arthur was under enormous pressure himself during their stay in the canyon, his concern for Molly was heartfelt. A strong, silent man for the most part, Foote rarely showed his emotions to others. He seemed happiest when engaged in hard physical work or in solving some engineering problem. Molly once said that his temperament demanded "activity at the rate of 40 miles a day on horseback." But he was also generous and kind-hearted, and during Molly's pregnancy, he helped brighten her days in a variety of ways. He made her a "lovely" worktable with a baby-basket on a shelf beneath and brought her a rose or two in the mornings. After she was up and walking again, he surprised her with a piano. It was moved into the house while she was walking outside with Tompkins. Through an open window she heard Nelly playing a Beethoven waltz, the first music she had heard since moving to the canyon. "We dont need a piano," she later confessed to Helena, "but it was a wise little extravagance of Arthur's. It is a rest to the soul in the midst of a landscape like this."

By November Molly had resumed many of her usual activities. She rode horseback again and worked on a new story. She should have felt pride and satisfaction when "The Fate of a Voice" appeared in the November issue of the *Century*, but she did not. The typographical errors in the story upset her, and she wrote to the editors rebuking them for failing to send her the proofs to correct. She was particularly disturbed by the error in the name of the protagonist: "The name of my girl was meant to be Hendrie and it comes out in print Hendric; a name which is no name at all, or rather one misspelled." She listed several other errors as well and ended with a plea: "Please, although I am so absurdly far away, dont forget me, again, until the last moment and then hurry in half-dressed."

Her annoyance soon gave way to delight when letters began to arrive from engineers, complimenting her on "The Fate of a Voice." In this and in her earlier work, Foote wrote about their profession in a way rarely found in nineteenth-century fiction. She described their work accurately and depicted them as bright, attractive, loving men. After reading this most recent of Molly's stories, one engineer wrote from Honduras: "I am unable to criticize your writing as literary productions. But this one thing I know, that for faithful portrayal of feelings and scenes dear to all of us who have spent our lives amid mountain and forest for a true appreciation of the lives of such as we are—they are unsurpassed."

Still, it was difficult for Molly to keep her spirits up for very long when news of the canal's future was so dismal and household worries continued to mount. In January her "best nurse" left for Boise with an ear problem and a new girl arrived, the seventh to stay at the Stone House since baby Agnes's birth. Molly finally shared her anxieties with Helena in the letter she wrote on March 6, 1887, wherein she movingly described the family's long ordeal.

> These last two years have been the sternest discipline *my* life has ever known. It is not a thing like sorrow, it is a steady strain and there has been no *limit* fixed—so long we must endure, and then—It has been a hope steadily deferred from day to day—Now and then rising to a climax of certainty—then being dashed down again, to resume the from day to day process.

In this and in subsequent letters, Molly expressed a fierce loyalty to Arthur's vision of western irrigation and a tender concern for his welfare. For a man of his disposition, she wrote, forced inactivity and the suspense of waiting "are simply the road to insanity." Yet he seemed in boyishly good humor, and his enthusiasm for the project was undiminished, even in the face of mounting criticism from landowners demanding to know when the canal was to start up. In Molly's eyes, Arthur was doing grand work by attempting to bring water onto arid lands.

> It is *making a country* as large as a small state—and if in its isolation and virgin barrenness it is so poetic a land—what will it be, with long lines of gleaming ditches traversing its vast levels with fields of alfalfa and herds of cattle, and rows of poplars marking the boundaries of the farms.

During this anxious time, however, Molly's assessment of her own work fluctuated between hope and disappointment. She continued to belittle her own talent and to praise Helena's, insisting that what she did was not art but an industry. And she now accepted her friend's premise, espoused in their girlhood, that art was not possible for a married woman. "She may use her gift if she has one, as a drudge uses her needle, or her broom—but she must be content to see the soul of it wither and the light of it go out." But in return, Molly avowed, the married woman "has the best thing that has ever been given to any woman—love."

Yet Foote never stopped trying to perfect her work. In the midst of this painful time of uncertainty, she conceived a series of illustrations that would bring her new acclaim as a western artist. She started work on the drawings the summer of 1887, while Arthur was in New York conferring with business partners. For background, she used the hills and bluffs that surrounded her, and for models she used friends and members of the family. She had completed four blocks by November 3, when she wrote to Richard Gilder suggesting that he publish her Far West illustrations in the *Century*, one to appear each month, accompanied by verse or text composed by a "collaborator." In the end Richard convinced Molly to write her own text, although poems by Edith Thomas appear with two of the published drawings.

Entitled "Pictures of the Far West," the series of eleven sketches, each accompanied by a short commentary, ran in the *Century* from November 1888 through November 1889. These pictures, depicting life she had observed in Boise Canyon, are among the best she ever drew. Attention to detail and delicacy of style resulted in a realism that is often poetic. Or, as Regina Armstrong observed in 1900, Foote "links the poetic and the actual in a manner which makes them inseparable." As an example, "Looking for Camp," the first illustration in the series, features a tall, slim man, with rifle resting on one shoulder, leading a horse down a hill slope at moonrise in search of camp. Details of the man's clothing, his riding gear, and the grassy hillside make this an authentic picture; suggestions of the man's dignity, the solemnity of the landscape, and the motion of the figures make it poetic.

The realism of Foote's illustrations goes beyond meticulous attention to detail. She shows the domestic side of U.S. expansion, which contemporary male artists ignored. Her images of women and children suggest that the West is a suitable place for building homes and raising families. "The Irrigating Ditch," among the best in the series, imparts a powerful sense of home life. In the foreground, a woman with babe in arms stands beside a water-filled irrigation ditch while in the distance a man regulates the flow. The tall trees in the background, which help define the figures, are signs of recent settlement. In "The Coming of Winter," Foote sketches a typical homesteader family in front of a crude cabin, the man with rifle in hand and his wife holding a baby. The exquisite detail—washtub, rub board, and mop hung on the outside wall, a large kettle on an outdoor table—is a reminder of the hard labor that awaits the homesteader woman.

Molly's pictures of the Far West are in stark contrast to those of Frederic Remington, a contemporary who painted dramatic scenes of Indian-white conflict and masculine adventure. In his illustrations for Theodore Roosevelt's "Ranch Life in the Far West," which also appeared in the *Century* in 1888 at the start of Remington's meteoric rise to fame, there is not a hint of domesticity. The drawings are of rugged men on horseback, cowboys fighting in a saloon, men in conflict over brands. This is masculine territory devoid of women and families. To many Americans, Remington's powerful images of a wild West seemed to depict the real West.

In the late nineteenth century, then, two competing visions of the West vied for public acceptance. Molly's domestic images of families and settlement offered a gentler vision of the West than Remington's more violent representations. The contrast is most apparent when two of Foote's Far West drawings, "Afternoon at a Ranch," which portrays her daughter Betty asleep on the patio of the Stone House, and "The Orchard Windbreak," featuring fruit trees, lush meadows, and a pretty woman standing near a tame fawn, are juxtaposed with Remington's well-known "Fight for the Water Hole" (1903), in which rough-clad cowboys blaze away at Indians to control an isolated water pool, or "Dash for the Timber" (1889), in which eight gun-wielding riders are pursued by a much larger number of Indians. Even Foote's male figures of engineers and farmers little resemble Remington's cast of gun-toting soldiers, Indians, and cowboys. But it was Remington's vision of the West—a vision that distorted the reality of western settlement—that gained in popularity as the old century ended and the new one got underway. This male view of a wild and violent West, perpetuated by such other artists as Charles Russell, Henry Farny, and Charles Schreyvogel, would eventually eclipse Molly's domestic version and come to dominate public imagery.

With Molly's work commanding good prices and news from New York guardedly optimistic as the year 1887 ended, the Footes began to talk of building a new house on the mesa outside of Boise. The Stone House had become "horribly cramped"after Agnes's birth. Finding a quiet spot in which to work had always been difficult, but now it must have been nearly impossible. In the Mesa House, Molly reported with delight, she would have for the first time in her life a room of her own in which to work. Rising above past frustrations and disappointments, the thirty-nine-year-old artist eloquently expressed an abiding faith and optimism in their western experiment:

> It is our fate to be always in these queer places—and I forsee [*sic*] the time when I shall long for them and be homesick for the waste of moonlight, the silence, the night wind and the river! There is nothing that will ever quite take its place! Dreamers we are, dreamers we always will be, and what is folly and vain imaginings to some people is the stuff our daily lives are made of. And there are thousands like us! If there never had been, there would be no great West. We may not be the ones who succeed, but to every one who dreams and realizes his dreams there must be a hundred or a thousand who dream and fail.

In the closing months of the year, Molly enjoyed visits with Bessie and with two or three recent arrivals from the East, among them Rosamond Dana Wild, the daughter of Richard Henry Dana, best known for his book, *Two Years Before the*

Mast. Letters from Helena continued to buoy Molly's spirits. But the contrast in their lives, now greater than ever before, left Molly wondering if a time would come when her friend would find her too provincial. While the Footes lived a life of solitude in the canyon, the Gilders continued to entertain a wide array of artists and authors in their New York City residence and in their summer retreat in the little village of Marion on the headwaters of Buzzard's Bay in Massachusetts. The Gilders also became friends with Grover Cleveland and his new young wife, Frances, late in the president's first term in office. In July 1888 the First Lady stayed with the Gilders at their Marion cottage; for the next two summers the ex-president and his wife returned to Marion, living in rented lodgings before buying a place of their own. The Gilders became part of a select circle of friends with whom the Clevelands exchanged enjoyable evening parties.

Helena never faltered in her loyalty to her western friend, however, always saying "just the right thing" when Molly's cares seemed about to overwhelm her, as they nearly did early in 1888 when the children fell ill and the house was crowded with visitors. After Christmas, Agnes's nurse had returned from Boise infected with measles, and Molly's three children and Birney Sherman, who was spending the winter with her cousins, all became sick. Thirteen people were jammed into the Stone House after Bessie came to help care for the youngsters and A. J. Wiley and Gerald Sherman arrived for a visit. The only place for little Arthur to sleep during the height of his sickness was on the sofa in the parlor. "It was a miserable evening," Molly wrote to Helena, "and I wished the house might be cleared of men with all my heart." Under the accumulated strain of the past three years, culminating with this outbreak of measles, Molly cried out to her friend:

> I am daily chopped in little pieces and passed around and devoured and expected to be whole again next day, and all days. And I am *never alone*, for a single minute! . . . I was brought up in a life where, you know, there was plenty of space and long solitary walks and not many people pressing

in. It is very bad for my disposition never to have the *room*, inside and out, to breath in.

In this same letter, Molly referred obliquely to another crushing worry: "I can not tell you, now, the principal causes of the strain which I feel sometimes keenly, that I wonder if I can bear it any longer." She may be hinting at Arthur's use of alcohol to escape the pressures under which he lived, a practice Molly first openly wrote about in 1889. She never revealed in her letters, however, the full extent of his drinking problem, but it was sufficient to cause her great distress.

Molly's ability to continue her work under these circumstances was remarkable. At the time of the measles outbreak, she was deep into the Far West illustrations and must already have started the third Leadville novel. Once the children were well, she returned to both projects, despite the cramped quarters and the uncertainties that swirled about her. A. J. Wiley, who, like Harry Tompkins, was almost a member of the family during the canyon years, later recalled: "The vast amount of work she produced under conditions that would have absorbed all the energies of an ordinary woman, is accounted for by the fact that she seemed not to be dependent upon propitious moods or favorable surroundings, but had the faculty of absorbing herself in artistic or literary work whenever the more pressing claims of family life relaxed."

The Last Assembly Ball, the third of Foote's Leadville novels, appeared serially in the *Century*, starting in March 1889, and in book form later that same year under the imprint of Houghton Mifflin and Company. The author uses the mining community to explicate for eastern readers the rigid class structure she found in western communities. In the opening paragraph she writes: "Among other unsafe assumptions, the East has decided that nothing can be freer and simpler than the social life of the far West." The frontier, she goes on to say, is in a "stage of fermentation," wherein its denizens are groping to establish proper relations among its classes.

The story revolves around Frank Embury, a young eastern engineer, who, disappointed in love, "hurled himself across the continent by the first train westward by railcar," arriving in Leadville during the mining boom. With his partner Hugh Williams, he finds shelter in the select boarding house of the widow Fanny Dansken. She establishes a homelike atmosphere for her young male boarders and becomes their self-appointed moral guardian. When Embury takes an interest in a pretty servant girl, Milly Robinson, and invites her to the "Assembly" ball, Mrs. Dansken protests, seeing the impropriety of their relationship. An idealist, Embury impetuously marries Milly, believing this will win her social acceptance. But Milly has a past unknown to Frank, who sees her only as a naive young girl in need of protection. In reality, she came to Leadville looking for the husband who deserted her, only to find that he had died. She soon gave birth to a child, who also died. Leadville socialites learn these facts before Frank does and subsequently snub the newly married couple at the ball. Embury's sins are twofold: he has married out of his class and to a woman whose background is suspect. He learns the truth only as he goes to defend his wife's reputation in a duel. Realizing that his hasty marriage was a mistake and that he can never present Milly to his mother, he seems to welcome the death that awaits him on the dueling field.

Although death seems a high price to pay for social improprieties, the author helps illuminate the complex social code that prevailed among the western elite. And even though her portrayals of Frank and Milly are weak, her characterization of Mrs. Dansken is masterful, as is her depiction of life in a boarding house. And she creates a delightful minor character in Mrs. Black, the minister's wife, who tells Milly that "when it comes to marriages—why, there's all sorts, and it's amazing how comfortable they turn out, spite of everything."

During her stay in the canyon, Molly's illustrations continued to appear regularly in *St. Nicholas Magazine.* A charming family scene, for which all three of the artist's children served as models, accompanied Washington Gladden's "Santa Claus in the Pulpit" (1887). Baby Agnes again appeared in an illustration for Mary Mapes Dodge's "First Steps" (1888) and in Molly's "The Baby's Sunny Corner," the frontispiece for the May 1889 issue. Two stories that Molly wrote and illustrated herself, "An Idaho Picnic" (1887) and "A Visit to John's Camp" (1890), introduced children to a West that was both authentic and appealing.

Despite the money that Molly earned, the Footes decided midway through the summer of 1888 that they could not afford to build on the mesa. For the same reason, they did not send little Arthur to a private eastern school as they had planned. But rather than spend another winter in the Stone House, they took rooms in Bessie's boarding house, where Nelly would look after Betty and Agnes in the mornings and hold school in the afternoons for Arthur, Birney, and a few select town children.

In September 1888 Molly traveled east alone to see her mother and to help settle the financial affairs of her father, who had died during the previous year. Molly's pleasure in returning to Milton after such a long absence was tempered by the sadness of dealing with executors and coming to terms with her mother's reduced circumstances. The old Hallock homestead was to be sold to pay off debts and Molly's mother was to live with Tom and his family. Still, Molly must have enjoyed the week she spent with Helena, now pregnant with her daughter Helena Francesca.

On this trip east, Molly handed over to Richard the manuscript for *The Last Assembly Ball*, a shorter composition than her previous novel. She soon learned that the *Century* agreed to pay her price of $1,000. But when the first installment appeared in March Molly's discovery of two "bad mistakes" upset her. Substitution of the word *heavy* for *heady* in the introduction, she fumed to Richard, "destroys all the sense of the whole business and is an absurdity, for it is the *heady* quality of the *light* air which, etc." The second mistake seemed less serious, *broad* instead of *board* sidewalks. But these matters, she insisted, "should be important, in a magazine of the Century's standing, and if a writer's work is worth publishing at all, it is certainly worth being treated with more respect."

The winter just ending had been particularly hard on Molly. Arthur had been ill, she reported to his mother, though the cause of his indisposition may well have been alcohol. Later, Molly was to write of this winter to Helena: "The *pressure* was terrible—and complicated, in ways I cannot describe to you. At times the least thing gave me such thrills of nervous irritability that I was frightened."

To escape the mental unrest that had tormented her for so long, Molly took the children to Victoria, British Columbia, a seaport on the south end of Vancouver Island, to spend the summer of 1889. By this time Arthur had accepted a government job with John Wesley Powell's survey of western water resources. After six years as chief engineer of the private canal project, Foote had turned control over to Harry Tompkins, though Foote remained as the company's consulting engineer. Molly, in fact, had urged Arthur to take the government job, even though the pay was small, because, as she told James D. Hague, "I felt it was suicidal for him, with his temperament, to live in inactivity and suspense any longer."

So Molly went off to Victoria for three months, where she rented a furnished four-bedroom cottage and began the experiment of living without Arthur. In addition to her brood, the cottage housed Agnes's nurse, who went along without salary merely to see something of the world beyond Idaho, an English housekeeper hired at $20 per month, and Maud Ahern, a young New Englander whom Molly had befriended in Boise and who was now on a round-about route home. The cottage was only a few minutes' walk of Beacon Hill Park, where on Saturdays the Marine band played and cricket, lacrosse, and baseball matches took place. Despite the lovely location, Molly felt lost without Arthur. She worked diligently on her drawings, however, reporting to her mother that she was trying "to make Victoria 'pay.'" And she became friends with Edith Angus, an Englishwoman who called one day at the cottage to meet the famous author. Thus began a lifelong friendship. Years later Molly recalled: "After this first visit we were friends. We both knew that the experience was exceptional." That Edith Angus talked to Molly about her own husband's battle with alcoholism must have strengthened the bond between them, and their walks together made Molly's days less lonely. In her reminiscences, Molly writes: "I shall always feel that I went to Victoria to meet Edith Angus."

But, of course, Molly had left home for other reasons. Clearly she longed to escape the pressures of her household, but just as clearly she wanted time to contemplate a longer separation from Arthur. She probably had in mind a move east to assure the children a good education. But in a July letter to Helena, written after several weeks in Victoria, she confessed her inability to endure such a long parting:

> This experiment has settled one thing in my mind. There is no use my thinking I could go anywhere with the children for their improvement and my own away from my old boy. I'm irrevocably committed to the part of an anxious wife.

So back she went to Boise—only to learn that Arthur had been on a spectacular drinking spree. Stunned and dismayed that he had jeopardized his job and his family's happiness, Molly cried out to her friend: "We are a family without a future." For now, life seemed most hopeless, their dreams turned to ashes. Sounding the depths of despair, she continued:

> One thing this summer has taught me. To think no more of homes, or of house building—anywhere—Our honor is built upon sand. I shall simply live as now with [Bessie], and share her *beds* and eat her cooking . . . . Anyway, the mesa is to me now a place with a blight upon it.

Undoubtedly, Molly reacted as many other wives of her generation did. Strong drink was a part of nineteenth-century society, and drunkenness was widespread. But the nation perceived alcohol abuse as mostly harmful to women and children. Women therefore joined the Women's Christian Temperance Union in large numbers and made temperance a popular reform. As wives and mothers, women were expected to protect society from drink. It is not surprising therefore that Molly lashed out against her husband's behavior.

Yet Molly remained "irrevocably committed" to Arthur and to his struggle to regain his self-respect. She had "a *mother's* yearning," she told Helena, "that he may keep strong and get through it creditably." Eventually they did build a house on the mesa and share good times again, but for the remainder of their years in Idaho happiness was always mixed with financial stress and family tension.

Richard Watson Gilder and Helena de Kay Gilder, from *Letters of Richard Watson Gilder,* edited by Rosamond Gilder (Boston, 1916).

The Leadville Cabin, 1879. This item is reproduced by permission of The Huntington Library, San Marino, California.

Capitol Hill in Leadville. At the center is the W. S. Ward house; next door on the right is the Foote cabin ca. 1879–81. Courtesy of the Colorado Historical Society, neg. no. F-5930.

“Court and Stair-Way of a Mexican House,” *Century*, November 1881.

"Indian Cart and Pottery Ovens," *Century*, March 1882.

Mary Hallock Foote and children in the Boise River Canyon, 1880s. This item is reproduced by permission of The Huntington Library, San Marino, California.

Arthur De Wint Foote in the 1880s. Courtesy of Evelyn Foote Gardiner.

The Stone House in Boise River Canyon, ca. 1886–89. This item is reproduced by permission of The Huntington Library, San Marino, California.

Boise River Canyon looking upriver. Courtesy of Idaho Historical Society, no. 2503.

"Looking for Camp," *Century*, November 1888.

"The Irrigating Ditch," *Century*, June 1889.

"The Coming of Winter," *Century*, December 1888.

Boise, ca. 1894–95. Back row, l. to r.: Mary Hallock Foote, Bessie Sherman, Nelly Linton; front row: Mary Birney Sherman, Agnes, Betty, and Arthur B. Foote. This item is reproduced by permission of The Huntington Library, San Marino, California.

"The Engineer's Mate," *Century*, May 1895.

The Footes at North Star Cottage. This item is reproduced by permission of The Huntington Library, San Marino, California.

Arthur Foote at home. This item is reproduced by permission of The Huntington Library, San Marino, California.

The North Star House. This item is reproduced by permission of The Huntington Library, San Marino, California.

Mary Hallock Foote, taken in Grass Valley on May 29, 1921. Courtesy of the California Historical Society, FN-16661.

CHAPTER 4

"I Was Not Happy That Summer on the Mesa"

FRIGHTENED and angered by Arthur's recent bout with alcohol, Molly resolved to gain some control over the family's future. On August 8, 1889, shortly after she returned to Boise, she wrote to tell Helena: "From this time on I shall keep my separate account. It is the only safe thing to do." Thanks to her checks from the *Century*, Arthur, Jr., was to enter St. Paul's School in Concord, New Hampshire, later that fall. Meanwhile, she and Arthur, Sr., managed to work through this painful episode in their marriage. He had been away on Powell's irrigation survey when Molly learned the disquieting details. But upon his return, Molly confided to her friend, he "made no concealments [*sic*], which is always the part most terrible to me."

Arthur's new job had taken him to the Grand Tetons to investigate matters pertaining to Idaho's water supply. He returned in good health and gave expert testimony before a senatorial committee, which was meeting in Boise. "Nothing could have been more becoming to him," Molly recorded, "or brought out better his peculiar line of work, for which he is suited." Their renewed intimacy during Arthur's short stay at home led Molly to exclaim: "We were very happy—though it was but for a little while."

For the remainder of the year, Arthur was often in the field locating reservoir sites while Molly and the two little girls lived at John and Bessie Sherman's boarding house. Both youngsters apparently spent a part of each day with Nelly Linton, which afforded Molly the time to draw and write. One day in September she rode to Boise Canyon with Harry Tompkins to make sketches for a story that was later published in *St. Nicholas Magazine*. By mid-November, however, she was "deep in my Irrigation story," a narrative she had been longing to write for nearly two years. She had planned to call it "The History of a Scheme" and to document from a woman's point of view the saga of the Boise irrigation project. Realizing her story would be unlike most other contemporary western fiction, she exclaimed to Richard Gilder: "It would be the best and uniquest [*sic*] thing I could ever hope to do and be an actual contribution to the history of the development of a new country, in a different line and perhaps more subtle, than the plains wagon and settlers cabin story of the Great West." Although she later deviated from her original story line, Molly was to write a powerful novel that drew on the heartache and disappointments of their prolonged stay in the canyon.

Early in January 1890, the Footes left the girls in Bessie's care and traveled east to visit family, friends, and business associates. Molly later described her time with Helena as "a complete and altogether happy visit for me." Their last stop was at the Tompkinses, where they received good news: a group of English capitalists had agreed to finance the Boise irrigation scheme. But Molly "could scarcely trust" this triumph, she later recalled. Years of suspense punctuated by disappointments led her to believe that "something else would go wrong."

On their return trip to Idaho, the Footes stopped in Denver where Arthur drew up contracts with William C. Bradbury to move the dirt on seventy-five miles of canal line. Before they reached Boise, however, they were snowbound on the Oregon Short Line, an experience that inspired one of Foote's most successful Idaho stories. But Molly scarcely lifted pen or sketching pencil during the two months following her return home. First, little Agnes fell ill and ran such a high fever that Molly sent for a doctor during the middle of the night. "I have no remembrance of anything that happened for a month after this, outside her sickroom," Molly later recalled. Then she and the children moved into new lodgings after the Shermans gave up their rental property and prepared to build a new boarding house across the street from the state capitol.

Arthur spent most of his time in the field, though his work for the irrigation survey ended later that year when, for political reasons, Congress failed to refund the project. Meanwhile, Foote had started building a house on the mesa about two and a half miles outside of Boise. Molly looked forward to the move. She would have her own study, and the children could roam the countryside to look for wildflowers and not be "penned in behind picket fences." Often she was struck by the beauty of the mesa. On one occasion she compared it to a great treeless moor, with sagebrush sticking up like tufts of heather. After spending two nights in the unfinished house, Molly wrote with enthusiasm to Helena: "The sunsets are magnificent and though we miss the river, the whole aspect is so much larger and freer than the canon [*sic*] that I know we shall be able to stay and to 'stand it,' solitary as it is."

Carpenters continued to work on the Mesa House through the fall, long after the Footes had moved in. By mid-October a newly installed windmill was pumping forty to eighty barrels of water a day from a 600-foot-deep well. A hired man was put to work plowing one hundred acres of Arthur's desert land claim, which was to be sown in wheat. And sometime later holes were dug for planting an orchard, and poplars were set out near the house and along the avenue leading to the property. Arthur was doing everything possible, in fact, to prepare the land to receive irrigation water in the spring.

After six long years awaiting financing, the smaller of the two canals that comprised the Boise irrigation system (the Phyllis Canal) was completed under Bradbury's supervision, and farmers above the Footes began getting water during the summer of 1890. In July Bradbury started work on the larger ditch, the New York Canal, which would include a section through the canyon and bring water to the Footes' property. Conditions looked so favorable that Arthur spoke optimistically of future development.

The cost of building on the mesa, however, frightened Molly. "We seemed to be spending money like water to get ready for water which was not even in sight," she later recalled. Her anxieties increased when she learned that Alfred and Katherine Rockwell, Arthur's cousins, had bought a large chunk of his canal stock to finance improvements. Arthur remained confident, however. He assured Molly that by sinking money into their "pioneer ranch," they would show potential investors what this desert land could do. Still, Molly writes in her reminiscences, "I was not happy that summer on the Mesa. I had seen so much trouble in families from mixing business and affection. The Rockwells did not need our scheme, but we needed them."

The summer held sorrows as well as anxieties. Molly's mother died in August and Helena's mother and brother Sydney a short time later. Amidst her grief, Molly wrote to Helena: "How short a time ago it seems that we all sat round the fire in the parlor at Kaywood [Helena's girlhood home]. Your mother with her sons, and how few we are left; there is no more Kaywood—no more Milton." The dust storms of the summer must also have contributed to Molly's sense of foreboding. The hot desert wind blew for days on end, with clouds of dust obscuring the sky and wind-driven particles entering the house through cracks in doors and windows. "My very blood seemed drying up," she recorded.

With these distractions, it is little wonder that by late September Molly had completed only three chapters of her irrigation story. But these she sent to Gilder, seeking critical feedback. In explanation for the dearth of material, she noted: "The summer has set all my thoughts adrift from my plans of work. There has been little continuity, except of heat—and you know how these waves of sorrow set everything afloat." One of the joys of summer, which may also have slowed her literary work, however, was her son's homecoming. When he left to return to school in August, after spending his vacation in Idaho, Molly lamented: "I miss him even more than last year because he is older and more of a companion."

But as Molly feared, troubles continued to plague the irrigation project. After Enoch Harvey, a prime backer of the enterprise, was killed in an accident in Liverpool in October, his English associates lost interest and failed to put up the promised funds. William C. Bradbury spent $208,000 of his own money to continue work on the New York Canal but was forced to stop in July 1891 after completing only six miles, leaving landholders like the Footes without irrigation water. Moreover, it was an unusually dry year. Without spring rains, the wheat on the Foote ranch did not sprout, and watering the orchard trees by hand from a hose cart was only a stop-gap measure. In the fall, they closed the Mesa House and went to live with Bessie in town. "It was the year of our private ruin," the author later recalled. That the Rockwells also lost heavily in the canal's failure deepened Molly's humiliation.

Harry Tompkins became another casualty of the canal's bankruptcy. In the spring of 1891, he suffered what must have been a nervous breakdown and spent a month with the Footes to recuperate. Heretofore Tompkins, still in his twenties, had been a pillar of strength to the Footes. Arthur trusted Tompkins completely, often leaving him in charge of both the household and the irrigation project when Foote was away on business. Molly once described for Helena her own indebtedness to Tompkins: "He has helped entertain and provide for sudden arrivals of strange guests, he has been my model, my critic, my 'coach' on my horse blocks, he has helped me nurse my sick children, and my sick husband, and my sick *self*."

Since their first encounter in Boise Canyon, Molly had enjoyed Tompkins's company and admired his physical grace. In a letter telling of a sketching trip to the bluffs, where Tompkins served as her model, the artist recorded: "Mr. Tompkins is our beauty. We always have one around somehow. He is six ft. four in. and is like one of those studies of very youthful male figures of Michael Angelo. A beautiful head and rather tragic profile." But the feature that most endeared the young man to Molly was his willingness to talk of poetry and novels.

Moreover, discussions about his own school days at St. Paul's had led the Footes to send little Arthur there.

Once he recovered from his illness, Tompkins traveled east to live with his family and then paid a visit to the Gilders. Helena needed no introduction to the young man who had received such glowing testimonials from her best friend. Most recently, in a letter notifying Helena of Tompkins's trip to New York, Molly had exclaimed: "He is a fine, in and out and all around strong character, and a friend for a life."

On a sadder note, Molly had informed Helena in the spring of the death of John Sherman. He had been in poor health for several years but lived to see the success of the newly built "Sherman House," which had opened its doors the previous fall. Although John's relatives invited his widow to make a home with them in Milton, Bessie preferred her independence. She stayed on in Boise to manage the boarding house and remained in Molly's eyes a perfect "saint."

In the midst of family grief and financial misfortunes, Molly persevered with her literary work. "The Gates on Grandfather's Farm," the first of three autobiographical accounts that were published in *St. Nicholas Magazine*, appeared in the April 1891 issue. "The Spare Bedroom at Grandfather's" followed in July 1892 and "The Garret at Grandfather's" in March 1893. These beautifully illustrated pieces provide a window to Molly's Quaker childhood.

Foote continued to illustrate the work of other authors as well. In 1891 her drawings accompanied Mary E. Wilkins's "Emmy" (*Century*, February), Laura E. Richards's "Vacation Days" (*St. Nicholas*, August), and Lucie A. Ferguson's "To the Summit of Pike's Peak by Rail" (*St. Nicholas*, November). She also revised a short story of irrigation, based on their life on the mesa, which *St. Nicholas Magazine* now accepted after initially turning it down. The acceptance letter, dated October 1, 1891, is worth quoting because it underscores Molly's capacity to rework material until she got it right: "We were very sorry to return the little story of 'A Desert Claim' last summer, but—thanks to you—our return of it then has now proved indeed a blessing-in-disguise for *St. Nicholas.* For in its new form, 'A Four-Leaved Clover in the Desert,' it is a real gem." Accompanied by four of Molly's drawings, this charming two-part serial was published in May and June of 1894.

Foote completed her adult irrigation narrative in midsummer 1891 and then dashed off a story to accompany a Christmas scene for the December issue of the *Century.* Entitled "The Rapture of Hetty," this slender tale of barely two and a half pages in print focuses on young Tom Basset, who, after having been accused of altering cattle brands, rides off with his true love in the middle of a Christmas dance. The full-page illustration depicts Hetty and her escort, Basset's rival, riding horseback across snow-covered hills on their way to the festivities. The drawing has more merit than the story, which Foote probably realized. She was certain that Richard would not like the tale, which she described to Helena as "a hateful thing." Still, when it appeared in the *Century*'s Christmas issue, alongside the work of Rudyard Kipling, Wolcott Balestier, and other well-known writers, Foote was pleased. "I am all puffed up with pride in *our* Christmas number!" she wrote to Richard.

Molly's irrigation story, retitled *The Chosen Valley*, was serialized in the *Century* the following year. She had revised portions of it during the spring of 1891, in accordance with suggestions of Robert Underwood Johnson, the magazine's associate editor. On May 12, Molly wrote to tell Richard: "You may announce my story as soon as you like." She had started writing the last chapter that very morning and planned to make revisions as the story was returned to her in a typewritten copy. "I can see the weak places better when I read the words not in my own hand," she explained.

In June she addressed a more formal letter to Gilder, requesting an advance of $300 on serial rights of the novel, which would pay for her son's trip home for the summer. She also informed Richard that, if he wished her to illustrate the story, she would try a new approach. She planned "to enlarge upon the locality and environment and not try to repeat the personal situations of the story already described in words."

Before the year's end, several western readers had responded to Gilder's pre-publication announcement by writing to Molly to wish the story "luck." They appeared "to be persons with Valleys of their own," Molly delightedly told Richard, "and I am Western enough to be superstitiously pleased with these good wishes for my coming voyage in the *Century* pages."

The Chosen Valley, illustrated by eight of Molly's drawings, was published in the *Century* in six installments, beginning in May 1892. Houghton Mifflin and Company brought it out in book form later the same year. As scholar Lee Ann Johnson has observed, this novel "represents a marked advance over its predecessors" for both its theme and characterization. Set in Boise basin, a locale with which Foote was thoroughly acquainted, it tells the story of two men locked in a lengthy battle over a scheme to build a dam in Boise Canyon to irrigate the nearby desert lands. Once friends and partners, Price Norrisson, the practical, profit-driven American businessman, and Robert Dunsmuir, the conscientious, high-minded Scottish engineer, have gone separate ways after Norrisson insisted that speed in building a dam took precedence over structural concerns. Having completed one small irrigation project, which he admitted had flaws, Norrisson has spent ten years attempting "to freeze out" Dunsmuir, who controls the best reservoir site in Boise Canyon.

Unable to raise development funds, Dunsmuir realizes that his water rights after all these years may not hold up in court, so he compromises. He accepts a small amount of stock in Norrisson's company and is named chief engineer. Norrisson, still in control of the project, calls upon his engineer son Philip to help with the scheme.

Once on the job, Philip sees his father as a promoter and does not quite trust him, but he admires the engineering skills and high principles of Dunsmuir. Together they set about to build the dam. But when the bedrock gives out, Norrisson orders them to build it on a pile foundation rather than expend more time and money in further excavation. The night before the formal opening, the dam gives way and Dunsmuir drowns.

A chastened Norrisson orders the dam rebuilt on solid rock and dedicates it to Dunsmuir. In a moving concluding paragraph, Foote underscores the price of western development.

> The ideal scheme is ever beckoning from the West; but the scheme with an ideal record is yet to find—the scheme that shall breed no murmurers, and see no recreants; that shall avoid envy, hatred, malice, and all uncharitableness; that shall fulfil its promises, and pay its debts, and remember its friends, and keep itself unspotted from the world. Over the graves of the dead, and over the hearts of the living, presses the cruel expansion of our country's material progress. . . . And those that are with it in its latter days are not those who set out in the beginning. And victory, if it come, shall border hard upon defeat.

Contemporary reviewers applauded Molly's novel, calling it "one of the best of her stories," "a book of singular power," "one of the strongest stories of the year." They especially liked her well-made contrast between Norrisson and Dunsmuir and her sensitive portrayal of Dunsmuir's Scottish serving woman, Margaret Dutton. One reviewer called the story "a piece of realism taken from the history of fierce competition in the country Mrs. Foote writes of."

The Chosen Valley, in fact, is steeped in realism, though Foote often thought of herself as an idealist or even a romantic. It portrays with great accuracy the Idaho landscape and documents the everyday concerns of western households. But most importantly it exposes the human cost of expansion and exploitation in the Far West. Although Foote applauded the work of Arthur and the fictional Robert Dunsmuir, men intent upon developing natural resources for the benefit of humankind, she also decried the "excessive greed" that often accompanied commercial development. In some of her later fiction, Foote spoke out against the destruction of untouched wilderness, but she did so from a domestic view and not as an environmentalist. She had witnessed both sides of territorial expansion and was in fact caught in the middle between her artistic appreciation of natural beauty and Arthur's professional goals as an engineer. Torn between the two competing impulses, Molly remained loyal to Arthur's developmental plans, which seemed to assure her family's survival as well as offer hope to pioneer settlers.

The Chosen Valley's success rests squarely on the fact that Molly's work, as she later observed to Richard, was "a helplessly faithful rendering into fiction of the experiences (my own and those of others) that have come under my own observation." Also lending credibility to the story are her finely crafted drawings of the basalt bluffs of the Snake and Boise river canyons.

As the "year of our private ruin" came to an end, Molly still found much to be thankful for. She had completed her fourth full-length novel, which paid for her son's trip home during the summer, and the *Atlantic Monthly* had asked for her next story, a gratifying request but one she had to turn down. As she explained to Horace E. Scudder, the magazine's highly regarded editor: "I am under a long standing engagement to the *Century* to give them the first reading of my few stories." But she was even more grateful to have "shut the door . . . on one dreadful trouble." Arthur, it appeared, had conquered his problem with alcohol, garnering Molly's sincere praise, for, as she observed to Helena, "it seems to be one of the hardest fights that men are called upon to fight." And, she concluded, "you can imagine that I can bear many disappointments to have that ugly shameful sorrow threaten us no longer." Their trials, in fact, were not over, and in following months the resilience of both husband and wife would be put to the test.

For Arthur, the long, frustrating struggle to find gainful employment continued. His testimony as expert witness in an important mining case that winter probably brought in little money. And two promising irrigation ventures he initiated during 1892 were to end in failure and disappointment.

To "ease my heart of wrath and bitterness," Molly recounted the fate of the first enterprise in a long letter to Helena. During the summer a young engineer by the name of

Clark "jumped" a reservoir site that Arthur was preparing to file on in the Land Office. This occurred after Foote had befriended Clark, a likable promoter much like Norrison in *The Chosen Valley.* After Clark professed to represent an eastern capitalist, Arthur shared with him maps and plans for developing the site. Clark's betrayal left Arthur dumbfounded because, as Molly explained, "[jumping] is almost unheard of between engineers." Without funds to contest the issue, Arthur had to stand aside and watch as construction began on the location he had discovered. With a calmness that escaped her when these events unfolded, Molly describes in her reminiscences how this tale of duplicity ended:

> [Clark] took A.'s idea for the dam and left out the essential feature, the "core walls," and the dam went out [in 1894] before the reservoir was half full. In other ways the scheme was mangled beyond recognition, and the whole piece of bad sportsmanship rankled with my husband the more that he had been fooled by a man of his own profession.

The second of Arthur's schemes was a proposal to build a new water system for Boise, with pipes and culverts to replace the "surface irrigation" then in use. Although he had the support of the city council and the commandant of Boise Barracks, the scheme fell through when the War Department refused to grant him a right away through the military grounds. In words that must have sounded all too familiar to Helena, Molly concluded her account of Arthur's venture: "the surveys were good work, the design was clever, and the maps are perfect, but it goes for nothing."

Had Molly wished to write another novel that focused on the human cost of developing the West, she did not lack for material. In the midst of Arthur's financial tribulations, the Footes received word of Ferdinand Van Zandt's suicide. After leaving Colorado, their former Leadville associate had married an English heiress and developed a prosperous mine in Montana. Collapse of the venture apparently led to his demise. "It was the usual Western tragedy," Molly confided to Helena; his wife's money was tied up in the mine as well as that of her English friends. Appalled by Van Zandt's death, Molly wrote in bitterness: "These schemes are all the very D—— for forcing a man off his balance, and mixing up his estimates of the relative value of things. Our canal is a perfect Frankenstein; it has a sort of life of its own and carries us along in tow. It amounts to a fate for this family."

Now, more than ever before, Molly's career was driven by economic necessity. With Arthur's work bringing in little or no income, Molly's earnings kept the household afloat. These dark Idaho years forced her to become a skilled businesswoman. In negotiating her own contracts, she apparently did not hesitate to ask good prices for her work. Nor was she slow to inquire when payments were delayed. As she explained in a letter to Helena: "I wish I didn't have to seem so mean and grasping about my work, but I have to make it count for as much as it will. I am mighty prompt sending in my bills, and I am working my poor wits for all they are worth."

Foote also became more assertive in controlling the texture of her manuscripts. She found Richard's editorial suggestions as valuable as ever but balked when another staff member toyed with her wording. "I do prefer my own adjectives, and as a rule my own construction," she told Richard. On another occasion, she took exception to the queries along the margins of the proofs but, when she discovered they were not Gilder's, wrote: "I am very glad you told me that the queries . . . were not editorial. They struck me as being on the school-teacher order."

After taking rooms with Bessie, Molly continued to juggle the demands of writing with those of her family. "I look back to that third-story bedroom at Bessie's, where my writing was done, as the best place for the purpose I have ever known," she writes in her reminiscences, "and my work in that room was blessed, if it be blessed to 'sell'—I am not so sure about that! The themes were the best that ever came to me, but if they had been returned and kept for ten years till they had ripened and settled on their lees, I might have poured a purer wine. But quick sales were very needful at that time."

She completed her short story "The Watchman" in this room late in 1891 and then sent it to Gilder, calling it "a sort of a ditch pastoral." She said it was inspired by the activities of the Phyllis Canal and playfully noted that she had wanted to call the heroine "Phyllis" but that her local critics—probably Arthur and Bessie—would not let her. Accompanied by four of Foote's drawings, "The Watchman" appeared in the November 1893 issue of the *Century*.

The story focuses on Travis, a hard-working young man hired by an irrigation company to patrol five miles of new canal to look for breaks. On his rounds, he encounters and soon falls in love with Nancy Lark, the pretty daughter of a poor farmer who bitterly protests the company's monopoly of water. Travis is baffled by a series of mysterious breaks in the canal until one night he catches Nancy's father digging holes in the ditch bank. Nancy comes upon the scene as Travis forces the old man into the water to help repair the breaks. Previously attracted to Travis, Nancy now can not forgive his humiliating treatment of her father. Later, after the entire ditch bank gives way and the nearby fields are flooded, Travis is held responsible and loses his job. But again the culprit is Nancy's father. In the end, Nancy reveals this fact to Travis, the company rehires him, and the young couple are reconciled and marry after the death of Mr. Lark. Although Foote relies on a conventional love plot to carry the story, two major strengths save it from mediocrity: its authentic details of western irrigation and its careful descriptions of the Idaho landscape.

By mid-February 1892, Molly had completed "On a Side-Track," which "the home critics say is my best to date," she told Helena. She later made revisions following Gilder's suggestions and illustrated her tale with two drawings, one of the female protagonist and the other of a snowplow engine. The inspiration for this story, which was published in the *Century* in June 1895, came from the Footes' last trip west when their train was snowbound.

"On a Side-Track" features an unconventional love affair between Phebe Underhill, a young Quaker traveling with her ill father, and Charles Ludovic, a fellow passenger who seems burdened by sadness. A heavy snowfall blocks their route soon after they cross the Wyoming-Idaho border. For a day and a half the train is idled on a sidetrack, giving Ludovic opportunity to woo the young woman. He desperately wants some sign of affection from Phebe before he leaves the train. In their final hours together Ludovic reveals the nature of his anguish: he is being taken to Pocatello to stand trial for manslaughter. He has killed a man in a fight involving the honor of his friend's wife and expects to spend time in prison. Phebe shows compassion, and a short time later, after a jury acquits Ludovic, he claims the young Quaker as his bride.

This story succeeds because Foote is able to build up tension until it reaches a climax with Ludovic's revelation and acquittal. She uses the same formula in the second tale she wrote in 1892, entitled "Maverick" (*Century*, 1894). Here an unorthodox romance involves a protagonist with a disfigured face and the young woman who rebuffs him. Foote creates a strong sense of place in the opening paragraphs with a masterful sketch of the desolate Arco desert of southeast Idaho where the tale unfolds. The aridity of the land is matched by the barrenness of Rose Gilroy's life. She lives with her half-crazed father and lawless brothers at an isolated stage station on the road from Blackfoot to Boise. Maverick, the county sheriff, had been taken in as a youth by old man Gilroy after Indians had mutilated Maverick's face. To escape the hopelessness of her situation, Rose makes a dash for freedom with a handsome young Swede employed on the premises. Maverick and a companion ride in pursuit, the Swede fires a pistol, and Maverick returns the shot, killing the young man. Distraught by thoughts of her imminent return to the station and of an inevitable union with Maverick, Rose begs Mavarick's companion to take her away. When he gently refuses, she "found a way" to escape the desolation of her life. She flees on foot into the nearby massive lava beds where certain death awaits her.

Molly found great satisfaction writing in her third-story bedroom, which she likened to the garret "of the poor artist with its atmosphere of solitude and concentration." From a window, she could gaze at the sky or at the treetops across the way on the capitol grounds. But financial matters often disturbed her thoughts. Shortly after completing "Maverick," Molly wrote to her sister-in-law, Mary Hague: "It is a pleasure to work. But I am always torn between the ideal way of working for the future on a sound basis and the necessity of making pot-boilers to meet current expenses."

The children's illnesses and other household concerns continued to interrupt her work. Early in 1892, for example, a case of diphtheria upset everyone in the boarding house. Anxious to protect Agnes and Betty from this contagious and often fatal disease, Molly consulted the post surgeon and beseeched Helena to quiz her own doctors about precautions she should take. A few weeks after the diphtheria scare subsided, a telegram from St. Paul's brought news that little Arthur had pneumonia. Although it was not a severe case, Molly spent several sleepless nights worrying about her son's well-being. Then in July nine-year-old Betty came down with scarlet fever. During a six-weeks' quarantine, Molly nursed and cared for her daughter in the Mesa House, where the caretakers, Mr. and Mrs. George Pinninger, provided meals and other services, though they stayed strictly apart from the stricken child and her mother.

It was a bad time financially for the Footes. Just weeks before Betty fell ill, Molly wrote to Helena: "We are in the most trying position out here . . . . The board-bill haunts me even in my dreams!" She itemized her expenses: $120 per month for food and lodging, $30 per month for other expenses, plus the cost of Arthur's schooling. "I just drudge at this desk till I am blue," Molly concluded. During the quarantine, she wrote a piece about Victoria because she needed to "bread-win" but doubted that *St. Nicholas* would publish it. "I am never fortunate when I write under strained conditions," she acknowledged.

When it was apparent that the Footes could no longer afford to keep Arthur at St. Paul's, both the Rockwells and Helena offered financial assistance. The Footes said no to both offers. For Molly, this was not a matter of pride but of "jealousy for our friendship." Helena's offer had touched Molly deeply, and she wrote in reply, "dearest friend of my whole life . . . . I cannot help crying, for pure happiness that you should love me so." But Arthur was to remain in school at least for another year. Dr. Henry Coit, the rector of St. Paul's, invited young Foote to stay on without cost to his parents because of his admirable record. "This offer was not ours to refuse," Molly later recalled, "the boy had earned it himself."

Living in Boise widened Molly's social contacts, even though she remained essentially a private person. She became good friends with the post commander and his wife, Captain and Mrs. Cunliffe H. Murray. The two women often walked together in the evenings after Mrs. Murray finished her French lessons with Nelly Linton. And on at least one occasion the Footes accompanied the Murrays to a military ball, which Molly enjoyed very much. She also joined the ladies Columbian Club, established to raise funds to furnish the Idaho Building at the 1893 Columbian Exposition in Chicago. "It's a great bore," Molly claimed and then admitted, "but there is a jolly side to it."

As the Columbian celebration got underway, however, economic disorder overspread the nation. Within six months of the fair's opening, hundreds of banks and thousands of businesses had failed, and unemployment skyrocketed. This depression, which began in mid-1893 and lasted for four years, was the worst financial disaster that the U.S. had yet experienced. During much of this period, Molly's literary work continued to support the family. Her short stories sold for at least $150, sometimes more, and her illustrations added to the family's income. She received $40, for example, for each of the drawings in "On a Side-Track." The amount of royalties she received from Houghton Mifflin is not known. She reported in February, however, that *The Chosen Valley* was selling better than she had expected, which, she added, was "very convenient."

Even with Molly's earnings, the Footes struggled to make ends meet. In a good year, her income greatly exceeded the average annual earnings of most American workers, about $415 in 1895. Yet the $ 150 Molly received for a short story, which in today's dollars would be roughly equivalent to $2,900, barely covered a month's expenses in the Foote household.

Molly's enthusiasm for writing remained undiminished as uncertainty hovered over her family and over the nation. In a reflective mood, she told Helena: "Middle age is the time to work, anyhow—one can't be young and lovely and a pleasure to the eye but one can do something, perhaps, at least one can try."

Arthur Foote never once stopped looking for gainful employment following the collapse of his irrigation schemes. But he would no longer play a major role in bringing water to Idaho farmers. Large-scale irrigation as Foote envisioned it finally came to Boise Valley early in the twentieth century after the U.S. Reclamation Service undertook to enlarge and improve the local irrigation systems started by private capital. On February 22, 1909, about three thousand spectators watched as water was turned into the much enlarged New York Canal. Two days later the *Idaho Statesman* published "An Appreciation" of Arthur D. Foote, written by D. W. Ross, in which Foote is given full credit for originating the Boise project some twenty-five years earlier.

For all practical purposes, Foote had severed his connections with the Boise irrigation scheme by the spring of 1893 when he went to Bakersfield, California, to interview for a job with a large irrigation district. But before the position was filled, Samuel F. Emmons asked Arthur to take charge of an onyx mine in Baja California. Eager to return to the field, Foote quickly accepted and then met Emmons in San Diego. Together they traveled by steamer down the coast to San Quentin and then overland by horseback to the quarries. Arthur's job was to oversee the mining operations and to locate and build a new port for shipping the onyx. Molly recalls in her reminiscences that "we had parted for two weeks" when Arthur went to Bakersfield but it would be several months before she saw her husband again. But at the start of his new venture, Molly was optimistic. "It does my heart good to think my dear old boy is afloat again," she wrote to Helena. "It will take ten years off his life. He is really an authority in his own line of work. And it seems so hard he should have been buried here so long."

But the economic cloud that hovered over the nation cast shadows on Baja California. Working in a harsh, demanding environment, Arthur missed his wife and children greatly. For a time, the Footes dreamed of moving the family to San Diego to be closer to Arthur's work. Molly loved the sea and would welcome the move. Writing to Helena from Boise, she avowed: "I have always hated the inland feeling, here. Idaho was never a place to choose for the home of a life-time; but only a place where we hoped to make money enough to be able to live where we pleased."

Still, husband and wife were both under strain. In April, Agnes came down with scarlet fever. "Twelve weeks in quarantine within one year!" Molly exclaims in her reminiscences. For six weeks Molly nursed and cared for Agnes in the one-room schoolhouse built the previous fall on Bessie's property. Several nights Molly went sleepless to give medicine to Agnes. And then, suddenly, Arthur's letters stopped coming, and Molly became nearly sick with worry. "I lay last night for hours simply panting with dread," she confessed to Helena. When a letter from Arthur finally arrived, it did little to allay Molly's fears. The stress of his job, his isolation and loneliness, apparently caused Arthur great mental anguish. "I have never known him to write me a letter like this in his hardest time," Molly confided to her friend.

Arthur Foote struggled courageously throughout the summer to "solve the problem" that he had been hired to conquer, which he did. But trouble dogged his footsteps. In the fall he lost $500 when the San Diego bank that held his savings failed. And soon afterward he was out of a job. As the depression deepened, the market for onyx dried up and the quarries closed. During this bleak time, Mary Hague wrote to Molly "bewailing" her brother's "continued unsuccess" and wishing that he "amounted to something." In reply, Molly wrote a spirited defense of her husband:

> You must remember your brother Arthur has *not* made a failure here, in the sense that there is anything against him, either professionally or against his character. The failure is one of over-confidence in our financial backers. We shall lose all our land, probably, and that means all our little stake which has cost a good deal in time and money. But we have gained quite the worth of that time in sobering experience; and you must not for one moment think that your brother Arthur amounts to nothing because he is not making money. He is making character, and is a better comrade and a tenderer, deeper, stronger man for his trials. It is only fine natures that can rise through bitter disappointment and unsuccess; and I have seen my husband progress grimly, in patience and silence, through bitter trials; and speaking as an outsider might speak I can say I have never admired him more than I have this past year. He has done a good summer's work, and it is only the hard times, coming as they have, which takes away the reward of success.

It is not known exactly how Arthur viewed his wife's triumphs when his own endeavors so often ended in failure. But the letters he wrote to Molly from Baja California that still exist are laced with words of affection and support. In closing a message dated April 23, 1893, he wrote, "Good night my brave lovely wife. Thee is all the world to me[,] more than thee was years ago when I first saw this bleak coast."

Molly's most recent successes included publication in the *Century* (1893) of three drawings, each featuring a well-dressed woman situated in an eastern wooded or seaside environment. "The Mourning Dove" appeared in February, followed by "The Hermit-Thrush" in June and "Sea-Bird and Land-Bird" in July. The last two were part of the lovely "Century Series of American Artists," which also featured drawings by Winslow Homer and Lydia Emmet.

These drawings helped to pay the board-bills that Molly was so worried about. But a deep-rooted conservatism, coupled with her own shyness, prevented her from accepting other money-making opportunities. Early in the year she turned down a request to give six talks in "select [eastern] houses" for $100 per talk. This way of making a living, she told Helena, though others might choose it, did not "seem lady like." And she added, "I had sooner take in washing."

By this time writing had become Molly's consuming passion. In February, deep into a new novel entitled *Coeur d'Alene*, she confessed: "I don't know why it should be so, but I have never felt so able to work." The story, which appeared serially in the *Century* starting in February 1894 and as a book later in the year, took as its theme the labor-capital "war" that broke out in the Coeur d'Alene mining district the summer of 1892. Although Molly had no first-hand knowledge of conditions in the northern Idaho mines, she was shocked by the violent nature of the dispute. Her natural sympathies lay with management and against the miners' union, to her a tyrannical mob that dictated the terms by which the honest poor made a living.*

Foote had written the first part of the story as a play before she submitted it to the *Century* in narrative form. C. C. Buel, the assistant editor, felt this dramatic style was one Foote

*In January 1892, shortly after the Northern Pacific and Union Pacific railroads raised rates for transporting ore out of the Coeur d'Alene district, members of the Mine Owners' Association (MOA) closed their mines in protest, throwing hundreds of miners out of work. Two months later, having obtained a repeal of the rate increase, the MOA planned to reopen the mines but with reduced wages for men who worked above ground. Consequently, the union miners refused to go back to work, which led the MOA to import non-union workers. Violence erupted in July after the union discovered an MOA spy in its midst. Unionists attacked mines, dynamited the Frisco mill, and captured non-union workers and their guards. Six men lost their lives. Afterward, the union allowed non-union workers, some with families, to leave the area. Later a band of armed men attacked these refugees while they awaited transportation on the shore of Lake Coeur d'Alene. During the conflict, the governor declared martial law and secured U.S. troops to help quell the violence.

should cultivate since it was "partly the source" of the story's vigor. Responding to Buel's inquiry about possible lawsuits stemming from her accusations against union bosses, Molly defended her accuracy. The story, she said, was pure fiction except where it incorporated the history of the Coeur d'Alene strike. She got her facts from court testimony in the trial of union bosses and from interviews with W. B. Heyburn, chief legal counsel for the mine owners' association, and with the owner of the Frisco mill, which was blown up during the dispute. Molly tried writing the last part of the story while in quarantine with Agnes but figured it would probably have to be done over. From the little schoolhouse, she wrote to Helena: "I am so shut up, and domestic, with my pails and beds and brooms and fires and washing and rubbing Agnes with Vaseline, and hanging my disinfecting clothes around! What an absurdity my work is, under the circumstances."

The story begins on a dark and rainy night when the heroine and her father, Faith and Frederick Bingham, seek shelter at the cabin of the hero, Jack Darcie, and his partner, Mike McGowan. Bingham, manager of the famous Big Horn Mine, is an alcoholic miscreant, who has misappropriated funds from the London syndicate that employs him. Faith has yet to learn of her father's flawed character, having been raised in the East by Bingham's genteel family. She instinctively knows, however, that Darcie is a cut above the common miner, and Darcie instantly is attracted to the beautiful and charming Faith. But the mining dispute that engulfs the Coeur d'Alenes in violence eventually upstages the central love story.

Jack Darcie, whose real name is John Darcie Hamilton, is the son of a British director of the Big Horn and has been sent to secretly investigate Bingham's running of the mine. Falling in love with Faith complicates his job. He writes two letters to the company, one resigning his position and another detailing Bingham's mismanagement, but he delays sending them until he sorts out his feelings for Faith. In the meantime, union bosses in the Coeur d'Alene district are gearing up for a showdown with the mine owners' association, which has refused to accept union demands for higher wages. Most of the mines are being worked by "scabs," except for the Big Horn, where the union works in cahoots with Bingham. Union workers suspect Darcie of being a company spy and set up an ambush in which he is wounded. His incriminating letter subsequently falls into Bingham's hands, who reveals its contents to Faith. Stunned by evidence that Darcie has been spying on her father, she agrees to break off all contact with him.

Soon union strikers blow up the Frisco mill above the town of Gem, kill some of the scabs, injure others, and completely overpower the non-union men. A friendly doctor who has given shelter to Darcie and McGowan warns Faith of the danger they all face when this lawlessness spreads. After reconciling with Darcie, Faith joins the train load of non-union workers, some with wives and children, who apparently have been given safe passage out of the war zone. She expects to meet up with Darcie and his partner at the Mission landing near Lake Coeur d'Alene, where they, along with the scabs, will board a steamer for passage to Spokane. A youth at the mission reveals, however, that unionists plan to massacre the scabs during the night. Though Faith shares this information with others, the unarmed workers can only scatter when the ruffians appear and start firing. Darcie, still suffering from his wound when he arrives in the vicinity, can take no part in the fighting. Order is restored when federal troops arrive and hunt down the marauders. A few months later Darcie and Faith marry and he assumes management of the Big Horn.

This is a fast-paced story that holds the reader's interest to the very end. Despite her anti-union bias, Foote accurately records many aspects of the Coeur d'Alene troubles—the wage dispute, employment of scabs, and destruction of the Frisco mill. In the climactic scene at the mission, she convincingly depicts the horror surrounding the July 11 attack on unarmed men. She titled this chapter "The Massacre," the term that was shouted from newspaper headlines shortly after these events unfolded. Area residents, in fact, commonly believed that several non-union men had been brutally murdered that day. Survivors of the attack told of fleeing terrified before the marauders and of being robbed of all their valuables. They also testified of seeing some men killed or wounded, but upon later investigation no bodies were ever discovered. Modern scholarship concludes that the motive for the attack was robbery and that nobody died that day, "though several of the victims suffered from exposure and shock." Foote probably read newspaper accounts of attempts to find bodies of the alleged murder victims. She chose, however, to leave the matter unresolved:

> Of the fate of those who fled up into the wild defile called Fourth of July Cañon much has been asserted and denied on both sides, but little will ever be known; the cañon and the river have been deeply questioned, but they bear no witness, and they tell no tales.

Still, in a final scene, which has no basis in fact, the author graphically depicts the hunting down of one terrified scab, who was robbed, turned loose, and then deliberately shot and killed as he attempted to swim to safety. Thus, Foote chose to portray unionists as murderous villains and to depict members of management as highminded captains of industry.

The reviews of the novel were mixed. A writer for the *New York Times* called it a "graphic, vigorously-told tale of the excitement in the Idaho mountains in the Summer of 1892" but cautioned readers that Foote had told only one side of the story. But the reviewer for the *Nation* criticized Molly for the tepid love scenes: "The serious labor troubles at the Coeur d'Alene mines lose actual and literary value by subordination to a tiresome love story." Still, the book seemingly appealed to many readers, especially those with anti-union sentiments. It was soon dramatized by Elizabeth W. Doremus, author of *The Circus Rider* and *Four in Hand*, and translated into French for a Swiss publication. Later, in 1906, the National Metal Trades Association of Cincinnati requested permission to serialize it.

While Molly was wrapping up the Coeur d'Alene novel, she received a telegram announcing her appointment as art juror at the Columbian Exposition. She delayed accepting only long enough to learn that jurors were to receive $500 plus expenses. The trip to Chicago would reunite her with her sixteen-year-old son after a two-year separation and might possibly lead to a reunion with Helena as well. Molly and "little" Arthur, in fact, toured the machinery exhibits together, but the former Cooper Union schoolmates missed seeing each other by a matter of days. On July 30, 1893, near the end of her three-week visit to the World's Fair, Molly wrote to her friend: "But how my heart aches to have you with me amidst all this beauty! It isn't right that we should not have it together."

Through a misunderstanding, Molly was assigned to "Group 143," the awards jury for etching. With little technical knowledge of the art, Molly claimed years later to have felt like a fraud in Chicago. But her fellow jurors, a congenial mix of artists and etchers, accepted her wholeheartedly. Molly especially enjoyed her association with the English etcher Francis J. Short, describing him in correspondence as "a genius" and the "most refined" man in the group, and with Emily Sartain, principal of the School of Design for Women in Philadelphia, as well as an artist and engraver, and, most importantly in Molly's eyes, "a very well-bred woman as well as a *clever one*."

The jurors spent their days in committee meetings judging the work of the world's greatest artists. But in the late afternoons, Molly and Emily Sartain often went out on the lagoon in a launch made available to the jurors. A night ride on the water with the nearby buildings illuminated by electric lights was for Molly a "never to be forgotten" experience. During this three-week interlude, she also went to concerts, attended dinners given especially for the jurors, and viewed an endless succession of art exhibits, saving her highest praise for English, American, and Dutch artists. By the end of her stay, she told Helena, she was "nearly dead with fatigue but so elated and excited and overjoyed with it all! It will do me worlds of good." Still, misgivings about her own work caused her to exclaim after she returned to Idaho:

> In Chicago—with real artists, with acres of real art before me—I was very sick at heart and half defiant as one must be not to be crushed; it is one reason why I am not happy among Artists; I'm just enough like them to feel the differences keenly. . . . Art is my stern, ironical task-mistress and she calls me a fool whenever I do my best; but I have to go on. It did hurt and humiliate me to have those artists think that I called myself an artist.

Molly failed to mention, however, that two of her drawings were on display in the Woman's Building, "The Letter of Resignation" from *The Chosen Valley* and "The Mourning Dove" (now retitled "The Wood Dove"), and that her novels were located in the library of the same building. Nor did she comment on the flattering attention she received in the official World's Fair publication entitled *Art and Handicraft in the Woman's Building of the World's Columbian Exposition, Chicago, 1893.* In the chapter on women illustrators, Foote is described as the pioneer "artist illustrator." And she is credited with having opened the way for other women artists: "About twenty years ago, we could count on the fingers of one hand all the women seriously engaged in this work; nor was it until the advent of Mrs. Mary Hallock Foote in the field, as the illustrator of her own charming stories, that illustration seemed to present an opening for women."

Upon her return to Boise, where young Arthur was to spend his vacation, Molly worried about her son's health. In the past year or so he had been ill with both pneumonia and mumps and now looked pale and underweight. Knowing of her anxieties, Captain Murray invited the lad to accompany the troopers from Boise Barracks on a three-week "Long March." He was to share the captain's tent and the officers' mess and to ride an officer's horse. Captain Murray promised Molly to bring her son back "as hard and brown as a trooper." Molly later reported that the boy had a glorious time, riding, boating, fishing, and hunting. He carried with him the beautiful rifle that the Winchester Repeating Arms Company had presented Molly for her frequent mention of the Winchester rifle in her novels. It was "an opportunity of a boy's lifetime," Molly writes in her reminiscences, "and never forgotten by our boy." At the end of this adventure, Arthur returned to St. Paul's, where Dr. Coit again waived tuition and residence fees because of the boy's accomplishments.

Little Agnes and Betty also benefitted from Captain and Mrs. Murray's friendship. The youngest Footes and the two little Murray girls became like sisters and spent much of their time together riding the Murrays' pony and roaming the hill-sides on the post gathering wildflowers. "The place is ideal for children," Molly avowed. The two little Murrays also attended Nelly Linton's select school, which helped make school life for Agnes and Betty "exceptionally happy." In writing about her youngsters in the summer of 1893, Molly confessed: "The three children have been just as happy and have had just as good advantages as we could have asked for them had all gone on wheels with us."

And finally there was good news to report about Arthur, Sr. Soon after the quarries closed down, his brother-in-law, James D. Hague, offered him a temporary job, which Molly hoped would "prove more than temporary." Hague had bought controlling interest of the North Star gold mine at Grass Valley, California, in 1887; over the next few years he and his associates acquired adjacent claims and then set about to rejuvenate the North Star. A new power system was needed for driving the machinery. So Hague sent Arthur first to Riverside, California, and then to the Calumet and Hecla copper mines in Michigan to examine recently installed electric power plants. By early January 1894, Arthur was back in Boise, where he wrote up his reports and awaited the "next news from California." In fact, Arthur spent most of that year in Idaho waiting to hear from Hague.

In the meantime, Molly's career soared. In this banner year of 1894, she witnessed publication of one novel, three short stories, and a collection of five previously published tales (*In Exile, and Other Stories*). And she received critical acclaim in some of the nation's leading journals. In February the *Critic* listed Foote as one of sixteen American authors who made a good living from their pens. In April an article in *Munsey's Magazine* reported that "Mary Hallock Foote stands, according to common avowal, at the head of American women illustrators." This same sentiment was echoed in Alpheus Sherwin Cody's vignette of Mary Hallock Foote published in May in *The Outlook*, though this is the piece, it may be remembered, that disturbed Molly because the author quoted her without permission.

Then in August *The Book Buyer* published an essay on Foote, as part of its series on author-illustrators, written by Helena de Kay Gilder. Molly was delighted that her friend had been commissioned to write the biography. Earlier in her career, she had shied away from publicity, but the family's precarious finances had brought about a change. In a light-hearted moment, she explained to Helena: "I am [now] willing to caper and prance in the columns of personalities, and show my middle-aged visage like the rest of us[;] if it will bring in any more dollars to my beloveds, what do I care!" And with Helena's name attached to the *Book Buyer* essay, "this scheme for publicity appealed to me as no other could."

Helena's biographical sketch is informative and insightful. After dwelling briefly on her friend's girlhood, Helena documents her rise to prominence as writer and illustrator. Helena still regards Foote as living the life of an exile, however: "In all her Western writings the homesickness of the exile can be read, the difficulty of the daughter of the soil, whose people for generations had lived in and loved the river country of the East, to adapt herself to her new surroundings." Molly read the essay with both pleasure and pain. Was she truly worthy of Helena's love and accolades? she wondered. The girl that Helena wrote about seemed a stranger, or "a younger sister or a daughter of the present me," Molly wrote in a letter to Helena dated August 10. And she added: "I dont know but I'm a little jealous of that Cooper Institute girl who had such good health and good spirits—but she wasn't half so tough as the old woman is."

In fact, at age forty-six the successful artist and writer had become a seasoned business woman. With the children growing up, Molly schemed to find ways to assure their education. Young Arthur had his heart set on studying engineering at the Massachusetts Institute of Technology, and Betty's artistic bent, Molly believed, warranted professional training. But these dreams would be realized only if Molly continued selling her work. "In the old days," she confided to Helena, "I used to regard my work as subsidiary to Arthur's . . . . but in these days, and for several years past, it has been the sole family income and I have to study to make the most of it."

During part of 1894, Molly worked to adapt *Coeur d'Alene* for the stage, figuring that a play would bring in more money than the published story. She even asked Jeannette Gilder, a successful writer and journal editor and Richard Gilder's sister, to help place the play in New York. By year's end, however, she had dropped the project. Critical feedback indicated the script needed additional work. So when Elizabeth Doremus asked permission to try to stage her own dramatization of the novel, Molly apparently agreed, with it understood that a third of any future profits reverted to the author.

Molly also secured release from her long-standing commitment to the *Century*. Starting in the fall of 1894, she was free to place her stories with other journals. This arrangement, Molly believed, would speed her work into publication. The sooner the stories were published, she explained to Helena, the sooner they could be collected into a book; "and each new book adds a little to one's income."

In August the *Atlantic Monthly* accepted Foote's two-part story, "The Trumpeter," which she had submitted "with a condition attached." Woven into the tale are scenes that occurred in Boise only a few months earlier when "Coxeyites" stood trial for violating federal law. The success of the story, she believed, depended in part "on the element of timeliness." The editor of the *Atlantic* apparently agreed; the story appeared in the November and December issues.

Molly called this her first army story, since the action takes place on or near an army post much like Boise Barracks. But as in many of her Idaho tales, a blighted romance ends in tragedy. Henniker, the popular trumpeter of K Company, is engaged to the lovely Callie Meadows, who lives with her family on the edge of the military reservation. The youngest in the household is sixteen-year-old Meta, a half-Bannock orphan raised by the Meadowses and treated like a daughter. Henniker suddenly awakens to Meta's beauty; though she initially rejects his advances, they secretly marry. Transferred to Fort Custer in Montana, Henniker leaves the pregnant Meta behind.

After giving birth to a son, Meta dresses in Indian clothes to obtain free railway passage to join her husband in Montana and travels partway with a party of Bannock women. At the end of the line, she must walk thirty miles in winter weather to reach the post, since no one will stop to give an Indian woman a ride. Henniker, recently discharged, passes his wife and son while making his way to the train station. He is too proud to claim the bedraggled Indian woman as his wife but hands the driver of the army transport a gold coin to give to her. Soon he learns that Meta died on the road and that the Meadows family has taken in his son. Seven years go by. Henniker, lame and homeless, joins a group of Coxeyites marching through Idaho and is arrested along with his comrades. Upon viewing the prisoners, Henniker's little son thinks they look like hobos, unaware that the fellow he calls a "dirty man" is his father. Humiliated and remorseful, Henniker later drowns himself in the Snake River.

Literary scholars have called "The Trumpeter" one of Foote's "most elaborately plotted" Idaho stories. It has other strengths as well, such as realistic depictions of military life, finely defined human relationships, and sympathetic treatment of the Bannock Indian tribe (despite the outmoded, racist terminology).

Foote's compassion for Meta, however, contrasts starkly with her contempt for Coxey's Army. For six or seven weeks during the spring of 1894, this band of unemployed workers had captured the nation's attention. Jacob Coxey, a wealthy businessman, headed a movement to pressure Congress to create jobs for the unemployed. To publicize the cause, he and his jobless followers marched from Coxey's home state of Ohio to Washington, D.C. Other contingents of unemployed westerners began the long trek eastward planning to join Coxey on Capitol Hill. Some tired marchers commandeered trains and were arrested; violence occasionally erupted when officials confronted the lawbreakers. In late May, Molly saw a group of these western Coxeyites in Boise where they had been sent to stand trial. In her story she pictures them as a lawless mob of dirty tramps, the very same image projected in the nation's press. Foote's political conservatism infuses this story, as it does in the novel *Coeur d'Alene*. In both narratives she lashes out at labor and reform groups that threaten the existing social order and expresses outrage at their use of violence to bring about change.

Months before she completed "The Trumpeter," Molly had sent a story to Richard Gilder that was unlike any other she had ever written because it dealt with adultery. At first she thought the theme was "too strong" for her to handle. But the dilemma of an unhappily married woman intrigued her. In the end, she called it a "moral tale" because the woman comes to grips with her sin and its ramifications just before she dies in an avalanche. Still, in a letter to Gilder dated January 15, 1894, Molly voiced her fears about the topic: "I am sending you a story which I'm afraid you will say won't do; but please don't say it till you've read it through. I know it's an ugly theme, but it would have to come in once, at least, in any true series of western tales."

The heroine of this tale, which Molly titled "The Cup of Trembling," is the beautiful Esmée, a coddled eastern woman, unhappily married to one of the richest mine-owners in Idaho. While he is away trying to sell his property, Esmée flees to a distant mountain cabin with Jack Waring, the sensitive superintendent of her husband's mine. Soon they are snowbound. Accustomed to having servants, Esmée is unsuited for "rough living," so Jack does all the work around the cabin. One afternoon, with a storm threatening, Jack snowshoes to a mine across the gulch, where he has arranged to pick up mail. In his absence, his brother Sid unexpectedly arrives, but Esmée is too frightened to let the stranger in. Unprepared for the coming storm, Sid wanders away and dies of exposure. Later that same night after Jack's return, the lovers realize that Sid had been the stranger knocking on the door. Jack goes to find his brother and returns with his body. A guilt-ridden Esmée begs for Jack's forgiveness. Equally guilt-ridden, Jack replies with brutal frankness: "Have I accused you? You did not do it. I did not do it. It happened—to show us what we are. We are impossible. We have broken with all the ties of family. . . . [Sid] is dead through my sin."

Late the following afternoon Jack goes for help to carry Sid's remains into town. Left alone with the body, Esmée goes through a spiritual crisis. At twilight, when another stranger arrives to warn of a probable avalanche, she realizes that God is giving her an opportunity. She refuses to abandon her watch over Sid's body, and shortly after the stranger leaves she and the cabin are buried in a snowslide. In death she expiates her sin.

Published in the *Century* in September 1895, the piece appeared later the same year in a volume entitled *The Cup of Trembling, and Other Stories.* Lee Ann Johnson singles out the title story as "the most arresting and the most finished" in the collection, which also includes "On a Side-Track," "Maverick," and "The Trumpeter." And she sees in these "dark romances . . . a grim working out of [Foote's own] fears and fantasies" during the difficult Idaho years. Perhaps this is true. Certainly Molly recognized that the stories belonged together, calling them her "perpetually gloomy Idaho tales." "I can't seem to think of any good wholesome jolly stories," she once remarked to Helena.

But Molly did not appear unusually dispirited the year she completed the final two stories that went into the collection. Her correspondence with Helena during this time continued to be a source of comfort and support. The two old friends exchanged family news, photographs of their children, and comments upon the books and essays they were reading. And in February Molly even wrote of having found a new peace. Her writing was going well, though she felt "hunted" by the need to make money for the children's education. In fact, like many other women her age, she viewed her children as the great hope for the future. On April 3, 1894, she wrote: "My keen consciousness is in the *three*, my new bodies, my youth three times multiplied; my hopes and fears are in them." And she confessed in this same letter to Helena that she had a "very wild" dream—to keep house for the three children in Boston while Arthur, Jr., studied engineering and Betty took art lessons. In the meantime, however, she prepared for her son's return to Idaho, where he was to spend the summer and the entire following year working in the field for A. J. Wiley, now chief engineer of the Bruneau Valley irrigation project, located about fifty miles south of Boise.

When not writing or sketching, Molly found contentment in a variety of commonplace activities, altering summer dresses for the girls, for example, and attending local Episcopal church services. The arrival of a new clergyman, one with seemingly "no intellectual curiosity," led Molly to comment upon religion more fully than was her usual practice. The new Episcopal rector, the Rev. Charles Deuel, it seemed to Molly, was wedded to church dogma and resisted any private interpretation. "I dont think I should be happy, even passively looking on, while such strange superstitions were poured into [Betty's] young mind, as opiates to dull its natural life of reflection and comparison." So she would wait to enroll the two girls in religious classes until they lived in a parish with an older, wiser, and more cultured rector. As for herself, Molly wrote: "I could never 'belong,' because though I believe in the immortality of the soul I dont know how to take the resurrection of the body. I am too old to be comforted that way."

Still, she went regularly to church, she told Helena, because "it is a good habit, and I wish I had had it earlier." And she took part in the church's charity bazaars, contributing some of her recently completed watercolors. She also remained active in the Women's Club of Boise, the former Columbian Club, which by the end of 1894 had started a free reading room and circulating library. Molly was enthusiastic about this project, noting that it would benefit Boise's homeless young men who had few wholesome amusements at their disposal. As a member of the book committee, Molly confessed, it was "great fun to choose within limits the books that so many of us need and so few of us have."

Earlier in the year, while they awaited word from Hague, Molly recruited Arthur to help with her copying work because she had not yet mastered the typewriter. "It was a great help," she avowed, "some 18000 words—and my writing is so bad I hate the look of my manuscript and am sorry for those who have to read it." For most of the year, however, Arthur remained without a paying job. In mid-September he traveled to Silver City, a recently rejuvenated mining camp in the Owyhee Mountains about fifty miles southwest of Boise, to inspect a mine. On the 29th of that month, he again left Boise, this time accompanied by Molly, and headed for Thousand Springs, where he hoped to locate a site that would provide electricity to the mines. Arthur had wanted Molly to see these magical springs, "one of the wonders of southern Idaho," since he first encountered them on the government irrigation survey. "It was one of our beautiful trips," she later reported to Helena. They were eight days going by wagon, stopping one day at Grand View on the Snake River, where their son and their nephew, Gerald Sherman, were working on the Bruneau project. During their four days at the springs, Molly sketched while Arthur hunted for power sites. The trip provided the inspiration for the last two of Molly's published

Idaho short stories, "The Harshaw Bride" and "Pilgrim Station."

A second trip to Grand View late in October at the invitation of A. J. Wiley interrupted Molly's writing, however. She and the girls may have spent two weeks there, staying in the company's two-story hotel, the only house on the site. In fact, the only inhabitants of Grand View were the men who worked on the irrigation project. Molly undoubtedly enjoyed evenings spent with her son, but her chief pastime during the day was working in watercolors. "It is restful to me to do something else than black and white," she explained to Helena; besides, she added, color was necessary to truly capture the countryside.

Among Molly's greatest pleasures that year was reading in the August 4 issue of the *Critic* Helena de Kay Gilder's "A Letter on Woman Suffrage," addressed to "Dear M." The Gilders were in the thick of New York progressive politics, supporting such civic concerns as tenement house reforms and better city government. But they opposed suffrage for women, as did many other well-educated and prominent personalities, including President Grover Cleveland and later journalist Ida Tarbell and Oklahoma progressive Kate Barnard. A New York state constitutional convention that convened in May 1894 caused the suffrage issue to be widely debated. Although the *Century* published essays both for and against women's suffrage, an editorial in the July issue, probably written by Richard, strongly supported the anti-suffrage stand.

Helena begins her lengthy letter to M. by referring to the "old summer days of our girlhood" when they denounced man's oppression of woman. For a time, Helena says, she had acquiesced in arguments for granting women suffrage, but after listening to the debates she wonders why no one has had the courage to say "women are *not* the equals of men in any sense applicable to government in a democracy." The proper sphere of women, Helena argues, is the home and those interests that stem from woman's natural inclinations, caring for the poor and the downtrodden, for example. In fact, anything dealing with philanthropy, education, and societal conditions is properly part of woman's domain. Suffrage would force women to do men's work as well as women's work. Like hordes of other anti-suffragists, Helena feared that giving women the vote would destroy the home and the existing social order.

Molly said she wept when she read this letter, for it expressed her feelings exactly. She gave copies to several friends in Boise and reported to Helena that it was "the thing we are all talking about." Molly never took a public stand on suffrage, but she shared with Helena a traditional view of womanhood, even though her behavior as family "bread winner" diverged from it. Despite her Quaker background, in which women were granted considerable freedom, Molly had grown up in a culture that believed women's nature and concerns were different from men's—that women's primary roles were as wife and mother. And she remained committed to these ideas long after she achieved success as a popular American author. In responding to an author's questionnaire from the Knickerbocker Publishing Company in 1905, she wrote:

> My work both as an artist and writer has been subordinated constantly, and I may say as a matter of principle, to my home life and its demands. With, to me it seems the happy result that I have been free from the pangs of competition and the urgency of that need of "success" which makes literature or art such a feverish business, for women. . . . it seems to me, as I look back, that this is the thing about my work I am most content with: that I never have allowed it to usurp the chief place.

Mary Hallock Foote was a conventional woman at heart, although she achieved public success in ways mainly expected of men. Nearly all her stories helped to perpetuate the status quo and to uphold traditional societal standards. Thus the realism she imparts in her fiction (as scholar Christine Hill Smith has observed) "suffers as a result of [a] self-imposed gentility." Never was she able to escape certain values internalized in childhood, a fact that influenced her creativity and limited the range of her vision. Although she was to remain productive as an artist for most of her life, the demands of family and household made it difficult—if not impossible—for Foote to develop fully her potential gifts as writer and illustrator.

The women characters in Molly's stories clearly reflect her ideas about being a woman. They may be assertive and self-reliant and demonstrate amazing energy and courage, but they follow prescribed roles for nineteenth-century women. Aware of the new opportunities opening for women as the twentieth century approached, Molly acknowledged the conservative personas of her heroines in a letter written in the spring of 1894 to Edward S. Holden, former president of the University of California and an admirer of her work:

> You gave me great pleasure—particularly in what you said about the 'girls'. . . . I have had it on my conscience that my stories do not preach a very advanced doctrine in this respect. My girls never have a "career"; never do anything to advance the "causes"; have not the missionary spirit; do not show any progressive spirit, even, as towards "man." I am glad if you can forgive them this and still can think them worthy to be known by your own daughters. To be honest, I am a sad recreant in these matters of woman's place in the future—the near future: in politics and the professions and in everything conspicuously progressive.

Later in the year, in responding to a letter from her old friend and mentor A.V. S. Anthony, Molly again reflected on her writing. After praising Owen Wister, whose western stories were just beginning to appear in *Harper's Monthly Magazine*, she wrote of the constraints that womanhood placed on her own work:

> I have a son nearly a man. I instinctively imagine my son reading my things, and the *maternal* point of view has no place that ever I heard of in art. . . . Yet an artist to be a great artist must know all there is to know about life, and no woman can know all there is about this life out here, unless

> she has a husband who spares nothing in his talk, and my husband is not one of that sort; I'm thankful to say.

Molly continued to write in a self-deprecating manner of her stories. Anthony had singled out "Maverick" for special praise, to which she responded: "I dont *at all agree* with you in your extremest words about Maverick. I shall never have the sureness of touch that some others, many others have." And in explaining why she persisted in writing these tales, she downplayed the joy she found in the creative process and stated simply that she did so "because I think them so worth while." Still, she found Anthony's praise immensely satisfying and helpful, isolated as she was from other writers. "It is very far away out here from the atmosphere which is supposed necessary to the function of artistic impulses," she wrote.

In both "The Harshaw Bride" and "Pilgrim Station," Molly remains true to her ideas about womanhood. Her female protagonists are resolute young women entangled in relationships that eventually will lead to marriage. Although they are not career women, they are talented artists who grapple with questions about love, deceit, honesty, and suspicion. "The Harshaw Bride" differs from Molly's other Idaho stories, however, because of its levity. She remarked upon this "new departure" in a letter to Helena written in the spring of 1895:

> I have finished a novelette called "The Harshaw Bride," and sent it to the *Century* for them to read. They are not quite "out" of my stories yet, and it may be they are not ready for a new one; but I like them to have the first reading of whatever of mine is a new departure, at least—as this is in a degree; being "in lighter vein," and written in the first person.

This is one of Foote's most successful stories. It was published in the *Century* in two installments, starting in May 1896, and was illustrated by ten of Molly's drawings. Later it was included in the 1903 volume entitled *A Touch of Sun, and Other Stories*. As the tale opens, the narrator, Mrs. Tom Daly of Bisuka, Idaho, is expecting the arrival of a young bride-to-be from England, Kitty Comyn. After a four-year engagement to Micky Harshaw, an English emigrant to the "wilds of Idaho," Kitty received a summons from "Harshaw" to come. When she arrives in Bisuka, she discovers that the cable had been sent by Cecil Harshaw, who wishes to force his cousin Micky's hand. Micky, in fact, has no intentions of marrying Kitty. She is mortified when she discovers the truth but is even more indignant when Cecil proposes marriage, supposing that the offer comes from a sense of duty.

Meanwhile, Cecil and Tom Daly talk of building an electric plant at Thousand Springs. Mrs. Daly persuades Tom to hire Kitty to draw pictures of the site for promotional purposes. So the four set out for Thousand Springs, where they encounter another artist, Miss Malcolm, who owns the property where Daly wants to locate the power plant. She refuses to lease or sell the land because Tom's plan, she feels, would destroy the scenic value of the Snow Bank waterfall. "The sight of it belongs to me," she says, "I will not have the place all littered up with their pipes and power-plants." Here Molly comes as close as she ever will to condemning the human destruction of pristine wilderness. And she projects her own ambivalence about the changes engineers impose on the western landscape onto Mrs. Daly. At first, Daly is glad Miss Malcolm resisted Tom's offer. Yet her love for nature must give way when it conflicts with her husband's schemes. "But I am not really glad," she confesses. "What woman could love a waterfall better than her husband's success? There are hundreds of waterfalls in the world, but only this one scheme for Tom." A new complication arises when Kitty learns that a third Harshaw, Micky's father, is on his way to Idaho to propose marriage to his "son's insulted bride." By story's end, however, Kitty realizes that Cecil loves her and Miss Malcolm is reconciled to Tom's plan.

Several memorable scenes and phrases grace this light-hearted narrative. There is a fine description of Thousand Springs, for example, and a delightful rendering of shared hilarity between Mrs. Daly and Kitty. And who will forget

Molly's description of Mrs. Daly as a "woman irretrievably married into the West" because it so aptly fits Mary Hallock Foote. Noteworthy also are Foote's three drawings of Kitty Comyn and her wonderful depiction of the Sand Springs waterfall, which had so delighted the story's young heroine.

"Pilgrim Station," published in the *Atlantic Monthly* in May 1896, takes its title from an abandoned stage stop on the route to Thousand Springs. The Reverend Withers, with three companions, goes in search of the station intending to erect a memorial on the spot where his son John was murdered two years earlier. The story focuses on relationships and false positions. The three central characters must each face the implications of their bogus stands: Daphne Lewis, the alleged fiancée of John Withers; Thane, his supposed best friend; and the Reverend Withers, who is willing to accept falsehoods to protect his son's memory. The story ends with Thane and Daphne parting, leaving to the reader's imagination the possibility of their future courtship. This slender tale was retitled "The Maid's Progress" when published in *A Touch of Sun, and Other Stories.*

While juggling the demands of family and editors, Foote continued to illustrate the work of other authors. Two of her drawings appear with William E. Smythe's "The Conquest of Arid America"(*Century*, May 1895) and four with his "Ways and Means in Arid America" (*Century*, March 1896). An irrigation visionary, Smythe later published a book entitled *The Conquest of Arid America* (1900), which historian Richard White claims "became the bible of a new crusade for an irrigated West." The female figures that appear in Foote's drawings suggest that women and children are central to a settled, irrigated West. Her illustration entitled "The Engineer's Mate" (May 1895) is the most striking in the series. It features a stylishly dressed woman standing on an isolated railway platform with several pieces of luggage at her feet. Her situation is uncertain, but her expression is one of anticipation. In a single drawing Foote encapsulates a lifetime of following an engineer-husband on his travels.

Arthur's situation, in fact, was still unresolved as the year 1894 came to a close. Molly admitted to Helena in a letter dated December 15 that "the question of finances is very serious." And once more she vented her frustrations with Boise society. As the holidays approached, she felt pressured into attending a round of teas and receptions, which to her seemed silly since "we all see each other all the time." And she added: "Mind you, it is the Western *town* I weary of, so that I feel almost crazed with the pettiness and dull monotony; it is not the Western country." Yet she enjoyed the supper and dance that Bessie Sherman hosted when their two sons returned home for the festivities. It was "a very pleasant Christmas," Molly reported.

And the New Year promised new beginnings for Arthur, Sr. Early in January 1895, James D. Hague summoned the forty-five-year-old engineer to Grass Valley to help install a pumping plant for the North Star. The position was temporary but Arthur was "hopeful and happy to be at work." Molly and the girls continued living with Bessie until April, when they fled to Grand View to escape the deadly flu that was sweeping through Boise. They spent an enjoyable spring and summer on the banks of the Snake River. For the girls there was a water tank behind the hotel to bathe and swim in and tennis and boat rides with the boys at day's end. "The evenings have the same beauty of our old cañon evenings, or on the Mesa," Molly observed. On occasion, they drove by wagon to the work site above the dam, where the artist seemingly stood for hours watching Indians spear salmon as the fish attempted to maneuver the fish-ladder. "It seemed impossible that art could have improved the composition," she wrote. "As the place itself is beautiful, and the figures most 'sincere' the whole makes a picture worthy of anybody who had the skill to do it, just as it is."

In late August, Molly and the girls returned to Boise to pack for a two-months' visit to Arthur, Sr., in Grass Valley. The trip marked a turning point in Molly's life, for she and Arthur were to spend the next thirty-five years and more in this lovely mining community. For most of this time they were financially secure and comfortable, though tragedy would strike when they least expected it. On that late summer’s day at Bessie’s, however, when Molly packed for her first trip to Grass Valley, uncertainty still hovered over the family. Arthur’s salary at the North Star was marginal, and James D. Hague gave no indication of what future work he might have for his brother-in-law. Molly nonetheless seemed eager to join her husband. Their son was en route to Boston to enter MIT, and Helena and Richard Gilder and their children were on an extended trip to Europe. Where Molly was to go after Grass Valley, she did not know; possibly she still thought of setting up a household in Boston. “I can tell better what to do after a good long talk with Arthur,” she confided to Helena in a letter dated August 30, 1895. For now, she would enjoy being on the Pacific Coast once more, “not on the sea, but in sight of the sea fogs filling the valleys of the coast range—as they used to at Almaden.” In her reminiscences, Molly poignantly describes this second trip to join her husband in California:

> The ends of the circle had met. Not a great harvest for a twenty years’ reaping, but some experience we had gathered, besides those two faces beaming at us in the seat opposite and the eighteen-year-old son on his way east to begin his life in precisely the way we might have hoped when he was our New Almaden baby.

CHAPTER 5

Grass Valley, California

GRASS Valley was a well-established mining town when Molly arrived with Betty and Agnes in the fall of 1895. Cornish miners and their families composed about three-fourths of the estimated 4500 people who lived there. The town boasted several churches, business blocks, and mansions, including the residence of Edward Coleman, one-time owner of the North Star mine.

Gold-bearing quartz had been discovered in Grass Valley in 1850. Development was rapid after that, and the region soon claimed some of the richest gold mines in all of California. But by the mid-1870s many of the mines were said to be "worked-out" and had closed. Marian F. Conway, a granddaughter of the Footes, writes in her history of the North Star that "only the Empire and Idaho were still producing in any quantity." And even the Empire was scheduled to close in 1878. That year, however, young William Bourn, Jr. (who was to become a good friend of the Footes), returned home from college and took over the family's business interests, which included the Empire. After sinking huge sums into the Empire and witnessing the discovery of new rich ore bodies, he bought the nearby North Star in 1884 to see if it too could be revitalized. But three years later he sold this mine to James D. Hague who, with the help of other financiers, took steps to rejuvenate the North Star and adjacent properties.

At first Hague envisioned constructing a large electrical plant to supply power for the planned developments. But Arthur Foote doubted the wisdom of using electricity at this time in wet tunnels and convinced his brother-in-law that compressed air would be cheaper and more reliable. So in 1895 Hague hired Foote to design and construct a new compressed air powerhouse. In her reminiscences, Molly comments upon how the two men complemented each other "in temperament" and "in the qualities and experience each brought" to the project. Foote had a talent for working with machines and subordinates, for instance, but was not a businessman. Hague, on the other hand, had a genius for raising funds but disliked working with machinery. "[James] hated a machine," Molly writes, "A. loved them and humored them and understood their little contrary ways."

When Molly joined Arthur in Grass Valley the family's future was still uncertain. Molly had no idea how long she would remain there or where she and Arthur would live once the power system was completed. At one point, Hague recommended Arthur for a position in South Africa; when that job fell through, Molly's relief was palpable. A week or so before Christmas, Hague examined the finished power plant and expressed his approval. Best of all, he wanted Arthur to stay on at least through the spring "to test his work and to watch it in operation." Even though the future was still uncertain, Molly told Helena she would no longer worry. "I am happy to tears, almost over Arthur's satisfaction," she wrote. "It breaks out of him in bursts of romps with Agnes."

Since arriving at the North Star Cottage, which was Hague's residence when he stayed in Grass Valley, Molly had kept busy reading proofs for *The Cup of Trembling, and Other Stories* and completing the last drawings for "The Harshaw Bride." She also finished a short story, "Diana of the Ditch Camp," which had been inspired by her stay at Grand View in Idaho. The fictional Diana was modeled on the daughter of the contractor who moved dirt on the Bruneau ditch line. She ran the men's boarding house and commissariat at the contractor's camp a few miles above Grand View. Her beauty, intelligence, and strong personality piqued Molly's interest.

Foote first submitted the story to *Harper's Magazine*, but when its editors were unable to guarantee immediate publication, she sent it to Robert Underwood Johnson of the *Century.* She asked $500 for the two-part story, which ran to about sixteen thousand words. She called it her "bicycle story" and said that it dealt with "contemporaneous subjects" and was in "a lighter vein." Molly knew she was taking a chance with this piece since she had never before attempted to write about "the emancipated girl." But the *Century* turned it down, apparently because Johnson felt Molly's attempt at "light heartedness" had not succeeded. Unwilling to abandon the manuscript, Molly wrote to Horace E. Scudder at the *Atlantic Monthly* early in April 1896 to ask if he would be interested in reading a story that the *Century* had rejected. "I have a sort of injured sense of having been taken on altogether too high and serious grounds by my friendly critics of the Century,"she confessed. And then she added: "I can't help feeling that there is *something* in this story." But "Diana of the Ditch Camp" was never published, and eventually it "went into the wastebasket."

Shortly after submitting "Diana of the Ditch Camp" to the *Century*, Molly was asked to contribute illustrations for Houghton Mifflin and Company's forthcoming multivolume reprinting of Bret Harte's poems and stories. Molly was delighted by the request. She called it "the opportunity of a lifetime," for Bret Harte had been among the most famous writers in the U.S. when Foote first won acclaim as a professional artist in the early 1870s. Although Harte's popularity in this country quickly dissipated, his reputation remained high in England, where he now lived. Like Molly, he had been born in New York and had moved to California, in 1854. His fame came from the local color stories he wrote about the Gold Rush. Molly had been reading his tales since before her marriage to Arthur and came to admire his style and poetic "distillations of the life of the mines," though she thought his writings were less realistic than those of Owen Wister. She once shrewdly observed: "Bret Harte gave his whole harvest in one incomparable vintage."

That she was living in "Bret Harte's old stamping ground" added to the appeal of the assignment. She wrote to her publishers: "Grass Valley is one of the oldest mining camps in [California]. 'Red Dog' is just over the hills and every night at sunset we look down on the Marysville Buttes. The pine woods are here, the old shafts and cabins, and windlasses, and all the accessories one could ask." She made a request of her own, however. "Please let me have a chance to do some of his women." Her first choice was to illustrate "The Idyl of Red Gulch." And she added: "I know the very background for the Schoolmistress and Sandy." She informed the firm that she charged "$50 for a full page drawing with more than one figure, less if there is but one." In an excess of enthusiasm, she conceded: "But frankly, this work is so charming, that if you dont want to pay so much, tell me what you will pay, and I dare say I shall be goose enough to come to your terms."

But a week later Molly withdrew her offer to accept less than her usual price. Upon "sober second thoughts," she realized she could not ask "one good firm one price, and another equally good firm a lower price—even to secure an exceptionally desirable order for work." So she restated her standard fees: $50 for a full-page drawing of more than one figure, $40 for a full page drawing of one figure with background, and less for a single figure with little or no background.

Soon she was hard at work on her illustration for "The Idyl of Red Gulch." She used Betty as her model for the schoolmistress and the nearby pinewoods for the background. Later she was dismayed when the Houghton Mifflin people objected to the dimensions of her drawing. In subsequent correspondence, Molly revealed just how much she had grown as a businesswoman. She insisted the mistake was theirs and not hers. Not once had they mentioned the size or shape of their book page, even though its narrowness, as she belatedly learned, imposed severe restrictions on the artist and called for specific instructions. She would make a new drawing to their specifications but only if they cared to "order it as a separate commission. . . . If I were as reckless of my time and strength as I once was I should offer on the impulse to present you with a new drawing, but one counts the cost of such impulses as one grows older."

In their reply to this offer, the publishers left "the matter of charge" for the second drawing to Foote's "judgment." But Molly shot right back: "[This] is not a question of my 'judgment,' but of a plain business obligation, which your House will decide." But if left up to Molly, "I will say frankly that, *this* time, I think you should pay for your own neglect." She reminded them that years earlier they had ordered a drawing of Mabel Martin when they really meant the subject to be Maud Muller, and she had sent a second drawing at no extra charge. "You owned that the mistake was yours, but you left the case in my hands then, as now, and I took back the drawing you ordered but could not use—choosing to act according to my taste in the matter and not make you any trouble. But this time I shall not let sentiment interfere with business." Still, in a postscript, she offered to complete another drawing at no extra cost if given additional time. "It is very unpleasant to be business-like—I had far rather be lady-like if I could." While seeming to capitulate, Foote nonetheless raised the expectation that as gentlemen the publishers would pay for the second drawing.

Still, it was the original illustration, slightly altered, that appeared in the published collected works of Bret Harte. A superb drawing, it shows Sandy reclining at the foot of Miss Mary, the schoolmistress, who is seated in front of a majestic pine tree. Molly contributed four other drawings to the collection, including a fine two-figure illustration for the poem "Her Letter." When the proofs of the drawings reached the artist in May 1896, she pronounced them "wonderfully perfect."

During these first months in Grass Valley, Molly revealed aspects of her home life in letters to family and friends. To Mother Foote she wrote about the "very pleasant home" that James had given them in the North Star Cottage, situated about two miles from the town proper. In the evenings, when

Hague was in residence, they often played "casino," with James and Betty pitted against Molly and Agnes (coached by her father). Christmas that year was a happy one. Cornish miners came to the cottage on Christmas morning to serenade the family. And a day or so later the Footes left for San Francisco, where they spent a "charming week" as guests of William and Agnes Bourn, the wealthy friends of James D. Hague.

Spring was exceedingly lovely. Although absorbed in her Bret Harte drawings, Molly took daily walks and helped to entertain Hague's guests at the cottage. On March 22 she wrote an especially cheerful letter to Helena, despite the uncertainty of Arthur's continued employment at the North Star.

> We are very, *very* happy here; and one gets used to suspense, as to everything else. One can bear suspense very well in surroundings like these. We have the peace of remoteness and freedom from social and conventional cares, yet we are (for a pair of "busted" irrigators from the Arid Belt) deliciously comfortable. Pine trees and electric lights; wood-paths and pine shaded roads and a snug little horse and cart to travel over them with; complete isolation, with a telephone to town and a watchman within call; and the roar of the stamp-mill distanced to the murmur of a cataract, mingling with the songs of meadow-larks in the falling valley at our feet.

But Molly's emotional equilibrium was jarred later that spring when she was asked to direct the Women's Art School at Cooper Union. Susan N. Carter, the school's long-time principal, was retiring and wanted Molly to succeed her. The Gilders also supported Molly's candidacy. But self-doubts assailed her, even though Hague assured her that her friends "would not be likely to encourage me to attempt something merely to fail." After laying awake most of one night and becoming nearly sick over the decision, Molly sent in her name as an applicant and then shared with Helena some of her reasons for doing so:

> The children must go East, or somewhere to school; East would be best, and New York as good as possible; and the income, though, as Mrs. Carter says, it is not large, is as much as I can make a year by my special work, even when I work hard and am blest in any subjects. Now it is time for me to stop writing. I feel it physically, and the work I do shows it. Mr. Johnson had to return my last story, and that is a warning, you see.

Still, the decision troubled her. Later she recalled how one evening she sat on the piazza "scared and tired and wretched"—even crying—thinking about going to New York with the girls "on a salary of my own, for perhaps three or four years." Witnessing his wife's anguish, Arthur spoke up for the first time. "[He] asked me if I couldn't have a little more faith in the future (in spite of the past) and trust to his being able to do things, etc. And he said right out that he hated to have me cut loose and set up with the children, and the West looked lovely to him in prospect. That was enough, of course." Resolving to trust Arthur and to abandon any thought of establishing a separate household (even for the children's sake), she withdrew her name for the Cooper Union job.

No sooner had she made this decision than Arthur was offered a job in Colorado. This apparently forced James D. Hague to act. The preceding months had given him ample opportunity to observe Foote's remarkable energy and ambition, his vast technical knowledge, and his managerial skills. For Hague these qualities prevailed over Arthur's record of bad luck in previous jobs. So he now asked Foote to stay on (at a modest salary) as superintendent of the North Star, an offer Foote readily accepted. Both Footes, in fact, were delighted with Arthur's new opportunity and the prospect of establishing a permanent home in Grass Valley. In following years, Hague's faith in his brother-in-law's abilities would be fully justified.

About the time Arthur took over as superintendent, the family's finances received a boost when the *Century* paid Molly for "The Harshaw Bride," although its method of payment distorted the comparative value she placed on her writing and drawing. The agreed price had been $800 for the story and $200 for the pictures. For some unknown reason the *Century* people sent a check of $530 for the story and one of $470 for the illustrations, which led Molly to respond: "It is a monstrous price for those drawings and I am jealous for my poor story in comparison, but if it suits you better to divide the thousand that way I certainly have no reason to complain."

But checks such as these were to be in short supply during the next couple of years, for ironically, with greater financial security, Molly found she was unable to write; ideas simply did not come to her. On September 7, 1896, she wrote to Richard Gilder: "The depressing fact [is] that I am an utter idiot when I try to write. Now that I have no longer that hunted feeling I have relapsed into a silly content." And the following March she lamented to Helena: "[When] I begin to write . . . a constriction binds me across the eyes and forehead; and a mental deadness settles on me." But she never totally stopped writing. "Without my work, my life is very very empty," she confessed, "I mean during the hours when Agnes is at her lessons and Arthur is at work." She published two insubstantial pieces during the year 1897: "Flower of the Almond and Fruit of the Fig," an allegorical children's tale set in California, which appeared in *St. Nicholas Magazine* in September, and "On an Old Plate," a vignette based on her stay in Victoria, which was published in the *Atlantic Monthly* in November.

During this dry spell, however, Molly was absorbing local scenes and dialects that would find expression in some of her finest work. One summer's day, for instance, she accompanied Betty and two of her friends into the mines, descending the 2,000-foot incline the way the miners did—in a flat car without seats or sides, feet braced against cleats, one behind the other, lying in each other's laps. And when Arthur had trouble with his eyes, Molly read technical reports aloud to him in the evenings, which added to her storehouse of knowledge about mines. Coming to the end of this fallow period, Molly observed: "I have to soak things in long and silently before I can make any fit-use of them. There is material here, but it requires strong and original handling—else it will go into the same rut with all other new eastern and mining stories, and there are enough of them."

During the time she could not write, nothing occupied Molly's thoughts so much as her children. She especially was concerned about their education and frequently reported on their academic progress. Young Arthur was doing well at MIT, she wrote to Helena, and would be spending summers in Grass Valley working for his father. Agnes was to be tutored by Nelly Linton, who rejoined the Foote household in the fall of 1896. And in August of this same year, Molly accompanied Betty, who was approaching her fourteenth birthday, to Berkeley where she enrolled in Miss Anna Head's private school for girls, "the best one out here," Molly avowed.

Mary Hallock Foote held strong opinions about her children's schooling. For the girls, "tone" and environment were as important as the subjects they were taught. That Betty's classmates at Miss Head's came from refined homes pleased Molly, as did the school's beautiful grounds and buildings. But some of the extracurricular activities disturbed her. She objected to the new craze of girls' competitive basketball, for example, because she felt the stress of the game was unnatural and interrupted the girls' fun. She also objected to girls of Betty's age writing for the school newspaper, believing they were too immature to probe deeply into the stories they wrote. For these and probably other reasons, Betty stayed at Miss Head's for only one school year.

After that, Molly entrusted Betty's education to her old friend Edith Angus, now widowed and tutoring a few pupils in Victoria, British Columbia. Edith Angus was "a cultured and wise woman, and very broad," Molly reported to Helena, and would provide the genteel role model that Molly wished for her daughter. Exercise under Edith Angus would be natural—golf, tennis, boating, and swimming—instead of basketball in a gymnasium. Molly admitted that her prejudices about competitive team sports did not apply to boys, "that is if we wish to cultivate in them the virtues of the soldier." So in August 1897 Molly took Betty to Victoria, accompanied by young Arthur. Although both son and daughter fell ill with malaria on the trip, Molly still enjoyed a round of dinners, teas, and drives. Writing to Mother Foote in November, Molly noted with satisfaction that all of Betty's classmates were ladies and that "there is no slang, no carelessness and slovenliness in speech or manners, and no reckless eating or excessive devotion to 'Athletics.'" Still later Molly summed up her views of parenting in these words:

> Well, it is middle-age with us. The time for planning and organizing the children's lives—the choosing of schools, which decides the choice of friendships, on which perhaps marriage—the whole future of a fraction of the race, depends! . . . We are our children's destiny, at this period. Later we fall off like the seed-pod after its work is done.

Despite her inability to write very much, Molly gained enormous satisfaction from her surroundings—the sunsets, the pine woods, the flowers (seemingly always in bloom), and the garden, which supplied an abundance of fruits and vegetables—so unlike Idaho where they had prayed "over a few square inches of grass!" Grass Valley, in fact, had many attractions that Idaho lacked, and before long Molly felt a sense of belonging that she had never experienced in Boise. She came to see Grass Valley as a home, and it was here, this writer believes, that she completed the process of becoming a westerner. Right from the start she sensed its possibilities and felt such confidence in her new surroundings that she was eager for Helena to visit. More than she ever did in Boise, Molly heaped requests on her long-time friend to come West. "I have never been in any place that to me seemed so home-like," she wrote to Helena on December 16, 1896, "so like a place to ask one's dearest friends to come."

And life in Grass Valley became more piquant after Molly established close ties with Agnes Bourn, wife of the millionaire mine owner William Bourn, Jr., a refined but unpretentious woman a little younger than Molly. Although the author had been a guest of the Bourns during her first winter in Grass Valley, the two women really came to know each other only after Agnes spent a week at the North Star Cottage early in January 1897. "She was a thoroughly unselfish and tactful guest; and I enjoyed our reading and talking hours exceedingly," Molly reported to Helena. It was soon after this that William Bourn commissioned the architect Willis Polk to design a cottage for his family above the Empire mine. Completed later that year on twelve acres of ground and with a floor area of 4600 square feet, the Empire Cottage resembled a mansion, though Bourn intended it a summer residence only. On her first visit to the cottage one Sunday in November, Molly described it as simply "lovely!"

Molly spent a good deal of her time in the evenings, as she had in Idaho, reading periodicals and the newly published works of leading authors. With two other families the Footes formed a magazine club, providing access to all the leading journals, including the *Critic* and Molly's beloved *Century*, which she avowed had "a certain scope and importance and works it seems to us on broader lines than any of them." She held a special admiration for the fiction of Henry James, a friend of Helena's since childhood whom Helena had met up with on a recent trip to Europe. But after Molly read his newest book, *The Other House*, she admitted that she did not like it very much.

But Foote had nothing but praise for the poetry and fiction of Rudyard Kipling, the India-born writer who was to live most of his life in England. Molly first became acquainted with Kipling when he wrote to request two drawings for the western section of *The Naulahka: A Story of West and East* (1892), which he coauthored with Wolcott Balestier. Kipling greatly admired Molly's contributions, telling his publishers "I've got two stunning Naulahka drawings out of Mary Hallock Foote." But when Kipling's father, an artist and author himself, failed to complete the eastern drawings, plans to illustrate the tale were dropped. Molly kept up a correspondence with both Kiplings for several years and was delighted when the younger Kipling offered to "introduce" her *Cup of Trembling, and Other Stories* in England. "It seems such an inconceivable thing for the Author of his books to be bothering about the Author of mine," she confessed to Helena in a letter dated June 28, 1896.

That winter both Molly and Helena read Kipling's newly published *The Seven Seas*; this and other of his work aroused in her such strong emotions that Molly wrote: "I confess it makes me wild, to read him! It fills me with such a longing for those strange roads once more." She was shocked to learn, then, that Helena felt differently, apparently finding Kipling's stories too strong, even "brutal." This led Molly to exclaim to her friend: "I should never be confident of being right when I differ from you on a question of Art."

During these early days at the North Star, Molly found additional satisfaction in the frequent visits of her nephew Gerald Sherman, a graduate of Columbia University. Like many other young engineers, Sherman first came to Grass Valley to work for James D. Hague, but he also was to work on occasion for William Bourn, Jr. Both before and after his marriage, in August 1897, to Lucy Huntoon, a young woman he had courted in Boise, the Footes treated him almost as a son. Prior to the wedding, Gerald's mother, Bessie, spent three weeks at the North Star Cottage in what must have been a happy reunion for the Hallock sisters. For several weeks afterward the newlyweds lived with the Footes while Bourn's company built them a cottage on the Empire grounds.

In fact, the Shermans were still at the North Star Cottage through the Christmas holidays. Molly's days now were taken up with household concerns and preparations for the festivities. She had a new German-born cook named Bena who turned out such marvelous cream soups, souffles, and other delicacies that Molly constantly sang her praises. A few days before Christmas, Bena worked overtime to bake the cakes that would be served to Christmas carollers. In a letter written to Helena on December 22, 1897, Molly vividly described the

Cornish traditions that the Footes would observe on this and later holidays. As superintendent of the North Star and the adjacent Stockbridge and Central shafts, Arthur would treat the miners on Christmas Eve to beer and soft drinks when they came out of the mines—"shift after shift, in their mud-soaked clothes." The men would stand around the shafts and fill "the great ringing place with the solid roar of their voices, singing the old Christmas carols." The next morning a group of picked singers would arrive at the North Star Cottage to serenade the superintendent's family and to be treated to cake, coffee, and more beer.

Household concerns continued to distract Molly as the new year unfolded. When Bena fell ill early in January, Molly hired extra help to do the hard work while Bena recuperated. And then James D. Hague arrived with a North Star director, both taking meals at the cottage and Hague living in a makeshift bedroom until Lucy and Gerald moved to their own house. "I have had a full-page drawing for the Century on my desk for two months," Molly confessed to Helena, "trying to get the right moment in which to finish it." But she was not disheartened, nor did she want Helena to think she was complaining. "This is Arthur's opportunity, and what woman would not put her own work aside for the sake of seeing her husband's powers in full play, after years of defrauded effort."

By April, Molly was at work on another story, and within the next two and a half years she would publish four short stories, one novel, and one collection of children's stories. Two of the tales, "The Borrowed Shift," published in the *Land of Sunshine* in December 1898, and "How the Pump Stopped at the Morning Watch," published in the *Century* in July 1899, draw on her knowledge of Cornish miners and conditions in the mines. Shortly before "The Borrowed Shift" appeared in print, Charles F. Lummis, editor of the *Land of Sunshine*, which featured the works of the foremost western writers in the U.S., issued his verdict on the fiction of Mary Hallock Foote:

> If those who have carefully followed American literature for the last ten years were bidden to make choice of the most typical series of Western stories written by a woman, I fancy a majority would promptly elect Mary Hallock Foote. Western in very truth of scene and "color" and outlook, marked by all the instincts at once of woman, artist, poet and story-teller, *The Led-Horse Claim* and its fellows are of a quality that refuses to be forgotten.

In "The Borrowed Shift," Molly uses dialect more, and with greater assurance, than she has in any of her earlier work. Her exceptional knowledge of mining technology and of the routines of her husband's employees add greatly to the story's credibility. At the start of the tale, a mining superintendent orders his foreman to let go four men. Unwilling to decide which of his fellow Cornish miners will lose their livelihood, the foreman has the men draw lots. Jimmy Dillon, widowed and with seven kids to support, fears he will jinx the outcome if he draws for himself and so leaves the mine, asking young Jack Dobell to draw for him. As luck would have it, Dobell draws a blank slip for himself and a marked one for Dillon. Despite his fiancée's objection, Dobell refuses to give the marked slip to the older man. The story eventually gets out, and Dillon confronts Dobell, who denies he has switched the papers but exacts a promise: that Dillon will allow the younger man to borrow the Monday morning shift to engage a rival in a drilling match. At the end of the day, during which Dobell proved his superiority with the drill, twelve fuses are lit at the bottom of the shaft and the signal given to hoist the four remaining men. But the cage will not move. As the seconds tick away and the engineer frantically works to correct the problem before the men are killed, Dobell takes the lead in pulling the fuses in the dark with his bare hands. "It was a nightmare in which seconds seemed hours." When he emerges from the shaft, Dobell is proclaimed a hero and gets his job back. He also marries his sweetheart.

"How the Pump Stopped at the Morning Watch" is one of Foote's shortest, yet most memorable stories. Like "The Borrowed Shift," it focuses on the murky world of the underground miner. This time, however, Foote's editors questioned whether her use of technical terms interfered with the flow of the story. Molly politely wrote back that she was "very fond of other persons' technical terms" and then pointed out that "the mining terms are now quite widely known. They are all in the Century Dictionary, for I took pains to look them up." Molly's instincts were correct; the story's success hinges on her understanding of deep mining technology and its associated dangers.

This story, in fact, is based on two actual events at the North Star mine, the tragic death on October 2, 1896, of the fifty-five-year-old pump-man, John T. Thomas, and the breakdown about four months later of a Cornish pump. As Wallace Stegner suggests in his study of nineteenth-century literary realism, fusing these two events into one allowed Molly "to arrive at a human truth larger than the factual truth."

The success of any mine, the author makes clear, depends on both the pump that draws water from its subterranean depths and the man who oversee the pump's maintenance. In the fictional story, "old John" Tiernay, the first and only pump-man at the Morning Watch mine, takes such parental pride in his pumps that—to his wife's consternation—he often skips Sunday services to look after them. When he emerges above ground, the narrator reports, he is coated in mud and grease and looks like "some old piece of mining machinery that has been soaked underground for half a century." In fact, old John has grown to prefer the darkness and solitude of the mine's interior to the light and society that await him above ground. Lately, though, he had appeared dazed and bewildered to the men who saw him. On the fateful day, a gardener knocks on the door of the superintendent's house and asks the mistress for an umbrella. She is surprised because it is a hot summer day with no rain in sight, but the gardener explains that the pump-man was struck by an empty car and badly hurt. The umbrella will shield old John from the sun as the boys carry him home on a mattress. Old John, the mining captain concludes, "wasn't all there" when he stepped into the path of the car; "he'd slipped a cog, somehow . . . . A man in a shaft he's got to keep his eye out. He can watch for forty years, and the minute he forgets himself, that minute he's gone."

After lingering on for three days, speechless and helpless, old John gives a final cry, vowing to get up because the pump has stopped. His distraught wife pleads for him to stop thinking of the pumps. But in fact at the same moment two miles away, the mine's watchman discovers that the crown wheel of the pump has broken. While the funeral sermon is preached, John's old enemy, "the water of the black deeps, was creeping up, regaining ground which he and the pumps had fought for and defended inch by inch and year by year." The mine closes, the paychecks stop, and, the narrator concludes, "the grave of ten millions [the value of the gold] is for sale cheap, with a thousand feet of water in it." By linking the worn-out crown wheel with the aging and disoriented pump-man, Foote creates a haunting tale.

Molly continued to deal with everyday concerns even while immersed in her writing. With typical candor she admitted to Helena her exasperation with local society, for among the matters that consumed her time—"interviewing butcher and baker—and milk-girl, discussing what we shall have for dinner . . . . studying over 'Best's' catalogue to choose a new jacket for Agnes, exchanging shoes that do not fit, nursing malaria and colds," she included "returning the calls of women as uninteresting as ever I have known." Yet she admitted that these "good and faithful" women had made a special effort to reach out to her, a perfect stranger.

In mid-February 1898, amidst the daily routine of their lives, sorrow entered the Foote household when a midnight telegram brought news of Mary Hague's unexpected death. The mother of three children and only a year or so older than Molly, Mary Hague died from complications following a hysterectomy. Her marriage to James had been troubled for many years, during which time she maintained a home in the East for the children while James traveled and worked mainly in the West. Despite this marital discord, James remained fond of his wife's brother and treated Molly with respect and affection. Later Molly reminisced in a letter to James about Mary's early influence on her own life: "At every turn in my life as a young wife and mother it was she, more than any other woman outside the relation of mother and daughter, who helped me most. Your house was the first to welcome us on this coast. She came to us at New Almaden to give me comfort and wisdom, out of her own youthful experience, in the critical time before my boy was born."

About the time Molly wrote these words, the U.S. embarked upon war with Spain to guarantee the independence of Cuba. War news was very much on Molly's mind, as it was with the rest of the nation, but Molly was to use the Spanish-American War as backdrop to one of her most successful stories, "Pilgrims to Mecca," in which she explores a theme she will return to several times—relations between parents and children.

Although "Pilgrims to Mecca" would focus on a mother-daughter connection, Molly's chief concern as she was writing this story was the possibility of her son going to war. On April 19 she exclaimed to Helena: "Well, thank the Lord, neither of our boys has enlisted as yet!" She thought that actual fighting might be averted, "even tho Congress does behave like cattle on a steamer-deck in a storm—stamping and bellowing and hooking one another." Still, she had written Arthur, Jr., a long letter apparently registering her concerns about the war and perhaps repeating what she wrote to Helena, that "it seems rather idiotic that we should throw away our soundest, sanest material in the way of future citizens, at the behest of those mad cattle of congressmen." Later that summer, as American casualties rose, the Footes dissuaded their son from enlisting in a company of army engineers being recruited in San Francisco. "He has been brought up to obey orders," she informed Helena. "And the orders from home were—not yet."

By mid-July she had sent "a little story which hinges on the war" to the *Century* and asked for an early reading. It was quickly accepted for publication, though one editor described it as "an interesting story in all its aspects, delicate, but not at all powerful." Still, he concluded, "it is too good to lose." Molly made a few revisions before "Pilgrims to Mecca" went to press, including a name change for a young man killed in the fighting. Richard Gilder apparently believed that Molly's selection of "Teddy" was inappropriate, or perhaps hackneyed, and so the fictional character appears in the story as "Billy Castant."

Published in the March 1899 issue of the *Century*, "Pilgrims to Mecca" features three of Foote's drawings, including one of young Elsie, for which Betty was the model. The story is about a western mother who accompanies her daughter east to a private school. On the Boston-bound train, Mrs. Valentin of San Francisco praises another traveling mother and daughter, their clothing indicating they are cultured and from the East, the type of people Mrs. Valentin hopes her daughter Elsie will meet and emulate. When they stop overnight in Chicago, news of the war catches up with them. On casualty lists posted on the station bulletin board, Elsie searches for the name of her admirer, Billy Castant, a college dropout who has enlisted in the Rough Riders.

Once in their hotel room, they are paid a visit from their old bishop, who sees that they are "pilgrims to Mecca." Mrs. Valentin admits that the purpose of their anticipated two-year separation from Mr. Valentin is to widen Elsie's horizons, although Elsie travels east only to please her mother. In an ironic twist, the bishop tells Mrs. Valentin that all the new girls entering Elsie's school, as well as the other girl on the train (a second-year student at the same school), are westerners like Elsie. In a carefully constructed scene, the bishop informs Mrs. Valentin that Billy Castant has been killed in the charge of San Juan. Upon departing, he advises her not to hurry Elsie's education. "With experience, as with death, it is the prematureness that hurts." Out of Mrs. Valentin's hearing, he adds: "It would be a happy thing if parents could always go with their children on these long roads of experience; but there are some roads that the boys and the girls will have to take alone." Awakened to the superficiality of her concerns about clothes and manners, Mrs. Valentin wires her husband that she is bringing Elsie home.

Although Molly assured Helena that the fictional Elsie was not her daughter Betty, still the author's preoccupations shaped the exchanges that occurred between the fictional mother and daughter. For all of her life, Molly equated genteel manners and upbringing with social acceptability, and she long regarded the East as the font of civilization. But like Mrs. Valentin, she had learned an important lesson: that the roots of the second generation were firmly planted in the West. When her niece Birney Sherman had been sent east to school, Molly told Helena, the homesick youngster wore a piece of Idaho sagebrush "as a Scots lassie might wear a sprig of heather!" Molly further remarked: "While we are striving in exile in order that we may one day take our children home, they are striking deep roots into this alien soil, and may not consent to call any other *home*."

Despite her worries about the war, Molly enjoyed most of the summer. With all three children at home, she made a special effort to become "acquainted" with her son and eldest daughter. Molly found keen pleasure in sharing with Betty some of her favorite books. "Reading Emerson again with Betty," she told Helena, "is like living over the days of our summer readings at Milton." To Molly's disappointment, however, she could not entice Arthur, Jr., to talk about himself or reveal his deepest thoughts, although he talked freely with his father about his work at the mine. Still, Molly was pleased that Arthur and Betty had become such good friends. And she especially enjoyed evenings at the North Star Cottage when Betty's former classmates came for a visit. On these occasions supper was served on the piazza under electric lamps in Chinese lanterns and Betty played the banjo. One of these summer visitors was to enter the Foote household as young Arthur's wife.

By early fall Molly was making plans to spend the winter in San Francisco so that Agnes could go to school with other children and Betty could enter art school where someone other than her mother would assess her talent. "I cannot judge if Betty's work is at all worth while," she admitted to Helena. "She seems to me to draw from life better than I did at her age, but to have less enthusiasm for the work itself."

So in November Molly and the two girls moved to San Francisco where they soon settled into a delightful boarding house on Leavenworth Street, which they named the "House of the Pepper Tree" because of the giant pepper tree that hung over the high garden wall. In describing the residence to Helena, she wrote: "You go up flights of wooden steps and landings from the high gate which opens on the street. There is a garden, and a glass-framed piazza with bamboo shades and tiger skins. The rooms we have are upstairs, and all the bedrooms cluster round a square hall where there is a big heater." Belle Miller, one of the two sisters who ran the house, was an exquisite pianist and played every evening in the parlor. Her music alone, Molly claimed, was worth more than their monthly board bill.

San Francisco captivated the two younger Footes. Despite earlier plans, Agnes soon began her studies at the Bourn mansion on Webster Street with the private tutor of Maud Bourn, the only child of William and Agnes Bourn. Betty also took lessons there but spent mornings at the Mark Hopkins Institute of Art (formerly the California School of Design). The Footes attended a variety of dinners, teas, and parties that winter, and Molly became reacquainted with women she had met nearly twenty-two years ago when she first went to San Francisco as a young bride. Christmas was an especially happy time since Arthur, Sr., came for a visit and the family went to Sausalito for a picnic. Molly's chief complaint was that the sisters kept the house too cold, forcing her to stay huddled by her bedroom fire or to go out for a brisk walk to keep warm. "San Francisco people don't know when they are cold," she grumbled.

Much of Molly's time in following weeks was devoted to her children—nursing their illnesses and orchestrating their activities. She accompanied Agnes to dancing classes and sat with the other mothers in a row against the wall during the lessons. Both girls took part in a fair instigated by Agnes Bourn that raised $1600 for the Children's Hospital in San Francisco. The Children's Hospital, in fact, was among the few civic organizations to engage Molly's sympathy. She was to dedicate the profits from *The Little Fig-Tree Stories* (1899), a collection of nine of her tales that originally appeared in *St. Nicholas Magazine*, to the hospital and also to serve on its board of directors. Included in *The Little Fig-Tree Stories* is a drawing of "The Lamb that Couldn't 'Keep Up,'" which Molly said was "supposed not only to illustrate the story of that name but to bear reference to the helpless children of the Hospital, the Lambs that couldn't keep up." Considering her busy social calendar and an unwavering devotion to her girls, it is not surprising that Molly wrote in mid-January: "I've got a writing streak on but I have no time to work it off—because of the little things—or rather because I *care* for the little things."

But Molly's life was about to take another turn when Agnes fell critically ill in March with malaria, her sixth recurrence since August. This time, when her temperature rose to 106 degrees, she became unconscious and responded only after Molly bathed her in ice-cold water. Fiercely protective of her daughter, Molly decided to take her to the East Coast to escape the California malaria.

Molly planned to go first to Boston to see her son and then to New Haven to visit with Mother Foote. From there she would go to her Cousin Alice's in Rye, where Agnes could romp in the countryside while Molly went on to Tyringham, Massachusetts, where the Gilders had a summer residence. She had not seen Helena in ten years and admitted to her old friend, in a letter written on April 3, 1899, as she was about to start out on her trip: "I come to you a bit shyly, after so long. I am old, my dear! Prepare yourself for a middle aged M.H.F.—not stout enough to be stately, not fresh nor fair but hopelessly the same inside."

A few letters provide sketchy details of Foote's nearly five and a half month visit on the East Coast. She later wrote of her reunion with Helena: "The Tyringham twilight walk will be one of the pictures of a life. I have it for keeps." By late June she had settled into a cottage with Agnes on Little Deer Isle, Maine—next door to the one kept by Mrs. Murray, Molly's best Idaho friend whose husband was now stationed in the Philippines. It was a very pleasant summer, enlivened by Arthur Junior's two-week visit following his graduation from MIT. "It is very sweet to sit here with one's son of an evening by our drift-wood fire," Molly confided to Helena, "Agnes upstairs asleep." During the nearly two months she spent on the island, she mulled over plans for her daughters' education. Arthur's cousins, the Rockwells, had invited Betty to spend the winter in Boston to continue her art studies, and Molly was delighted when her daughter accepted, for she hoped that more would come from this stay than mere drawing lessons: "Ostensibly the object will be the Art lessons; but all the lessons of life are what we want for our young folk. Lessons in pretty behavior, manners and mental culture. Meeting fine people—no matter if they do have a few cranks and queernesses [*sic*]." Agnes also was to spend the winter in the East, possibly with Cousin Alice in Rye where she would attend the local school. Before returning to Grass Valley at the end of October, Molly continued her visits to family and friends and helped both daughters settle into their new surroundings.

Yet leave-taking was difficult. Back at the North Star Cottage, she wrote on October 28: "I was rather broken up by the partings, especially with Agnes, who looked to me somehow wistful and bewildered." So she spent her first day at home "prowling about alone unpacking and putting things away." She concluded this letter to Helena by declaring: "It has been a wonderful summer for me. . . . For the girls it is equally important—and that must be my consolation for I miss them dreadfully."

But Molly accomplished a great deal of work that summer, much of it on Little Deer Isle, though she failed to mention this to Helena. In July she sent to Richard Gilder "The Golf Bonnet" sketches, which appeared in the November 1899 issue of the *Century* as illustrations for a poem about a pretty woman's golfing bonnet. Sometime that summer she also completed an illustrated short story, "A Touch of Sun," published in the *Century* in January and February 1900, and a novel, *The Prodigal*, which appeared as a serial in the *Atlantic Monthly*, starting in September 1900, and then later that same year in book form under the Houghton Mifflin imprint.

In both short story and novel, Foote continued to explore the dynamics of the parent-child relationship. "A Touch of Sun" deals with Margaret Thorne's dilemma when she learns that her son Willy is engaged to a beautiful heiress with a flawed reputation. Should she keep silent about Helen Benedet's youthful indiscretion, perhaps jeopardizing her son's future happiness, or tell the truth and possibly incur his wrath? The story is situated in a mining community modeled after Grass Valley during a summer heat wave, "a touch of sun" blighting vegetation as well as human souls. The unhappy Mrs. Thorne cannot keep silent and writes to Willy of Helen's elopement with a dashing cowboy seven years earlier. Once into their flight, the rebellious teenager had lost her illusions about her companion, however, and appealed to a stranger to help her escape. Mr. Thorne was the anonymous stranger who came to her rescue and later shared this tale with his wife, never dreaming that their son would later fall in love with this girl. Helen makes an unexpected visit to the Thorne cottage to explain to Mrs. Thorne why she has kept her past from Willy and to announce her intention of breaking the engagement. By the end of their conversation, Mrs. Thorne comes to admire the young woman and regrets her interference. But Willy arrives, explains that he has always known of Helen's past, and apparently convinces her to marry him anyway.

In this as in her earlier work, Foote's masterful descriptions modeled on people and places she knows most intimately add to its strength. For example, Molly portrays the sights and sounds of the mining area with precision, although this is not a story about miners. Mr. Thorne, the mining superintendent, resembles Arthur Foote in occupation and in his "stout" physique and the clothes he wears; and the fictional couple, after thirty years of marriage, are comfortable in each other's presence, much like Molly and Arthur had become. The reader senses also that Molly writes from personal experience when Mrs. Thorne says of her husband: "His larger help she needed, but he had seldom known how to pet her in little ways."

The Prodigal is one of Foote's shortest but most highly praised novels. Charles F. Lummis proclaimed it "one of the very best, both as to its humanity and its art, that she has ever written." And despite the recent appearance of Frank Norris's highly acclaimed *McTeague* (1899), which centers on San Francisco, Lummis declared of Molly's book: "No one, I think, has ever written a more compelling story of San Francisco." The opening paragraph of *The Prodigal* makes clear Foote's acquaintance with the city's waterfront, which is the story's principal setting: "An August fog was drifting inland from the bay. In thin places the blue Contra Costa hills showed through, and the general grayness was tinged with pearl. San Francisco dripped and steamed along her bristling water-front; derricks loomed black, and yards and topmasts reddened, as a fringe of winter woodland colors up at the turn of the year."

The prodigal is Clunie Robert, son of a wealthy New Zealander, who, after being shipwrecked on the coast of Mexico, becomes engaged to the lightkeeper's daughter, mainly it seems to keep living off her father. Doubting the lad's repeated claims of wealth, the lightkeeper forces him to work on whalers to repay his debt. Clunie eventually works his way to San Francisco, where he arrives hungry, half-clothed, and penniless. He applies for money at Bradshaw & Company, one of the oldest shipping houses in the South Sea trade, with which his father does business. But the elder Robert wishes to teach his son the value of money and has authorized the firm to advance him only fifty cents a day. Borrowing money from the firm's shipping clerk, Morton Day, Clunie bets on a boat race and then fritters away his winnings on liquor and gambling.

Day loans Clunie additional funds to start work as a harbor boatman, and the prodigal's redemption begins. Thereafter, he gets involved in two situations that show the strength of his character. The first involves a tramp steamer consigned to the Bradshaws that carries a human cargo of 1500 Chinese "coolies." When smallpox breaks out on ship, the captain convinces Clunie to smuggle his pregnant wife ashore. The mother dies, and the surviving baby is placed in the care of the mother's sister, Annie Dunstan. Clunie soon falls in love with Annie and gives up drinking. The second incident occurs some months later after Clunie has won a position with the Bradshaws. He discovers that his former fiancée, the Mexican woman named Concha, has booked passage on the *Parthenia*, a steamer he deems unseaworthy. He suspects that the light-skinned child accompanying Concha is his son. Now he must confront his past and possibly jeopardize his relations with Annie Dunstan.

On the day the ship is to depart, Clunie goes aboard to find the woman and vows to remain on board if he cannot persuade her to leave. But she does leave and tells Clunie, to his surprise and relief, that she is happily married to a ship's steward. The *Parthenia* sinks as it clears the Golden Gate. Unfortunately, Annie Dunstan has been told that Clunie is on board and is panic-stricken when she witnesses the ship going down. But she soon encounters Clunie and Mort on a narrow cliff path as the two men go in search of help; she later consents to marry the New Zealander. While this action takes place on the California coast, Clunie's father has traveled to England where he falls critically ill. But Clunie holds out hope that once his father regains his health he will join the newlyweds in New Zealand. By the story's end, Clunie Robert has triumphed over his past and exhibits a largeness of character that the elder Robert would admire.

The critics called *The Prodigal* "remarkably lifelike," "a good character sketch," and "a realistic tale." A writer for the

San Francisco Bulletin praised Foote's descriptions of the city's waterfront, adding that "Mrs. Foote writes of the great West as no other writer." Yet Molly had been so unsure of the novel's suitability for genteel readers (because of Clunie's "implicit sexual liaison" with the Mexican woman and his excessive drinking) that she delayed seeking Richard Gilder's opinion until after she returned to Grass Valley from her summer in the East. In a letter dated November 19, Molly's fifty-second birthday, she confided to Helena:

> I have just been taxing Richard's friendship and time. . . . I wanted his moral and sensitive judgement on an ugly piece of work which has some bits of realism in it which I would fain preserve but whether to pay the price! I shall trust his judgment as it were an edict. I had the whole thing with me at Tyringham in my trunk but it jarred whenever I thought of it.

Originally entitled "When He Came to Himself," the story met with Gilder's approval but for some reason the *Century* did not publish it. When Bliss Perry at the *Atlantic Monthly* offered $300 for the tale, Foote politely bickered over the price, saying that "$300 is just $200 less than I call my lowest price per [10,000] words." She suggested a compromise of $400, which Perry accepted. Still, after *The Prodigal* appeared in print, Foote voiced concerns similar to those she had raised earlier about the constraints that womanhood imposed on her writing:

> It is not a woman's story. *How* I wish I had a son who would put his name to my stories. One could write so much better if one were not a woman—a wife and mother of young girls. The fields beyond where only men may tread. I know as much about the men who tread those fields as a man could—more—but I dont know the fields, and dont wish to appear to.

Like many other women writers of her generation, Molly never shed an inbred reserve that prevented her from dealing with societal problems head-on. Although she wrote about adultery and sexual dalliance, for example, she did so with great restraint, oftentimes forcing readers to infer her meaning. It was, she felt, neither genteel nor ladylike to write as a man might about such topics.

One commission that Molly accepted while on Little Deer Isle eventually fell by the wayside; yet its fate demonstrates how difficult it was for some women to carry on their art. Molly had been delighted when Houghton Mifflin asked her to contribute illustrations for a new edition of Nathaniel Hawthorne's stories, for the island provided a perfect background. But after selecting four of his tales to illustrate, she notified the firm in mid-September that she was unable to complete the drawings on time. Betty was en route to New York from San Francisco, she wrote, and "for a few weeks I shall be immersed in the domestic side of things." She promised to send the first drawing, one of "Rappacini's Daughter," in a month. Yet the delays continued. Sometime after returning to Grass Valley, Molly took charge of Lucy and Gerald Sherman's one-year-old twins when Lucy fell ill of typhoid fever. Ashamed of her tardiness, Molly offered to resign from the project, expressing at the same time a fear that her work had fallen out of fashion. In reply the art editor at Houghton Mifflin wrote a strong letter, in which he reaffirmed her talent and asked her to reconsider:

> Only a day or two ago I was admiring for the hundredth time your charming drawing in the Subscription Longfellow illustrating the "Hanging of the Crane," and comparing it with some of your recent drawings in magazines. I was more than ever impressed with the fact that you have, while retaining all your skill never lost its youthful freshness. You are therefore quite mistaken in supposing that any one, least of all our firm, considers your work old-fashioned. . . . As long as you are willing to make pictures we are unwilling that any illustrated Edition of our leading authors' works should be issued without something from your hand.

The firm extended the deadline once more and increased her pay to $75 for the one picture of "Rappacini's Daughter."

But the drawing that Foote submitted was not to her satisfaction; in offering to send another, she pinpointed the difficulty: "I had to send you a Rappacini's daughter begun as to the face with enthusiasm—carried out as to the figure (in the absence of my model) with less assurance, and, as to the background, a complete fizzle." But time may have run out; none of Molly's work appears in the Houghton Mifflin edition of Hawthorne's stories.

Ironically, about the time the Hawthorne project fell through, Molly received critical acclaim in the *Critic* for her work as an illustrator. Writing in the August 1900 issue, Regina Armstrong began her essay on women illustrators, "Mary Hallock Foote is almost the first name that occurs to one when women are mentioned in connection with illustration," and then went on to call Foote "the dean of women illustrators."

In December, Molly's literary work was singled out for praise by Kate Chopin, author of *The Awakening* (1899), in a review essay published in the *St. Louis Republic* entitled "Development of the Literary West." In heralding the fiction of modern western writers, such as Ambrose Bierce, Owen Wister, and Octave Thanet, Chopin led off with this observation: "What pleasure have we not all felt, for instance, in reading the stories—so genuine—of Mary Hallock Foote? Hers is excellent work, with a fine literary quality, damaged somewhat by a too conventional romanticism. But she knows her territory and leaves in the mind of the reader no inclination to question." Here Chopin identifies the main weakness in Molly's early stories, the use of predictable love plots. But she also recognizes Foote's major strength as a local colorist, her accurate portrayal of western scenes and personalities.

By the time these two essays appeared in print, Foote's career as an illustrator was near its end; her creative energies now would be focused mainly on writing. Regina Armstrong attributes this change to the difficulty Foote had in securing models and in establishing studios in her western homes and to the ease with which she could take up pad and pencil for writing. Then, too, stories could be mapped out during sleepless nights and on long walks in the countryside. But another factor influenced the direction of Molly's dual career. In the early twentieth century, her novels would cease to be serialized, which meant that she lost the opportunity to illustrate her own stories for the journals. And after the Hawthorne failure, Foote accepted very few commissions to draw for other authors. Still, her artistic talent continued to be praised. Some years later, at the end of his own distinguished career as a western illustrator, William Allen Rogers wrote in his memoirs:

> If Mrs. Foote were not so identified with her work as a novelist she would be better known as one of the most accomplished illustrators in America. There is a charm about her black-and-white drawing which cannot be described, but it may be accounted for by the fact that, more than any other American illustrator, she lived the pictures from day to day which she drew so sympathetically.

For most of the year in which Molly was touted in the press, Helena was in Europe and their correspondence lapsed. But on the last day of the century, December 31, 1900, Molly sent a special message to her friend now at home in New York City. Molly's children were at the forefront of her mind. Agnes had spent the fall attending school probably in San Francisco, or perhaps Berkeley, but fell seriously ill from a smallpox vaccination when she returned home for Christmas. This dampened Molly's holiday spirit, she admitted, and scared her "out of a month's sleep." Betty was in Boston enjoying a second year at the art school, and Arthur was in Grass Valley working full-time for his father. All three children had spent the summer at home, which made for lively times. Molly especially enjoyed Saturday afternoons when Arthur Junior's friends came for tea and tennis and often stayed for supper. In a reflective mood, Molly concluded: "The century that was ours is over and now our children step to the front; and they will have some rousing questions to decide. . . . I wish for my children three things and no more! Health, Work, Love!"

Like most mothers, Molly felt a pang of regret whenever a child of hers left home. This was true even when a son had reached maturity. In May 1901 twenty-four-year-old Arthur, Jr., sailed for Korea where he was to work as an engineer for three years. Luckily for Molly, the empty space he left behind was filled temporarily at least by Gerald Sherman and the twins. She had volunteered to keep the three-year-old girls during Lucy Sherman's confinement. "I am a sort of vice-grandmother for Bessie," Molly confessed to Helena, and then added, "they are such dear little things and the feeling of them in ones arms makes the baby-hunger which is in our blood, I suppose, as women whether mothers or not." Betty spent that fall and winter at home, but Agnes went east to school. Even with the absence of two family members, Molly wrote with conviction on December 30: "We are perilously happy this year, somehow. I don't know why. It's dangerous to be so happy at our age, with three hostages at large."

Despite domestic concerns and the social obligations attached to her husband's work, Molly continued to write and to draw. Not all of her efforts were successful. Both the *Century* and the *Atlantic Monthly* turned down a short story entitled "In Extremis," which she had first submitted to Richard Gilder in October 1900. But her work as an illustrator led to a significant, although somewhat improbable, friendship with short-story writer Margaret Collier Graham. Both women had arrived in San Francisco as young wives in 1876; Molly moved to New Almaden while Margaret and her husband took up residence in Pasadena, California, where she began her literary career. Graham's story, "At the Foot of the Trail," with an illustration by Mary Hallock Foote, appeared in the June 1901 issue of the *Century*; Molly also contributed three drawings for Graham's "The Wizard's Daughter," published in the *Century* in April 1903. Through their letters, the two women established a deeply felt bond, although they possibly never met in person. They shared a lively sense of humor and a love of writing, but they were quite different in other ways. The widowed and childless Margaret, for example, was active in civic affairs, gave numerous public talks on literature, and worked diligently for women's suffrage. Sadly, their friendship was cut short when Graham died in 1910 at age sixty, after a three-year illness.

Since returning to Grass Valley from her recent stay in the East, Molly had worked steadily on a new novel, the plot of which she had discussed with Richard during a visit to the Gilder household. The working title was "The Impostor," later changed to "Sapphira" (the name of the female protagonist in an early draft), and still later to "The Desert and the Sown," the title it carried when published by Houghton Mifflin in 1902.

Foote had hoped to sell serial rights to "The Desert and the Sown" to the *Century* for $2,000, but the firm announced that it now bought serial rights only if it also obtained book rights. Since Molly had already offered the book to Houghton Mifflin, her long-time publishers, she sent the manuscript to Bliss Perry, hoping he would serialize it in the *Atlantic Monthly.* But in December 1901, much to Molly's disappointment, Perry rejected the story for serialization. He told the author that it lacked the periodic dramatic climaxes necessary for installments and that its unpleasant topic might alienate ordinary magazine readers. On the other hand, the story's powerful plot, in which "the psychological interest never flags," its "admirable character drawing" and fine workmanship, made it perfect for publication as a book. He had recommended it to Houghton Mifflin, in fact, and was authorized to offer Foote a royalty of 15 percent instead of the 10 percent royalty she had received on her previous novels.

Still, it was a blow not to receive a cent for serial rights. "So far as royalties are concerned," Molly wrote to Helena, "it is almost like giving it away unless its fate be very different from that of its predecessors." Facetiously, she vowed that her next book "shall be of love pure and simple. No more problems in wifehood and widowhood. They dont pay." She related how Betty kept saying, as she copied the manuscript for her mother:

"It's good! It's blazing good!" And so "her mother was childish enough to be influenced by the prattle of a child. Yet it *is* good too. I'll be hanged if it isn't." And she added: "I shall never do anything better or duller."

But the novel was not the least bit dull to the critics. Most reviews were favorable, one writer's verdict often echoed by others: "It is a book of such compelling interest that once started, it is laid down only as one turns the last leaf." *The Desert and the Sown* is a complex narrative that touches on issues of class and parent-child relationships. The plot is built around the story of an older couple, Emily Van Elten and Adam Bogardus, who had played together as children on the Hudson Valley farm of Emily's wealthy and tyrannical father, Abraham. Motherless since the age of four, Emily came to idolize the older lad, first a chore-boy and then a regular hired hand on the Van Elten farm. Disinherited after she eloped to the West with Adam, Emily despaired over her new life of poverty but was too proud to complain. When their son Paul was two, they moved by wagon south from the Wood River country of Idaho and camped for the night at One Man Station. While Adam was away hunting for his strayed mules, the station keeper made such rude and suggestive remarks that when Adam failed to return, Emily accepted the offer of a ride from her husband's friend passing through on his way east. Although she left behind a letter of explanation for Adam, she never again heard from her husband and believed him dead. Meanwhile, she went to work in a hotel, bore her second child, Christine, and almost died from strain and overwork. Eventually Emily became independently wealthy after inheriting the New York estates of both her uncle and her father and turning them into profitable enterprises.

This is the story that Paul Bogardus, the son of the hired farm hand, tells his fiancée, Moya Middleton, at the start of *The Desert and the Sown* to explain why he is committed to helping the poor. The opening scenes take place at Bisuka Barracks in Idaho where Moya's father, Col. Middleton, plays host to Emily Bogardus and Christine, on hand for the wedding. Just weeks before he is to be married, however, Paul departs on a hunting trip that will lead to the unexpected reunion of his parents.

When the hunters fail to return in a timely fashion, Col. Middleton sends out a rescue party. With a hard winter setting in, the soldiers stumble across Paul's companions, who have fled for their lives in the face of a storm, leaving their severely injured guide behind. Paul alone chooses to stay with "Packer John." During their long ordeal, as Packer John and Paul approach death by starvation, they learn they are father and son. Packer John tells Paul that twenty-odd years ago when he returned to One Man Station to rejoin his family, the keeper so enraged him with lewd taunts about his wife that a fight ensued, in which the keeper fell against a bedframe and broke his back. To spare Emily the infamy of being married to a murderer, Adam lost himself in the Idaho wilderness.

When they are finally rescued, Adam Bogardus convinces Paul that his mother must be given the opportunity to choose not to recognize him since their lives have become so divergent. Ushered into his presence, the shocked wife instantly knows, but refuses to acknowledge, that this grizzled old man is her long-lost husband. With this rebuff, Adam again flees into the countryside. This denial places a wedge between Emily and her son, who soon departs on his wedding trip with Moya to find his father. Eventually mother and son, father and daughter-in-law, wind up at the Van Elten estate in New York, where Packer John, or Adam, now mentally unstable, finds a familiar lair in which to die. In a haunting scene, the little son of Paul and Moya leads his grandmother to an old tower bedroom where they find the emaciated and foul-smelling old man. Repenting of the mistake she made in Idaho, Emily now acknowledges Adam as her husband and sits with the dying man in his last hours.

At least two reviewers called *The Desert and the Sown* the best novel that Foote had ever written. Others described it as "a well-wrought and strikingly original piece of fiction," "the ripened fruit of years of experience both in literature and in life," and "bold in conception, fearless in execution . . . . It will repay a second reading." But most critics failed to probe the significance of the title, which Molly took from a stanza of the *Rubáiyát* of Omar Khayyám, wherein the poet refers to a strip of herbage "that just divides the desert from the sown" where the "name of Slave and Sultan is forgot." In this novel, as never before, Foote means to expose the artificial barriers of class. Modern readers will be struck by the author's insight into the human condition and by her superb character sketches, especially of Emily Bogardus, a proud, strong, yet flawed, personality. Readers also will enjoy Foote's flashes of wit, the suspense she evokes in several scenes, but especially in the hunting episode, and her exquisite descriptions of the Hudson Valley and Idaho landscapes.

When *The Desert and the Sown* was released in May of 1902, Molly was on the East Coast helping to console Alfred Rockwell and his daughter Diana after the death of Kate Rockwell, Arthur's cousin and benefactor. Molly spent about five months away from home, visiting a host of relatives, including Mother Foote and sister Phil, as well as Helena and Richard Gilder. She also met Owen Wister, author of the recently published and best-selling novel *The Virginian*. Long an admirer of Wister's fiction, Molly had written to his editor in the mid-1890s praising his western stories, a gesture that Owen Wister valued. Later, in the preface to *Members of the Family* (1911), Wister acknowledged his indebtedness to Foote: "It was a happy day for the tenderfoot when he read the first sage-brush story by Mary Hallock Foote. At last a voice was lifted to honor the cattle country and not to libel it."

In the fall Molly returned to Grass Valley with Agnes, where the youngest Foote was to spend the winter. "Ah, how sweet and small and remote the dear little Cottage looked when Agnes and I returned!" Molly exclaimed in a letter to James D. Hague. "It has been a happy, tho' hot home for us, and our children love no place so well." Adding to Molly's pleasure upon her return was a visit from "dear old Bessie Sherman," who had traveled to California to see her grandchildren. Later that year, after much planning and many family discussions, Betty left home to enroll in Emily Sartain's School of Design in Philadelphia. And then about mid-November, Molly fell ill with influenza, which left her incapacitated for almost a month. She had not yet fully recovered when a letter arrived from James D. Hague bearing joyous news. Because of recent successes, the North Star company planned to bestow a generous Christmas gift on each of its employees. Arthur's share was a block of stock in the company. When Arthur read this letter aloud, Molly later told her brother-in-law, "it made me weep." She thanked James for this "splendid Christmas gift" and then added: "If we could have lived by your advice all our lives, our foolish sanguine temperaments would not have got us into scrapes. You pulled us out of the worst one, and placed a roof over our heads."

Even with domestic preoccupations, Foote found time to work on a new story. On February 13, 1903, she wrote that she had just finished "a twaddling thing, interrupted by the grippe," which she was sending to Florence Bates at McClure and Phillips since Bates had been pestering her for a story. But it was "not a fit in that direction." Responding to a politely worded letter of rejection, Molly assured Bates that she was "too old to be very sensitive about what befalls the paper and ink side of my life." Yet she still wanted to see the story in print and toyed with the idea of sending it to Bliss Perry at the *Atlantic*. But the fate and the title of this story are not known for certain. Perhaps the tragedy that soon overwhelmed the author and her husband accounts for its disappearance from her correspondence.

Still, the year 1903 held days of happiness and contentment for the author and her family. *The Desert and the Sown* was selling well, Molly reported to Helena in February, at least "for a *book of mine*." And Houghton Mifflin was to publish later in the year *A Touch of Sun, and Other Stories*, collecting under one cover four of her published tales: "The Maid's Progress," "Pilgrims to Mecca," and "The Harshaw Bride," in addition to the title story. The San Francisco critic George Hamilton

Fitch wrote a flattering review, in which he asserted that the stories were "so saturated with the Western spirit that they would be recognized by any expert as written by one who had put into them bits of her own intimate knowledge of the country west of the Rockies."

In the spring Molly and Agnes spent a week in Berkeley and a second week with the Bourns in San Francisco. During this pleasant interlude, the author witnessed a military review near the Presidio in honor of President Theodore Roosevelt, lunched with her brother-in-law James in the Call Building, and attended a luncheon at the Bourns'. "I've never seen Mrs. Bourn sweeter or more charming in her unaffected, warm-hearted way," Molly later recalled.

The affairs of her growing children continued to dominate much of Molly's thinking. She worried about her "shy unexpressive" son in Korea and about Betty's first serious romance in Philadelphia. During the summer Molly returned to San Francisco to work out details for Agnes to study with Maud Bourn's former tutor during the winter. So while the youngest daughter soon left the North Star Cottage for school, the oldest returned to escape the attentions of a rejected suitor. Of Molly's parting with her youngest child, she wrote days later: "Still, though we knew it was best, we parted with groans—inward—on my part—and on hers a few brief tears which by now are gone and there is plenty to smile over." The summer, in fact, had held many enjoyments for the family. Molly's niece Birney Sherman came for a visit, followed by one from Billy Hague, the only son of James D. Hague. And then came Professor Robert Richards from MIT with his wife, "the Mrs. Richards who is a bacteriologist and chemist" [Ellen Richards, the founder of home economics; also the first woman admitted to MIT and subsequently a chemistry instructor there for many years]. Molly enjoyed the Richardses immensely and after their departure wrote Helena, "we really have needed and shall always need the Eastern influence out here."

Among the literary delights of the summer was reading Mary Austin's *The Land of Little Rain* (1903). In October

Molly wrote to this new western woman writer to praise her for writing of the West as no one had before. Austin's spiritual identification with the wilderness, which she expressed in lyrical prose, struck a deep chord in Molly's inner being. "No one can live in those Lands of little rain," Molly wrote, "without having moods that correspond to the nature that hath us in thrall, a nature without mercy—in its unspeakable beauty and its power of awakening longing and unrest." And so she encouraged the younger writer to "write! And keep on writing!" and thanked her "many times for what you have already done."

Christmas that year was a time of mixed emotions for Molly. She shared Arthur Senior's pride in the continued success of the North Star; for the second year in a row, the company was distributing "a splendid Christmas present" among its employees. Having both girls home for the holidays, of course, was a special delight, but rumors of war in Korea increased Molly's anxieties about her son. And then a telegram arrived to further dampen her holiday spirits. Alfred Rockwell had died unexpectedly and his daughter Diana, on the verge of an emotional collapse, requested Betty to come stay with her through the spring. So the Foote cottage soon emptied of its youngest occupants, Agnes returning to school in San Francisco and Betty heading to Boston to stay with her cousin.

But the spring held out promise for renewal with shrubs and flowers rushing into bloom. Molly was in high spirits on April 10, 1904, when she wrote Helena of recent events. Gerald Sherman's decision to accept a position with the Copper Queen mine at Bisbee, Arizona, had left the assistant superintendent's place at the North Star vacant. Arthur, Sr., had cabled his son to ask if he wanted it. Molly reported with glee that when their son wired his acceptance, Arthur, Sr., left work to share the news with Molly—only to find her in the bathtub. "Agnes came and shouted the words through the key hole, and when Arthur came up the path at sound off, with the sunset behind him there was great joy in his 'Well Girl!'"

But Molly's happiness in anticipation of her son's homecoming soon turned into unspeakable anguish after Agnes suddenly was stricken with acute appendicitis. A surgeon and a nurse rushed to Grass Valley from San Francisco to operate. Aided by two local physicians, Dr. Carpenter of Lane Hospital pronounced the operation a success. But days later complications developed and Agnes fell unconscious. A special train speeded the return of Carpenter and another physician, but their combined medical knowledge could not save Molly's last-born child. Agnes Foote died on May 12, 1904, at the age of seventeen. Four days after the funeral, the grief-stricken mother finally summoned strength to write Helena of these awful events. Molly's pain reaches out across the years.

> My dearest Friend—
>
> If I could have written to you in the first of this it would have been easier but there was no time. It was all so quick. This is all there is to tell—that is, all the Doctors can or will tell us. . . .
>
> The Doctors left us about sunrise. It was over at 4 in the hot afternoon. Her poor father had seen her last as she lay on the table awaiting her ordeal. Then she had said "Dear Daddy," and kissed her finger to him as he looked back at her. He could not bear the last part. But just at the last he came and saw the beautiful white dream of peace on her face. She was unconscious long, long before the end.
>
> Some mysterious "shock" the Doctors called it, following the operation, one of the rare cases, not to be accounted for. Not a mental shock for she was not afraid. A shock to the system, fastening upon the weakest organ; with her the liver, weakened by repeated malarial fevers. In the end it went to her brain.
>
> She was buried on Saturday. She died on Thursday, May [12th]. The miners lined the road for a quarter of a mile on her way—and as they brought her down to the gate under the cherry-trees—the men sang "Welcome! Welcome!" one of their carols she loved and the one they sang at Central Shaft last Christmas when we were there—so happy!

The hymn we chose for the one to close the service was the "Pax Tecum" that was sung at Tyringham that dear Sunday with you—when Agnes held the book with me, and her hand held mine, and she squeezed hard at the words: "Peace, perfect peace, and loved ones far away," for that morning we had talked of a second winter in Boston and she had meekly owned it was best and consented to go through with it. Oh, I am so glad we sent her nowhere that winter, but kept her home with us.

Now, the experiments in "education" are over. *Our* education will begin now.

There is not so much to regret. It is more a passion of love[,] fearing it did not express itself fully enough while yet there was time. Your loving Molly

An outpouring of sympathy helped Molly through this terrible ordeal. But as a letter she wrote nearly two decades later indicates, life would never be the same. In reflecting upon the "immeasurable grief" that had befallen another couple, the seventy-six-year-old author observed: "They will get over it of course and have many happy years but it will change them though they may not realize it themselves. I dont believe courage has anything to do with the secret influence of a great grief." Still, Mary Hallock Foote needed all the courage she could muster to face life without her youngest child.

CHAPTER 6

"The Pain and the Sweetness"

MOLLY and Arthur Foote, in fact, did have many more happy years together, but pain and sadness filled their days immediately following Agnes's death. Reflecting on her "one great sorrow" nearly six years after her child had died, Molly said it "remains an extra heart-beat big and heavy that throbs once and sinks again like a great wave striking the shore that comes from far away. It is sure to come again." But life did go on; Molly coped with routine household matters and found solace in her family.

Even while Molly grieved for her child, Helena was faced with a similar crisis. After an illness of several months, Richard suffered an acute attack of appendicitis in July 1904. Molly first learned of Gilder's danger from the *San Francisco Chronicle* and immediately sent a telegram to Helena extending "our love and sympathy to you all in this dreadful suspense." Gilder's quick recovery brought relief to everyone. But about eight months later, when Margaret—the cook at the North Star Cottage—fell violently ill with appendicitis, Molly was forced to relive the nightmare of Agnes's ordeal. Two surgeons arrived to operate, but Margaret seemingly hovered at death's door for some days. Later, Molly confessed to Helena that the experience had left her "nervously undone," even though Margaret recovered. "To be the victim of such coincidences" was almost more than she could bear.

But Molly found comfort in having both Arthur, Jr., and Betty at home. And it helped also to have other youthful spirits in the house. When Julia Roberts, a family friend, came for an extended visit in the fall of 1904, the young people spent their evenings dancing and playing the piano, purchased recently with Molly's "story money." "We make no point of doing what is conventional in the circumstances," Molly admitted, "because the two we have left must live." The greatest thing of all, she said, was having "another girl" in the house "with a waist to put one's arm around—someone with a laugh and a gleam and a gift for silence as well as happy casual words."

A short time later, Molly shared some of her reflections on sorrow and grief with Margaret Collier Graham on the occasion of the death of the author's mother. After extending "loving sympathy"to her friend, Molly referred to the sameness of "the great human griefs" which take "an infinity of forms." She went on to assure Margaret that she was not "solely lost . . . in gloomy thoughts." Still, Molly was capable of writing only a brief Christmas letter to Helena that year. "It is not possible to write," she explained, "what is here is nothing at all of what I would say."

A visit by Diana Rockwell in the spring, which coincided with Margaret's bout with appendicitis, helped to relieve some of Molly's strain. And other visitors that summer were welcomed diversions. The writer Arthur Colton appeared one morning with a letter of introduction, followed by David Atkins, a mining engineer from Wales. David's brother Henry, a partner in a San Francisco art shop, had volunteered to design a marble monument in memory of Agnes Foote, having lost a younger brother with the same unfulfilled promise. Sometime later that year, Arthur and Molly left Grass Valley "to recruit" at Byron Hot Springs, a small resort to the east of the Contra Costa hills. Molly did not enjoy the crowd very much and stayed only one week, leaving Arthur to continue his "hot soakings and thrice a day drinkings."

This was the same year—1905—that the North Star company built a new house for the Footes on a beautiful wooded knoll not far from the cottage. Designed by Julia Morgan at the start of her stunning architectural career, the North Star House, as it was called, was an imposing two-story structure built in a "U" shape around a courtyard and a small pool. The lower part of the exterior walls was of local stone, the upper part was shingled. On the first floor was a reception room, sitting room, and dining area—all paneled in wood and with wood floors and ceilings; on the second floor were bedrooms, guest rooms, and several bathrooms, sufficient to accommodate company officials when business brought them to Grass Valley.

Julia Morgan, who later designed the Hearst Castle at San Simeon, often visited the site during construction. At some point she must have encountered Mary Hallock Foote, though such a meeting is not recorded in Foote's correspondence. But in October, just after the Footes moved into the North Star House, Molly indicated in a letter to Margaret Collier Graham that she and Arthur had played a role in its final design.

> "The Company" has been most generous in building us a big cool lovely house, and is letting us do it ourselves, instead of building it over our heads . . . . We rejoice in its spaciousness, and in the absence of *things.* We have put our things away, the so-called ornaments. We have adopted the Japanese idea of the "go-down," and only the things we really care for are around.

By mid-January 1906 Molly felt sufficiently comfortable in the new house to extend yet another invitation for her best friend to visit. There was plenty of room and the view was stupendous. "Outside of our big end window lies *all* the valley and the buttes beyond rising clear from the mist of the Sacramento—all is miles apart but to us as we see them the Buttes lie just beyond the dark sharp ridge of pines and the coast range is just beyond the buttes." With a touch of her old wit, Molly acknowledged that the upstairs plumbing needed work. The pipes in the new bathrooms, she wrote to Helena, "make such a roaring through the house that Betty quotes 'Piping down the valleys wild,' whenever we hear the tumult begin."

There is no indication that Molly attempted to write anything other than personal letters for at least two years following Agnes's death when her grief was most intense. She did oversee publication of "The Eleventh Hour," however, which was published in the *Century* in January 1906. This probably is "the twaddling thing" that Florence Bates rejected in 1903, for Molly never would have written such a tepid romance after the tragedy. The tale, in fact, centers on a mother's concern about a daughter's choice in marriage, the very issue that Molly had wrestled with when Betty went east to Emily Sartain's School of Design. The fictional Mrs. Durbrow, a widow, fears that her daughter Katherine will accept the proposal of David Cameron, a rich and powerful older man who will swoop her away to a different lifestyle. She confides her fears to young Tom, a protégé of the deceased Mr. Durbrow, who is smitten with Katherine. But when the mother asks Tom to declare his feelings, he refuses, saying that Katherine must be free to accept or reject Cameron's proposal. Now the mother regrets her interference, knowing that Tom will avoid Katherine altogether. The two young people are subsequently thrown together but neither seems capable of saying what she or he feels for the other. At the last moment, when Tom is about to leave for a job in Valparaiso and Cameron is on his way to propose, a riding accident allows the two young people to discover their mutual love. Cameron, who witnesses the scene, soon "passed out of their private lives forever." Molly's appraisal of this story is accurate; "The Eleventh Hour" is one of her least substantial tales.

A few months after this story appeared in the *Century*, Molly's thoughts turned to the great tragedy that befell San Francisco on the morning of April 18, 1906. At about 5:00 A.M. the city was struck by a massive earthquake that would have measured about 8.25 on the Richter Scale (developed later at the California Institute of Technology). This shock and the tremors and fires that followed literally destroyed the Bay City. Like everyone else, Molly was horrified by the extent of the devastation. As reports trickled in, she learned the fate of some of her friends: the Bourns' house survived, Mrs. Ashburner was homeless, Mrs. Bennett's family was sleeping out of doors. Survivors streamed into outlying communities. Grass Valley took in its share of refugees, or as Molly reported to the Gilders, " the poor seem to have gathered in so many of the still poorer."

Molly sent word to friends in San Francisco that the North Star House would also accept refugees. The Richardsons, who had saved their house on Russian Hill and then turned it over to a homeless friend, soon accepted Molly's invitation, as did at least two other San Franciscans. Another refugee couple was housed in the cook's house at the North Star Cottage, which now served as quarters for a handful of bachelor engineers. To her friend Margaret Collier Graham, Molly admitted: "We are most comfortable—and half ashamed to be here unscathed when so many [others] are in strange straits." Yet Molly recognized the heroism and unselfishness of so many caught up in the tragedy; later she was to weave their stories into her tenth published novel, *The Valley Road* (1915).

Among those left homeless was Ina Coolbrith, the unofficial poet laureate of California and former assistant to Bret Harte, editor of the *Overland Monthly.* The Spinners' Club, a group of society women dedicated to literature and the arts, decided to hold a fundraiser to aid the beloved poet, who also suffered from arthritis. They solicited short stories from such leading California writers as Mary Hallock Foote, Mary Austin, Gertrude Atherton, and Frank Norris, with proceeds from the anthology to go to Coolbrith. Although the poet realized little from this effort, *The Spinners' Book of Fiction*, published in 1907, contained some remarkable tales. The story that Molly contributed, "Gideon's Knock," represents (as Lee Ann Johnson avows) "the transmutation of her recent sorrow into a piece of haunting fiction."

Melancholy pervades the story from beginning to end. The narrator, a young mining engineer by the surname of Othet, arrives at the Consolidated Resumption mine to take over as manager. He shares the manager's house with Joshua Dean, the mine's cashier. On a stormy night in February, Othet seeks answers to a mystery that has bothered him. Never does the watchman knock at the front door to deliver the late evening mail; rather, the Chinese cook rushes outside to gather the mail before the knocker is lifted. And Othet is mystified also by the large quantity of mementoes that the previous manager and his wife, Mr. and Mrs. George Fleming, have left behind. So seated before a roaring fire with a storm raging outside, Joshua Dean tells the young manager the story of Gideon's knock.

The previous watchman, a man named Gideon, had been devoted to the Flemings. He brought the mail each evening, aware that they lived for letters from their children, a son stationed in the Philippines and a daughter, Constance, at school in the East. On a summer's vacation in the West, however, Constance met and fell in love with a handsome foreigner. Six months later, he took her away to live in San Francisco.

The daughter's letters continued to arrive; but something was wrong. The mother became increasingly agitated, walked the floors, snapped at her husband, and then apologized. Finally one night, there came a knock on the door. It was Gideon's knock. But when Fleming opened the front door, no one was there. This strange knocking came a second and a third time, with the same result: no one appeared when the door was opened. Joshua Dean, who lived with the Flemings, telephoned the post office and learned that Gideon had started for the mine an hour and a half ago with an important telegram; further investigation revealed Gideon's horse and cart in Fleming's stable. Joshua set out to find Gideon and located his body in an abandoned mining shaft into which he had accidently fallen. Before he died, however, he snagged his mail sack to a protruding pine-root. So the telegram was saved and eventually reached the Flemings. The message was from Constance in the city. It said "come to me, mother . . . . I need you." And so the Flemings were driven to Colfax, the nearest railroad junction. "And were they in time?" the narrator asks.

> "To bid her good-by," said Joshua. "There was no hope for her but in death. Of course, they never explained. She simply fled from—we don't know what. As long as she could she

> bore it without complaint, and then she came home. She had them both with her and she knew them. . . . The logic of her choice was death. They saw her free, without a stain, without an obligation in this life, even to her child, for it lay dead beside her."

The watchman who replaced Gideon was ordered "to leave that knocker alone." But the silence of the house was more than Mrs. Fleming could bear and so they left. On this note Joshua ends his story. The narrator refuses to believe what it appears Joshua believes, however—that Gideon had willed the knocking while lying in the shaft. To Othet's suggestion that he has lived in the house too long and consequently developed an unhealthy state of mind, Joshua replies that he prefers to keep his mind unhealthy—"if by that you mean the tendency to project it a little farther than reason . . . . Healthy minds are such as accept things—endeavor to forget what gives immeasurable pain. I prefer the pain."

While grappling with the reality of Agnes's death, Molly had written to a friend: "If matter be indestructible, spirit must be too." In her fictional tale, she does not attempt to explain the force behind Gideon's knock. By leaving this phenomenon unexplained and other questions unanswered, Foote forces readers to draw their own conclusions. And so the story lingers on in one's mind. What drove Constance from her husband? the reader wants to know. What finally killed her and the baby? Although "Gideon's Knock" was to be the last of Foote's published short stories, it "offers ample evidence that [her] skill remained undiminished by her personal tragedy."

Several months would elapse before Foote took up her pen to work on a longer piece of fiction. For the time being, family and household concerns absorbed her energies. In August 1906 an upstairs bedroom served as an operating room when a surgeon arrived to remove Arthur Senior's ulcerated gall bladder. After Foote was out of danger, Molly wrote to tell Helena: "We are a thankful house this morning." And before many more days elapsed, Molly took pleasure in announcing her daughter's engagement to Rodman "Tod" Swift, one of the North Star's junior engineers, whose family lived in Massachusetts. The newlyweds were to live in the North Star House after a June wedding.

But the winter was to be a difficult one for Arthur D. Foote, and Molly would share his concern. Miners at the North Star were threatening to strike because of the eight-hour day issue. Yet the usual Christmas festivities took place at the mines, and Arthur announced the company's decision to grant an eight-hour day to all of its employees. The men voted to strike anyway, and other Grass Valley miners did the same. "Not a miner in the whole camp is at work," the local paper reported. Still highly critical of unions, Molly believed that the "ill-omened" Western Federation of Miners had spurred on the unrest. A lengthy shutdown, she feared, would bring misery and bitterness to the town. But the dispute was settled by the end of January, and "gloom turned to great rejoicing."

Despite an unusually wet and cold spring, the North Star House continued to attract visitors, including Tod's mother, who made an extended visit before the wedding. Betty's uncle, James D. Hague, and her cousin, Diana Rockwell, also arrived for the ceremony. Betty, who shared her mother's fondness for the old customs, had wanted a Quaker wedding. But when the bride and groom belatedly learned that such a marriage would be illegal in California since neither was a Quaker, they were married by an Episcopal clergyman. Still, they followed Quaker custom by having Uncle James read the marriage contract after the ceremony, which the guests signed as witnesses. The letter Molly wrote to Helena in mid-June was filled with news of Betty and Tod, still on their wedding trip to Bear Valley. Molly keenly missed both daughters. "I am rather haunted by visions of [Betty] about the house," she confessed. "But there are places more haunted still. The silent woody places where I used to see my little Dreamer, her eyes with the light in them that came with her thoughts when she was alone."

Molly liked her new son-in-law right from the start. In a subsequent letter she asserted: "What a supreme mercy, that

[Betty] took this boy, so nice to live with, so proud in big ways; and so simple and unfretful in little ways. Suppose he had been unwilling to come here with her, and make one family!" When the young couple returned from Bear Valley, the Footes and the Swifts soon settled into a routine. Tod and Betty lived upstairs in two rooms where they took breakfast alone, but the two couples met for evening meals, along with Arthur, Jr., and spent much of their leisure time together. That Molly enjoyed sharing simple tasks with her daughter is evident from such notations in her letters to Helena as this: "[Betty] sits writing on one side of the table, I on 'tother, and we smile at each other across."

Later that summer, Molly's spirits soared when Helena's sons, Rodman and George, paid a visit to the North Star House. She still longed for Helena to come, however, missing the comfort of talking little things over with her long-time soulmate. "Come dearest friend," she wrote several weeks after the brothers had departed, "and walk the long walk—to the asparagus bed—with me, and talk about clothes and servants; and I shall want to talk of the better things, too, for who is better to talk of them with than you." But it was Bessie Sherman, rather than Helena, who walked the garden paths with Molly that fall, during a brief stopover on her way to spend the winter in Arizona with Gerald and Lucy. The two sisters no doubt had a tearful reunion, for much had changed in Molly's life since their last meeting.

Some weeks after Bessie's visit, Molly shared with Helena the news that Betty was pregnant. As the weeks went by, however, Molly grew increasingly apprehensive. The winter had been especially happy, she wrote to Helena in February 1908, but such times as these made her fearful since "out of such a [clear] sky fell our stroke." Although little Agnes Swift, born on May 14, the anniversary of her namesake's funeral, was a healthy baby, her mother was stricken with a dangerous infection shortly after giving birth, which kept her bedridden for several days. Still, by mid-June, with Betty fully recovered, Molly would bask in her new role as "Granny."

During the worst heat of the summer, the Footes received word that James D. Hague was seriously ill. He and his son William ("Billy") had been to Grass Valley on business just before the baby came; his old friend Louis Janin, of whom Molly was so fond, was there at the same time, which made for "a lovely visit." But Molly knew that James's attack was a warning; "everybody is getting so old," she lamented. Still, the news of Hague's death in August at the age of seventy-two must have come as a shock. James had been Molly and Arthur's benefactor since the early days of their marriage, and his charm and erudition had always made him a welcome guest. "There was no man of his generation Arthur loved so well, or got so much comfort out of," Molly told Helena after Hague's death. The work at the North Star would continue, with George B. Agnew of New York succeeding Hague as president and Billy Hague as managing director.

Sometime during the latter half of the decade, Molly began writing a long historical novel. That she did not refer to the manuscript in her correspondence until it was nearly finished is not surprising. Writing came in the quiet moments, when no one in the family was ill or facing a crisis, when questions of servants and household supplies had been dealt with. She continued to believe that her literary work was of lesser importance than her responsibilities as wife and mother, and therefore not something to write about. And a lifelong modesty no doubt kept her from discussing her fiction-writing with Helena, once perhaps even more artistically ambitious than Molly but now totally devoted to affairs of her husband and children.

With *The Royal Americans* (1910), Molly capitalized on a literary craze for historical fiction that had swept the country around the turn of the century. The Revolutionary War was among the most popular topics, as attested to by S. Weir Mitchell's successful *Hugh Wynne* (1897) and Winston Churchill's best-selling *Richard Carvel* (1899). For her Revolutionary War tale, Foote spent a good deal of time in careful research, for we know she consulted William L. Stone's *The Life and Times of Sir William Johnson*, John Fiske's *Dutch and*

Quaker Colonies, General Philip Schuyler's official records, and the diary of Baroness de Reidsel, wife of the general in command of the German auxiliaries. She also enlisted the aide of Helena, herself a descendant of the original Dutch settlers in New York. Did Helena know, she inquired, if the correct term among the old Dutch Calvinist families was "godmother" or "witness"? And could she locate among her relatives the equivalent of the English Prayer Book? That these questions concerned only a few sentences in the entire story underscores Foote's concern for historical accuracy.

Foote sent selected portions of her manuscript, the parts of which she was most unsure, to Richard Gilder sometime in the fall of 1909. Although Gilder gently rejected the story for publication in the *Century*, he "generously" asked to read the entire manuscript. Molly never regretted her decision to spare him this lengthy chore, for her long-time friend and literary mentor died of heart failure on November 18, 1909, at the age of sixty-five.

With sorrow in her heart, Molly reached out to console Helena, as she had so many years before when the Gilders had lost their first-born child and still later when a newborn son had died. Molly's first written acknowledgment of Richard's death is no longer extant, but on January 1, 1910, she wrote to her friend: "I think of you intensely all the time, when there is a time sacred enough to be near you in your sacred sorrow." Further on, Molly confessed that she had her "own private pang for the hours of [Richard's] time" that she had taken recently with her manuscript. She recalled the "exquisite letter" Richard had written in return, "showing his perfect art of saying, 'I dont want it'—without in the least discouraging the one who offers, or missing one single merit or point of significance in the work itself." A year later, Molly was able to tell Helena that *The Royal Americans* was a "financial success . . . probably because I followed some of [Richard's] advice which wasn't really advice, but a light cast on dark places."

The Royal Americans is a complex historical romance that follows the life of Catherine Yelverton, from her birth on the eve of Montcalm's victory at Fort Ontario in 1756 to her marriage at the conclusion of the American Revolution. When Catherine's mother dies soon after giving birth, Catherine is raised in the home of Adrian Deyo, a Calvinist minister, while her father, Lieutenant Edmund Yelverton, serves in the British army. Among her playmates is Bassy Dunbar, a neighbor boy of apparently lesser social status. Later Catherine is sent to England but returns to America in 1773, eager to rejoin her father after living among relatives unsympathetic to colonial interests. En route to the Deyo house, however, she meets and falls in love with the Quaker Francis Havergal, a former childhood acquaintance. Their romance is thwarted, however, by religious differences, and the engagement is broken.

Meanwhile, Edmund Yelverton, recently reunited with his adopted daughter Charlotte, arouses gossip when he brings her to live on his estate in the northern wilderness. He is joined there by Bassy Dunbar, now a man of wealth and of good reputation, who has agreed to manage the older man's estate. Belatedly and wrongly, as it turns out, Dunbar learns that Catherine is pledged to Havergal. Although Bassy secretly loves Catherine, he asks Charlotte to marry him to stop the slanderous gossip that threatens to destroy Yelverton.

The American Revolution soon engulfs the Dunbars and the Yelvertons. Entrapped in a loveless marriage, Bassy goes off to fight in the patriot army while Charlotte supports the royalist cause. Catherine, now living in her father's household, also is thought to be a Tory because of her father's loyalty to the old British army. When fighting intensifies, Yelverton is jailed and eventually exiled to Canada. Charlotte and Catherine, with the Dunbars' infant son, are sent to British lines where they come under fire in the fierce battle that rages around Saratoga and Charlotte is killed. Eventually Catherine, the little boy, and the boy's father are reunited at the Albany mansion of Catherine's godmother, Madame Schuyler. In the final pages of the novel, Catherine and Bassy declare their love for one another and pledge to marry at the war's end.

The outstanding feature of this novel is Foote's superb characterizations of both historical and fictional characters. Reviewers singled out for praise her depictions of old Colonel Yelverton, his daughters Charlotte and Catherine, and stately Madame Schuyler. Critics also lauded her special talent for description. "Mrs. Foote has the gift of presenting in words a picture almost visible to the reader," a writer for the *New York Times* avowed. "Her description of Madam Schuyler asleep in her dining room, for example, is as clear in every detail as a Dutch painting." But the story's remarkable authenticity comes from the author's ability to weave historical details into the fictional story. Real-life figures, such as Madam Schuyler and her nephew General Philip Schuyler, Ethan Allen and Benedict Arnold, and Baroness de Reidsel, serve as backdrop to the fictional protagonists. The credibility of the novel also derives from Molly's familiarity with the Hudson Valley, where much of the action takes place, and with Quaker customs that set apart the Havergal family.

The success of *The Royal Americans* must have spurred Molly to start right in on her second historical novel, *A Picked Company* (1912), although being a grandmother probably interfered with her writing. Molly adored little Agnes, "the most gleeful baby I ever handled," she told Helena, and she took pleasure in caring for the baby in the afternoons so that Betty would have a chance to ride or spend time with her husband. But there were other distractions as well, including the many friends, relatives, and company officials who visited the North Star House.

Toward the latter part of 1910, the Swifts left Grass Valley foı the East Coast, where Tod had accepted a position with the Submarine Signal Corps. They settled into a small cottage in Hingham, Massachusetts, but soon built a larger house overlooking the water, calling it "The Wharf-House," the house in which Molly and Arthur Foote were to spend their final years. For the present, however, the North Star House felt empty without Tod, Betty, and the grand-baby, and, much like Mrs. Fleming in "Gideon's Knock," Molly lived for the weekly letters that arrived from her daughter. Still, by the end of the year, the Foote household had expanded to include yet another newly married couple, Billy Hague and his wife Bessie, awaiting the building of their own house.

Despite household disruptions and other diversions, Molly found time to work on her second historical romance, a portion of which she sent to Betty for comments in January 1911. Foote made revisions during the late summer, and then sent the story off to Houghton Mifflin, which published it the following year. Although *A Picked Company* is less complex and less compelling than *The Royal Americans*, the author's penchant for historical accuracy is still very much in evidence.

A Picked Company tells the story of a group of New Englanders who migrate to the West in the 1840s and help establish America's claim to Oregon Territory. Action centers on members of two families, Reverend Yardley and his son Jimmy, and Silence and Alvin Hannington, their daughter Barbie, and their orphaned niece, Stella Mutrie from Jamaica, who lives with them. The beautiful Stella disrupts the community with her flirtatious behavior and arouses Barbie's resentment when she wins the attention of Barbie's young man, Jimmy Yardley. Stella's lack of moral fiber is apparent when the Hanningtons make plans to join Reverend Yardley and his band of Congregationalists on their overland trek to Oregon. To avoid making the journey, Stella accepts an offer of marriage, then breaks the engagement when she meets Capt. Bradburn, the dashing older man who will guide Reverend Yardley's wagon train. Seduced by Bradburn on the trip, Stella becomes pregnant, a catastrophe that threatens the harmony of Yardley's picked company. Bradburn, a married man, refuses to bow to Yardley's demand that Stella's betrayer step forward. Nonetheless, Yardley orders Stella to leave the company. Cured long ago of his infatuation with Stella, Jimmy volunteers to accompany her back to Fort Hall, Idaho, where she is to spend the winter. Bradburn reconsiders, confesses his responsibility, and then rides to intercept Stella and Jimmy, only to die in a duel when Jimmy refuses to release his charge to Bradburn without his father's authorization. Having been told by Bradburn that the Reverend expects Jimmy to return to the company, Stella and Jimmy reverse their course, with Stella suffering a miscarriage soon after rejoining her aunt and uncle.

The last part of the novel is a working out of private destinies. Barbie and Jimmy marry and begin their own family in Oregon, the hardworking Silence becomes ill and dies, and Stella leaves the community for California to locate the gold that Bradburn had told her about. She ends up as a prostitute in San Francisco but marries a good man when she begins to lose her health and beauty. Hard times cause her to resume her old habits, however, whereupon her husband kills her and shoots himself.

The first part of *A Picked Company* is well done; it contains historically accurate details of overland travel, good dialogue, and a complex characterization of Stella Mutrie as temptress and victim. Foote also successfully builds suspense, starting one page-turning chapter in this way: "It was early on the morning of the second day;—these were days, every circumstance of which was to fix itself in the memory of those who lived them." But the novel's second part is less satisfying. Stella becomes a caricature of the bad woman fallen on hard times. And the reader gains little sense of the community-building that goes on once the Hanningtons and the Yardleys reach Oregon. Although reviewers focused on the novel's weaknesses, the author picked as a major strength its crisp writing. "All I did feel sure of was that I had stripped the style pretty near of verbiage," she wrote to Helena shortly after the book was published.

The spring before Molly completed *A Picked Company*, she made her first trip to Hingham to see Betty and her family. She planned to stay through August to see her daughter through her second pregnancy and to greet Helena upon her return from Europe. But Molly cut short her visit when her son sent word that Arthur, Sr., had suffered a severe attack of neuritis and was not responding to treatment. The few days she spent in Hingham had been "lovely beyond words," however. She had enjoyed exploring the town and nearby beaches with Betty and little Agnes and took delight whenever the child called out, "Ganny, come!" After returning to Grass Valley, Molly fell ill with bronchitis and pleurisy and was confined to bed for several weeks. Both "invalids" finally recovered, but Betty's pregnancy was to end sadly in a stillbirth.

Possibly the only bright spot for Molly that summer was news of her son's rollicking trip to Lake Tahoe in his Ford roadster. Already a popular vacation spot, the lake could be reached by rail over Donner Pass year around but heavy winter snows kept the motor road closed until the summer thaw made it passable. To gain publicity, the Tahoe Tavern, a resort located on the shores of Lake Tahoe, offered an elaborate silver cup to the first motorist to reach its doors in the summer of 1911. Arthur Foote and four friends accepted the challenge. They set off from Grass Valley on June 2 for the sixty-four-mile trip, with Foote's Model T Ford loaded with tools and supplies. For the next eight days they pulled, pushed, and maneuvered the car through snowdrifts and across the raging Bear River where a bridge was out. Thanks to their engineering skills, they beat out their competitors and claimed the silver cup on June 10.

Later that fall Molly had a "week of great fear" when Arthur, Sr., suffered two painful attacks of an unknown cause. After consultation with his local doctor, Foote spent nearly a week in San Francisco undergoing further examinations. When Molly received word he was to undergo surgery, she and her son motored to Vallejo, where they caught a boat for the city, arriving in time, she later reported to Helena, "for two lovely quiet hours with our dear man before he went to sleep." After a two-hour operation, during which a tumor was removed from Arthur's intestine, the surgeon assured Molly that the patient would fully recover. "So it goes, at our age," Molly mused. Referring to her husband, she continued: "The years of peace and prosperity and honored achievement for him have not been many compared—and they came just too late to count for what such years might have been had we been spared our three [children]: but who *is* spared." Despite Molly's steadfast loyalty to Arthur and their regard for one another, Arthur's penchant for schemes and strong drink were to cause Molly heartache in the near future.

In the meantime, the couple spent a pleasant Christmas in Grass Valley entertaining their niece Marian Hague and enjoying the snow-covered landscape. "It is the weather for open fires, new books, the old ones too, and for piazza-pacing at sunset," Molly noted in a letter to Helena. The reading of fine literature, in fact, remained a constant pleasure in Molly's life. Over the past several months, she had read works by John Galsworthy, Mary S. Watts, and Anne Douglas Sedgwick, and she was soon to read books by Mary Austin and about Mark Twain. Molly admired each of these writers, but she singled out Anne Douglas Sedgwick for special praise. Molly had "devoured" *Tante* (1911), one of Sedgwick's most successful novels, and believed that the author was "quite one by herself among the writers who just miss being the greatest."

Anne Douglas Sedgwick was among the few writers that Mary Hallock Foote ever met. Like Henry James, Sedgwick was an expatriate, who spent most of her adult life in England and explored in her fiction the contrast between American and British ways of life. At age twenty-nine, she had spent two weeks or more at Richard and Helena Gilder's summer home at Tyringham. It was there that Molly and her daughter Agnes met the author in June of 1902. Sedgwick held very decided views about Americans, finding many to be thoroughly nice and sympathetic but others, "crude, yet so very 'cultured,' so provincial yet so travelled, so absolutely unconscious of any lack in themselves." The day before she was to meet Molly at Tyringham, she wrote to a friend in England asking if she had read Foote's books. She went on to present her own impressions, gained largely from reading Foote's fiction but also undoubtedly from her conversations with the Gilders.

> [Mary Hallock Foote] is not nearly well enough known, and yet she is really an exquisite artist. She has had a queer life out in the West with her engineer husband,—she a delicate, idealistic, Emersonian, intensely righteous little person. Her stories will give you a better idea of her than I can,—do read them—the short ones—especially the one called 'The Cup of Trembling'; —do read it.

Many of the women authors that Molly admired lived their adult lives in radically different family arrangements than Molly. Anne Douglas Sedgwick, for example, married Basil de Sélincourt at age thirty-five; she continued to write but the couple had no children. Mary S. Watts married at age twenty-three but also remained childless. Mary Austin, who married, then divorced, had one daughter, whose severe mental retardation caused Austin to commit her to a private institution. And Willa Cather, one of Molly's favorite writers in later years, never married. Undoubtedly the careers of these women were affected by the stress and strain of daily living, but the point here is that Molly belonged to what must have been a small corps of successful late-nineteenth- and early-twentieth-century writers who had children and found satisfaction in marriage. In her family life, Foote more closely resembled women authors of an earlier generation, such as Harriet Beecher Stowe, Elizabeth Oakes Smith, and Caroline Lee Hentz, all married and raising children at the time they were writing. For Molly's generation or the one that followed, there are many examples, besides those already mentioned, of successful authors who never married (Alice French [Octave Thanet], Sarah Orne Jewett, Mary Murfree, Constance Fenimore Woolson), who remained childless after marriage (Mary Wilkins Freeman), or whose marriage either was a disaster or ended in divorce (Gertrude Atherton, Edith Wharton, Charlotte Perkins Gilman).

Except for the publishing of *A Picked Company*, the most pleasurable event for Molly in the year 1912 was a trip to Hingham in the fall. This allowed opportunity to visit Arthur's sisters Kate Coe, now widowed, and Elizabeth Jenkins and her husband, Edward, in New Haven, as well as Diana Sumner, née Rockwell, in Manchester, and Helena Gilder at Tyringham. It had been ten years since Molly and Helena had last met; in the interim, each had suffered a terrible loss. Molly approached the reunion with some shyness, writing to Helena beforehand: "We must give ourselves a little time for the first settling of the waters which will wash to and fro when we come together again. But you cannot be other than yourself, and soon we shall find each other just as always, except externally you will find your old Molly fatter and more battered."

The reunion was memorable but also painful, as the two old friends recalled their last meeting at Tyringham when Richard and Agnes were both present. There were happy moments together, of course, and Molly had time to become reacquainted with Helena's daughters, Francesca and Rosamond. Afterwards she penned these words to Helena: "I am simply unable to write from the conflict of feelings. The pain and the sweetness of that visit. The young lives around us and then ourselves—your rooms, your bedside, your garden, the meadow where I left you, to go back alone." She must have found it just as difficult to leave little Agnes when she departed for Grass Valley. On her last day at the Wharf-House, Molly reported, "a little voice calls 'Ganny why can't we play ball!' . . . I go to play ball, the infant of 65!"

Back at home, Molly's newest diversion was an Airedale puppy, named John Michael, which soon captured a part of her heart. Christmas that year was spent quietly with Billy and Bessie Hague and their infant son, and on New Year's Day the Footes hosted a traditional visit from the older men and officials of the North Star. The new year was to bring many changes to the Foote household. But before these came about, Molly's niece, Mary Foote, had on display at the New York Armory Show a picture entitled "Portrait," which some scholars have attributed incorrectly to Mary Hallock Foote. At this revolutionary exhibition, which opened for one month on February 17, 1913, about thirteen hundred American and European works of art were on display, including the works of

Cézanne, Gauguin, Van Gogh, Matisse, and Picasso. Molly never wrote about Mary Foote's contribution, but she and Helena both despised much of the modern art exhibited at the show. Molly especially lashed out at the Italian Futurists, calling their work "immoral, monstrous exhibitions of coarse egotism."

Molly's social activities that spring centered on her family and the obligations that came with being the wife of the North Star's superintendent. One day, she and Arthur motored down to Sacramento with Billy and Bessie Hague and their guest to attend the opera. A few weeks later she helped host a lawn party for visiting company officials. About this same time, however, Arthur, Jr., succeeded his father as the North Star's chief officer, with Arthur, Sr., staying on as consulting engineer. The sixty-four-year-old Foote, though, was not content to rest in retirement and was about to get involved in a project that was to eat up his savings and perhaps trigger another bout with alcohol.

Late in 1911 the elder Foote and his associates had purchased the Tightner mine, situated high up in the Sierra Nevada at Alleghany, about forty miles northeast of Grass Valley. The mine was reached by a terrible road that was closed by snow in the winter. As president of the Tightner Mines Company, Foote helped negotiate an agreement with public officials and other mine owners to build a new all-season road. Having faith in the project, he took the contract himself and began construction late in 1913. But when actual costs far exceeded the original estimate, Foote used $50,000 of his own money to finish the job. Local residents later referred to the road as "Foote's Folly," but others considered it a "marvel of engineering skill." A portion of it, in fact, has been described as "America's most spectacular mile of mountain road." Still, as Rodman Paul points out, the significance of this monetary loss to the Footes was far-reaching, coming as it did at a time when the sale of Molly's work contributed less and less to their income: "Unlike their recovery after the Idaho disaster, this time there was no chance to rebuild their personal fortunes and thus provide money that would make possible travel, independence of their children, and assurance against the inevitable uncertainties and expenses of old age."

Still, Molly and Arthur Foote lived fairly comfortably at the North Star House for several more years while their son was the resident manager. Their income, in fact, was sufficient for them to visit Hingham occasionally and to take trips away from Grass Valley to escape the summer heat.

About the time that Arthur, Jr., assumed management of the North Star, Jeannette Hooper, Betty's former roommate at Miss Head's school, paid the Footes an extended visit. By mid-August 1913 Jean and Arthur were making plans to wed, much to Molly's joy and relief, for she had worried for some time that her son would remain a bachelor and bury himself in his work. Earlier in the summer Arthur, Jr., had driven Jean and his parents to Lake Tahoe. The "four of us . . . had a perfect time," Molly later reported, "[Arthur, Jr.,] and Jean on the front seat, my old boy and I behind, comparing our locomotion with other times and other methods of getting over the ground."

By September 1, however, Molly and Arthur had packed up and left for Seattle, where Bessie Sherman now lived with her daughter Birney and her lawyer-husband, Bamford Robb. On the advice of Arthur's physician, they had fled the intense heat of Grass Valley and gone north "for coolness and salt water and friends near and good doctors if needed." After a few days rest in Seattle, they moved on to Hood's Canal on Puget Sound, where they stayed in a small cabin with a fireplace and spent their days fishing and taking long walks.

The Footes returned to California in time for Molly to have a new dress made for their son's wedding, which took place in San Francisco on October 23, 1913. Soon afterwards, the senior Footes left on a trip to Hingham, where they would see for the first time their new granddaughter Sally Swift, born the previous spring. They must have visited the New Haven relatives as well, and Molly spent some time with Helena. But all too soon they departed for home, taking the southern route that gave Molly her first glimpse of New Orleans.

Once back in the North Star House, a new routine was quickly established—or as Molly reported to Helena: "We have retired from the head of the table, we old Footes." Molly gladly relinquished to Jean the supervision of that large house and its staff of three servants. All seemed perfectly fine as the new year got underway, at least on the surface. But Arthur, Sr., must have been laboring under tremendous strain. He had stepped down from a job that had brought personal fulfillment and public praise and now was caught up in a road project, the difficulties of which probably were apparent already. And increasingly he was feeling the effects of his age. For whatever reasons, Foote turned to alcohol. As in the past, Molly did not immediately share this new trial with Helena. But this time her daughter-in-law witnessed Arthur's behavior and thought he was having a stroke. How often Arthur drank to excess is not known, but it happened more frequently than Molly notes in her correspondence. Finally, late in the year of 1914, Molly confided in her friend.

> I . . . never feel safe to have [Arthur] take journeys without me. A great trial in my life lifts and seems to pass away for long periods. Yet I am never free from the secret dread; and the risk to him, of these repeated fatal experiments—at long intervals—perhaps a whole year—increases with each one. The last took almost the form of a "stroke." This is very shattering—or undermining to my old nerves. I am a damaged piece of furniture, upholster myself as I may.

Molly must have felt this "secret dread" strongly when she and Arthur traveled eastward in September 1914. They stopped first in New Haven, where Arthur consulted with Edward Jenkins on a business matter, and then went on to Hingham for a long visit with Betty and her family. In the following days, Molly exchanged messages with Helena to arrange a brief visit. But for one reason or another, the two friends were not destined to meet. At first Molly put off making the journey to Tyringham because of a cold and then because of the threat of bad weather. "I simply felt chilled to the bone and had taken cold already in the first stages and dreaded a big one," she explained to Helena. On the return trip to Grass Valley, Molly wrote from Chicago seemingly to apologize for the missed opportunity and vowing that next year she would make "a two-year visit in one." Sadly, there were to be no further reunions for Molly and Helena.

It was only after Molly reached home, however, that she told Helena what really had been troubling her. Her recent letters, she said, had all been "off key." There had been no legitimate excuse for staying away from Tyringham, "only a sudden feeling that I could go into no more deeps [*sic*] of feeling. 'I love her, but just now I cannot see her merely for a short-agitating, unsatisfactory few hours.'" In New Haven, her sister-in-law Elizabeth had demanded a report on her brother's battle with alcohol. And Betty, "my very self, the core of my being," had to be told of Arthur's recent relapse. In writing of her "secret dread," Molly concluded:

> You must not think this means now what it meant when the children were younger. It cannot hurt them now. It does not hurt me as it did. I have gained a different point of view. But it is certainly true that in hardening oneself in one direction simply to hide and bear—one loses poise, [fairness] of discernment towards others, from day to day.

While still in Hingham, Molly mentioned in a letter to Helena that she had "incidently written another novel," for which Betty had served as "first reader and critic." She must have started writing it about the time that *A Picked Company* was published. After her return to Grass Valley and further revisions, she sent the manuscript to Houghton Mifflin Company, which published it in the fall of 1915. The firm selected the title, *The Valley Road*, from a short list of names that Molly had submitted. Later, she was delighted when reminded by Helena that Richard had used the same title for one of his poems. "I am sure my dear friend, your Richard, who was my guide in such things," she wrote in September, "would not mind that I have instinctively as it were, put his own choice phrase on the title page of my latest and last book."

More than once, in fact, Molly proclaimed *The Valley Road* was to be her last book. "No more," she told Helena. "This could never have been written since the war." The fighting that erupted in Europe the previous year had stunned the author. The daily war news, which she avidly read, sickened and discouraged her. In the novel's preface, penned in July 1915, Molly told her readers that she had written the story before the start of the conflict. But even so, she continued, "it has seemed strange enough to be going on with mere mechanical revision—seated, as it were, with one's knitting at the spectacle of the world's agony since August of last year."

In this story, set in the Sacramento Valley, the author continues to explore the nature of parent-child relationships. The action centers on the Scarth family and their San Francisco cousins, the Ludwells. Caroline Scarth, born and raised in New England, follows her engineer-husband, Hal, to California with two small children. They take up residence near Marysville, where Hal oversees the Torres Tract, a mining-irrigation project financed by eastern capitalists. The story quickly moves to the year 1904, which finds the middle-aged Scarth grappling with poor health, his engineer-son Tom preparing to leave wartorn Korea, and his youngest child Engracia studying music in the East. Tom arrives in San Francisco the day his father dies following emergency surgery; Engracia returns home a short time later.

Now Caroline and her adult children must reassess their financial situation while they cope with their loss. Tom becomes interim manager of the Torres Tract, Engracia works briefly as a social secretary, and Caroline immerses herself in her children's affairs. Meanwhile, Hal's wealthy cousin Tom Ludwell, his wife Anna, and their daughter Clare hover in the background. Eighteen-year-old Clare toys with the idea of acquiring young Scarth as a lover, though she really loves a playboy named Dalby Morton and Scarth loves an American girl whom he met in Korea, Mary Gladwyn. The Scarths soon have as a houseguest forty-something-year-old Gifford Cornish, sent from New York to inspect the Torres Tract. During his lengthy stay, he falls in love with Engracia, who rejects his proposal of marriage because of its suddenness and the difference in their ages.

The San Francisco earthquake helps to resolve relationships. At the request of her mother, Tom locates Mary in the city where she is nurse to Dalby Morton after his appendectomy. Tom convinces the pair to accept refuge at the Scarth residence in the countryside. Clare Ludwell, now homeless, soon joins them, which complicates matters since Dalby, who unhappily had parted with Clare months earlier, is now engaged to another woman. When Dalby and Clare rediscover their love for one another, they attempt to elope but are thwarted. Angry at Dalby's deception, Clare's father demands a two-year separation before he will bless their marriage. Meanwhile, Tom and Mary wed and return to Korea, where an engineering job awaits him. Cornish appears unexpectedly at the Scarth residence and convinces Engracia to marry him. Near the close of the story, with the future of her children assured, Caroline Scarth moves east to live with a maiden cousin. She wisely has declined invitations to live with her children, explaining:

> And it cost her no great pang in one way, for she wanted silence and peace; and if there should be problems in these young lives they were not her problems;—and she could not at her time of life bring to a new set of problems the courage she had brought to her own. Nor does the understanding of one generation fit the needs of the next. No; she wanted to lie at anchor in some quiet haven and dream her own dreams and think over her life—with him. And more than art or clothes or clever talk, though she had loved these things in her youth, did she love her personal life apart, the solitude she had grown used to and learned to need;—room for the lonely soul which each of us must bring to our last account with life, in preparation for what we trust will come later.

In this heartfelt declaration, Foote projects her own hard-won wisdom onto her fictional counterpart. In fact, *The Valley Road* is largely autobiographical, for Molly incorporates into it many of her own experiences and points of view. Caroline and Engracia, to cite one small example, dealt with their grief after Scarth's death in a manner similar to that which Molly and Betty adopted after Agnes's death, "they drugged themselves with books." A more startling example, because of the sensitive nature of the issue, is Foote's treatment of alcohol abuse. Caroline and Anna Ludwell have had to come to terms with their husbands' drinking. And when Clare Ludwell angrily tells a drunken Dalby that she never wants to see him again, her mother shows more sympathy and tells Clare: "He's no different from the others—in this respect . . . .The very same thing . . . might have parted me from your father once. But we cared for each other and I had faith."

Most reviewers liked this novel. One critic called it "a wholesome human story of normal people leading normal lives." Another said that it was "full of quiet power, of respectable people with strong characters well delineated." As with most of Foote's stories, the locales and characters are finely drawn, and the romantic scenes are handled with restraint. Although *The Valley Road* did not become a best-seller, Molly's publishers soon reported that it "had a very respectable sale in its first period and seems to have made many friends."

In July, shortly before *The Valley Road* appeared in print, Molly and Arthur fled the Grass Valley heat and set up camp near the fishing village of Pescadero, forty-seven miles south of San Francisco. It was "the place of our dreams," Molly reported to her sister-in-law, Kate Coe. They had the ocean in front of them, vegetable gardens stretching out behind, and beaches curving away on either side. Best of all, it was "incredibly solitary"—no house in sight, no chattering hotel crowds. The cool foggy mornings and the crashing of the waves delighted Molly. They had arrived in a motorcar driven by a Grass Valley young man named Archie, who also served as their "swamper," and had carried all their camp gear in a specially built trailer. "We, of course, go into camp prudently, at our age," Molly wrote to Helena from the campsite, "and with the comfort experience teaches one how to achieve." Their own large tent held two cots, two chairs, stove, camp trunk, tripod washstand, rubber bathtub, and one set of canvas shelves. The Footes so enjoyed their "Camp at Pescadero Beach" that they returned there the following two summers, and Molly was to write about it in her twelfth and final novel, *The Ground-Swell* (1919).

After the Footes returned from their "sea-camp," their daily routine was punctuated by a few pleasurable events. Their daughter-in-law Jean gave birth to her first child, Janet Stanwood Foote, on September 4, 1915. And later in the month Molly and Arthur stayed a few days at the Hotel St. Francis in San Francisco, where Arthur attended a congress of engineers, meeting old chums he had not seen in forty years. Molly enjoyed the small group of friends that met almost nightly to attend the banquets together. But a high point upon her return to Grass Valley was a visit from Helena's daughter Rosamond, who had just finished compiling a volume of her father's correspondence. It was shortly after Rosamond's visit that Helena wrote to ask if Molly would consider writing an introduction for the book. Molly demurred. Although she would love to do this for her friend, she told Helena it was a task for a writer of greater stature or someone who shared in Gilder's civic work. But then in a single sentence, which would have made a fitting opening for Rosamond's book, Molly summed up her feelings about Richard: "He was more than a critic, more than an editor, more than a good business-man, more than a poet, more than a perfect friend: he was human, and he was spiritually human; warm to the best in each one of us but never deceived as to what was the best."

As the old year ended, Molly's thoughts increasingly turned to the war in Europe. Like many of her friends, she was impatient with President Woodrow Wilson's diplomacy. "We are all words," she lamented, and later she signed a petition urging

Wilson to close the German and Austrian embassies. She reported to Helena with pride that her daughter-in-law cared for her own baby and gave the wages of a nursemaid to the Belgians. "We live in the war news," Molly added.

The new year began inauspiciously when Molly read in *The Nation* a notice of the death of Jeannette Gilder, Richard's literary sister. Rain and snow storms soon blanketed Grass Valley, nearly stopping all motor traffic and bringing an end to Molly's walks. But disturbing news continued to reach the North Star House. Helena was operated on for appendicitis, probably sometime in March. "I cant bear to think of your precious strength wasted in bearing and recovering from this kind of devastation," Molly wrote to her friend. And soon after, a telegram arrived from Seattle with news that Birney Robb's husband had been killed in an accident. "My poor Bessie Sherman," Molly lamented, "[her] heart bowed by her daughter's grief." But joy also came into the house when Betty and little Agnes arrived for a six-week visit. On Easter Sunday, Molly wrote a long letter to Helena, chatting about books, little Agnes, and tulips and roses. There were more serious comments about Wilson and the war and about Willa Cather's *The Song of the Lark*, which she called "a fine, fresh vital thing." She closed, urging Helena to work hard to regain her health. "For all our sakes! . . . We love you so! There is no one else but you." These are among the last words that Molly wrote to her friend of fifty years.

The *New York Times* tells us something of Helena's final days. On May 19, 1916, she witnessed the marriage of her daughter Dorothea to Dallas D. K. McGrew, a minister's son. Because of her recent illness, the ceremony took place at Helena's apartment on Gramercy Park with only a handful of relatives in attendance. But she never regained her strength. Helena de Kay Gilder died on May 28 at the age of sixty-nine.

Molly must have started right in on a tribute to her "perfect friend"—her eleventh novel, written and published in less than one year. Dedicated to Helena, *Edith Bonham* (1917) is a memorial to their friendship of half a century and incorporates incidents from their Cooper Union days and from Molly's life in Idaho.

In the story's opening scenes, Foote contrasts the lives of the narrator Edith Bonham, raised in an artistic and literary family in the city, and Anne (Nanny) Aylesford, the daughter of a Hudson Valley farm couple. When they met at Cooper Union, it was "as much a case of love at first sight," the narrator declares, "as if one of us had belonged to the 'opposite sex.'" Nanny marries first and follows her husband, Douglas Maclay, to Idaho, where he manages mines near Silver City. The two friends next meet when Nanny returns home with her infant daughter Phoebe. Nanny tells how she and Douglas had given up a dream of living on the mesa after financial difficulties shut down an irrigation project. So Nanny now lives in Boise while Douglas works at the mines. Moved by Nanny's apparent loneliness, Edith promises that when freed of responsibilities to her widowed father, she will move west to become a governess to Phoebe.

Four years go by. When the elder Bonham departs for Tahiti on an artistic quest, Edith arranges to join the Maclays in Idaho. But when she arrives outside of Boise, she is stunned by news that Nanny has died after giving birth to a son. Grief-stricken, the twenty-seven-year-old Edith plans to keep her pledge to Nanny. The next few weeks are a trial for nearly everyone, as Maclay stays away at the mines and Edith must deal with household staff and his daughter's grief. Eventually Edith wins Phoebe's affection. But a new ordeal awaits them when Phoebe contracts scarlet fever, and she and "Aunt Edith" endure a six-week quarantine in what was to have been Nanny's dream house on the mesa. Douglas pays daily visits, keeping a safe distance from Edith and the child. He finally stuns Edith anew when he proposes marriage. Angered by this insult to Nanny's memory, Edith refuses. Only later does she discover that Maclay had been trying to protect her from the town's gossip about her "unchaperoned status."

The awkwardness between Maclay and Edith is temporarily resolved when she and the children go to live with the

Aylesfords in Nanny's childhood home. For the next five years, Douglas fails to visit, although he writes weekly to Phoebe. Mrs. Aylesford finally sends for her son-in-law when she sees that his letters thinly conceal a love for her daughter's friend. Douglas and Edith eventually resolve their differences, marry, and return to Idaho, where Edith will give birth to two sons. In an epilogue, the adult Phoebe looks back on her stepmother's life. To the modern reader, this segment seems unnecessary, but it gave Molly a final chance to write of her sacred friendship with Helena. Phoebe describes her Aunt Edith (Helena) as the "queen of all mothers, perfect in love, in friendship, in magnanimity, the soul of friendship, which came as natural to her as vanity and selfishness to smaller natures." Phoebe concludes that her own mother (Molly) "would have asked for no praise beyond the fact: 'Edith loved me as I am.'"

Within a few months of its publication, Houghton Mifflin notified Molly that *Edith Bonham* had "made a very good start." One reviewer, for the *Boston Transcript*, believed that *Edith Bonham* would "probably be considered [Foote's] most appealing novel." Another wrote that her style "as always, with its quiet clarity, offers grateful refreshment to ears which may be a trifle weary of the din and 'punch' of the current literary mode." But what Foote makes clear in *Edith Bonham*, more so than in any of her previous stories, is that she has fully accepted the West as a place in which to live and raise a family.

Much to Molly's delight, the size of her own family at the North Star House continued to grow. Jean gave birth to Marian Hallock Foote on December 3, 1916, and to Evelyn Norwood Foote on Christmas day of 1919. Shortly after Marian's birth, the *Grass Valley Morning Star* announced in bold letters that Boise, Idaho, had recently honored a local resident. During a "Mary Hallock Foote Week," the Boise public library exhibited a selection of her drawings, watercolor sketches, and illustrations, and a daily paper ran serially *The Chosen Valley*, the best of her early Idaho stories. One suspects that the author did not place great value on this public acclaim, however, especially since events unfolding in Europe clamored for the nation's full attention.

Molly may have been visiting Betty in Hingham when President Wilson asked Congress, in April 1917, to declare war against Germany to make the world "safe for democracy." Edith Angus, Molly's old friend from Victoria and now living in London, soon wrote to Molly and Betty at the Wharf-House to extend her greetings to "our new Allies." "Your President's speech was magnificent," she avowed, and she thanked mother and daughter for sending her copies of the *Atlantic Monthly*, which her military son shared with other men in the service.

But closer to home, many families would forever be changed by America's entrance into the war. The Footes' nephew Billy Hague had obtained a commission in the Engineers Reserve Corps and was called into service soon after the declaration of war. He spent time at the Presidio in San Francisco and at Vancouver Barracks in Washington before being shipped to France sometime the latter part of 1917. That same winter, Molly knitted socks for American soldiers and wrote frequently to Billy's little son "Jamesy," now staying with his mother Bessie in San Francisco. In a letter dated December 26, she described for him the little Christmas party staged for her two small granddaughters. But all too soon the family was in mourning. Lieutenant William Hague died on January 2, 1918, of pneumonia at the Red Cross Hospital in Paris. The bereaved wife and son soon left for her family's home in Massachusetts, but Molly's letters to little Jamesy were to continue for several years.

The war served as backdrop to Foote's final novel, *The Ground-Swell*, which Houghton Mifflin published as the author approached her seventy-second birthday. Like *The Valley Road*, Molly's latest story depicts the complexity of parent-child relations, and like *Edith Bonham*, it is a first-person narrative, told from the perspective of a woman protagonist. *The Ground-Swell* opens in California, where during the summer of 1914 the narrator Lucy Cope and her just retired husband, General Charley Cope, hunt for the perfect site on which to build a home. The story focuses on two of their three daughters, the oldest Cecily, married to a San Francisco socialite named Peter Dalbert, and Katherine, unmarried and committed to helping the poor in New York.

While camped on the coast below San Francisco, the Copes discover Del Refugio Point and plan their dream house. But disturbances both within and without the family reach their isolated "sea-camp" much like the ground-swells they observe off the coast. "A mother's thoughts at my age," Lucy Cope muses on a solitary walk, "are so often a review of her own mistakes with her children." But she cannot refrain from intervening in their lives.

When Katherine arrives for a visit, Lucy introduces her to Tony Kayding, overseer of the large Del Refugio ranch on which they are camped, and secretly hopes the two will wed. At the mother's urging, the young people ride nightly together; Tony falls in love, but Katherine rejects marriage to return to her work. Meanwhile, Lucy unexpectedly observes her son-in-law Peter Dalbert arguing with a disreputable woman high on a cliff above the sea. The woman slips and falls to her death when Peter fails to help her. Horrified, Lucy orders Peter to go away and plans to keep this ghastly secret to herself. But when he continues his self-indulgent behavior, Lucy threatens to speak out unless he changes his character. He deserts his family instead, but Lucy cannot bear to explain his absence to Cecily.

The elder Copes spend the winter in New York where the talk is of war. And here they encounter Katherine's liberated friends, women who smoke, forego marriage for idealistic causes, and question the concept of "my country right or wrong." Baffled by their behavior, Lucy describes them as belonging to a "third sex." Katherine soon leaves to aid the war effort, and the Copes return to California where Tony Kayding , now owner of the Del Refugio ranch, has built them their dream house. Before the story ends, Peter becomes an ace in the U.S. air service (partly redeeming his character),

Charley is recalled to active duty, and Katherine dies of grippe in a French hospital where she has nursed the wounded. "Her death, we say to each other," the mother concludes, "was not a mistake, it was a necessity of her previous life and her whole attitude toward life; and it was that in her which counted. . . . And now that she is gone there is no more to say about us as a family."

Foote's literary talent is manifest throughout *The Ground-Swell*, which must be acclaimed the very best of her novels. Her realistic portrayal of a mother's anxieties about her children is heart-rending. From beginning to end, the reader is caught up in the Copes' quest for an idyllic retirement and concern for their adult offsprings' happiness. Lee Ann Johnson believes that in the character of Katherine Cope, Foote meant to capture the spirit of her daughter Agnes. Here, at the end of her writing career, Molly successfully dealt with the issue of the modern woman. Certainly Katherine Cope is light years removed from Cecil Conrath, the heroine of Foote's first novel. And as one reviewer noted of this exquisite study of human character: "The book ends, but the story goes on. So real is she [the mother] that we know it goes on."

In four of her novels written early in the twentieth century, in fact, Foote created a handful of memorable older women protagonists. In Molly's earlier stories, her heroines almost always are bright, young, and beautiful and involved in complicated relations that will lead to marriage, as, for example, Cecil Conrath in *The Led-Horse Claim* and Josephine Newbold in *John Bodewin's Testimony*. But gradually, with the wisdom that accompanies experience, Foote devised more complex and more interesting older female characters—wise mature women who attempt to impart their wisdom to the younger generation. Emily Bogardus in *The Desert and the Sown*, Caroline Scarth in *The Valley Road*, Edith Bonham in the novel of that name, and Lucy Cope in *The Ground-Swell* are such strong personalities that they linger in the reader's memory long after the books are put aside. And we readily see in these stories the benefits of having an older woman author explore themes of such universal appeal as parent-child relations and family tragedies and triumphs.

While working on *The Ground Swell*, Molly continued to cope with the everyday concerns of the household. She usually took daily walks with her dog, occasionally donning a raincoat to tramp through the pasture in a soft rain and always admiring the flowers bursting into bloom. In late December 1918, a second wave of the worldwide flu epidemic swept over the North Star House, and Arthur, Sr., and the two grandchildren came down with mild cases. While Arthur spent New Year's Day confined to bed, Molly listened in the downstairs hall as North Star personnel toasted the health of the mine and the memory of Billy Hague. Although Molly's enthusiasm for writing remained unabated in the following months, *The Ground-Swell* was to be her final published work of fiction.

CHAPTER 7

The Final Years

MIDWAY through the year 1920, Mary Hallock Foote wrote to thank her publishers for the "very good sized cheque" she had received from the first sales of *The Ground-Swell.* She continued to write for the next decade or so but her stories now would remain unpublished. By late 1923 she had four long short stories piled on her desk, which, she told her sister-in-law Elizabeth Jenkins, had been "sent back with polite expressions but no check." The first of these, "On Trust," a story about labor and capital, had been rejected by four magazines. She had then sent it to Ferris Greenslet at Houghton Mifflin for his advice and to inquire if the firm might publish it as a little book.

She also told Greenslet that a Mr. James Scherer, "one of my old readers," had an idea that her stories might have promising "material for moving pictures," and she asked for permission to continue these negotiations. Scherer also had expressed the opinion, however, that no magazine would print "On Trust" because of the subject matter. Greenslet answered right away, wishing Scherer "Godspeed in his effort to sell the motion picture rights" of some of her stories. Houghton Mifflin, he told Molly, "has tried it without much success." And after reading "On Trust," he pinpointed the problem. The story, he said, "has all the customary Mary Hallock Foote quality and charm," but because of its awkward length it would be difficult to sell to a magazine. "It's too long for one number, and hasn't got quite the substance to be a two-part novelette." And he rejected the idea of publishing it as a small book, since, he said, book stores would have little chance of making a profit on it. But he generously offered to send the story to the editor of the *Atlantic Monthly* for consideration. The verdict was the same; the story remained on Molly's desk.

Still, Molly wrote Greenslet that his comments had been a great help, especially "if one is to go on doing anything, at my age. "She was hard at work on a second story and confessed that "condensing is the hardest work to do." Later, when all four stories had been rejected by the journals, she again inquired if Houghton Mifflin would consider publishing them as a book. She reminded Greenslet that he already had read and praised "On Trust" and "Our Invisible Host"; the two he had not read were "The Miniature" and "In Quarantine." His reply was brief and negative: "Short stories are notoriously sticky merchandise."

By this time, however, the seventy-five-year-old author was in the midst of completing her autobiography, the first chapters of which she had sent to Greenslet in May 1923. Writing one's "Rems," she told the editor, was "one of those things we swear we never will do! I have yielded to the temptation[,] of course, as we always end by doing those things we are vowed never to do." Tentatively entitled "Backgrounds with Figures," Foote's reminiscences would be in three parts: Eastern Homes, Western Camps, and Camps that were Homes. She had completed about half the manuscript but expected to do her best work when she tackled the Idaho irrigation section. "Irrigation is big," she said, "[and] that ten years was worth remembering." Idaho and Grass Valley, she told Greenslet, "were the two greater camps which became to us in every sense of the word Homes."

She then asked the editor a series of questions. Did the manuscript hold his interest? Would he agree to publish it? "And if so, would you rather wait till I am dead so to speak? There is no need to be delicate about it—I am talking from a business point of view." In fact, although Molly clearly intended this as a family chronicle to leave to her grandchildren, she was too good a businesswoman to ignore the possibility of profit, as her next question to Greenslet indicates.

> Finally, if you think the whole idea and the work itself worth while, would you try if the Atlantic or whatever magazine you think best, would publish parts of it that the author might realize something on it that way? . . . The serial idea is purely mercenary of course. I am in no hurry to have it in print. But I'd like to get the price of my railroad-fares out of it and then I'd come on and have a last talk with you (and incidentally see my daughter at the Wharfhouse).

About two months went by before Greenslet replied. Both he and another reader had read Molly's manuscript. "The reader, a very competent one of the younger generation, was very appreciative of the delicate flavor and charm of your story," Greenslet told Molly, "but was doubtful about its having much appeal to the public." Although Greenslet admired Molly's work, he decided to withhold a final opinion until he saw more of the manuscript. He sent the segments he had read, however, to the editor of the *Atlantic Monthly*, but his appraisal was about the same as the Houghton Mifflin reader: "It really goes against the grain to return these chapters. First, who would not like Mrs. Foote, and, second, who would not think these chapters well written? But it would be very difficult to persuade many people to begin a serial of this kind."

Although the reply was discouraging, Molly told Greenslet that she would continue to work on her reminiscences. She had almost completed chapters on Leadville and Mexico but would not immediately send them to Greenslet. "That which is unfinished is nothing," she wrote. And she added that her daughter Betty now urged her to "forget the publishing part; cease to regard it as anything but a family document."

But Betty continued to bolster her mother's spirits. In a letter to her dated September 20, 1924, Betty referred to her mother's friendship with "Aunt Helena" as having a certain romance "and a kind of glory like that the Greeks took in their epic friendships." And now she discovered that Rosamond Gilder shared some of these same feelings.

> The riches thee has in thy past! Now will thee believe me about the Rems. Rosamond and I cant both be mad *and* Aunt Bessie [who had read part of the manuscript]. It's the most strange and beautiful life that you could imagine. Every kind of love in it—of friends and family, their husband[s] and children and all kinds of people and country — the basic loves yet not like anybody else's and not told as anybody else would.

Betty commented also on Molly's drawings that would accompany the text. Surely the pictures would entice Houghton Mifflin—or even the Century Company—to publish the manuscript. "Nobody has rems with their own illustrations. *Mais* what a lovely strange work it would be! Yes I think that's a grand scheme."

Molly continued to work on her autobiography in the following months. In 1929 Betty told her Aunt Elizabeth Jenkins that "Mamma" had written it "partly for the grandchildren's reading . . . and partly because, being a business woman, she knows that there are revivals, as it were, of authors, often, after they are dead . . . . She is looking out for posthumous pennies for her descendants, you see!" The following year Rosamond Gilder showed Molly's "rems" to a new publishing house. By this time, Molly had revised the manuscript, taking out parts that some members of her family said were too personal and shortening it in other ways. Betty's comment to her mother undoubtedly was correct: "Of course, thee has weakened all the principal characters, paradoxically, by leaving out their weaknesses." But Molly's manuscript remained unpublished until 1972, when the historian Rodman Paul oversaw its publication by the Huntington Library. His excellent introduction to Foote's *Reminiscences* informed a new generation of readers about this exceptional woman, whose lifework had helped mold America's memory of its western heritage.

Foote's autobiography ranks among the very best stories she ever wrote. The lyrical quality of her writing suffuses the text, her talent undiminished by the passing years. But she made no attempt to give a balanced account of her life. About one-fifth of the memoirs is devoted to her childhood and her education at Cooper Union and two-fifths to the early California and Leadville years and the excursion to Mexico. These were the chapters she wrote while still envisioning their serial publication, and she no doubt tailored them for a public readership. She must have felt, for example, that the public's interest in exotic places justified the disproportionate amount of space she devoted to the Mexican interlude. The eleven years or so that the Footes spent in Idaho receive full coverage but very little is said about their experiences in Grass Valley, where Molly was to live more than thirty-five years. In fact, the autobiography comes to an abrupt end with Agnes's death in 1904. The author's explanation for this brevity provides an effective closing and brings to mind the way in which she ended *The Ground-Swell*, in which Katherine Cope dies in France:

> All that has happened here since [Agnes's death] would be too difficult to tell for one so deeply implicated through her relations to the chief actors, yet so powerless, as myself. The next generation took the lead in household and mining affairs and made their own decisions, as we made ours . . . . But the North Star House now has its own flock of children, little Californians to whom this place will always be home; its memories will haunt them as the desert wind and the sound of that cañon river rising to our windows at night has stayed with our own children all their lives.

How accurate are Foote's memoirs? Rodman Paul notes some factual errors in his edited volume. And in her final paragraph, Foote herself acknowledged the subjective nature of her observations:

> These fragments of my past are presented merely as backgrounds and the figures upon them are placed by instinct in a selected light and seen from a certain point of view. To that extent I suppose I am still the artist I tried to be, and the old romancer too. And everyone knows the magic perspectives of memory—it keeps what we loved and alters the relative size and value of many things that we did not love enough—that we hated and resisted and made mountains of at the time.

Certainly time softened the most painful of Foote's memories. Paul states, in fact, that "virtually every aspect of the Footes' experience [in Idaho] is decisively understated." Yet Foote is surprisingly candid, and a careful reading of her letters to Helena and other family members substantiates the bulk of her autobiography. Two of her most admirable traits had always been her modesty and honesty, both of which helped to shape this beautifully written memoir. It is quite possible, of course, that Molly had access to the nearly six hundred letters that she wrote to Helena over the course of their friendship, which would account for her remarkable memory of past events.

Molly continued to find satisfaction in her work into her eighties—writing at her desk situated in the Footes' downstairs sitting room, adjacent to their bedroom, and surrounded by her books. She had stopped illustrating long ago, the last known of her published work appearing in the March 1906 issue of *St. Nicholas Magazine.* Her habit of writing long letters to her family continued, however, through the 1920s and early 1930s. She often was poetic in these epistles, as in this description of a winter landscape near the North Star House, which she sent to Elizabeth Jenkins:

> The pasture moss-green yet streaked with snow. The pine-trunks black with rain—and printed with what looks like finger-works of bright serpent-green, as if by fingers dripped in fresh paint! And the pine-needles that make the floor of the woods the most effective copper color—and the manzanitas pale sage-green, silvery with dampness.

After 1923 or 1924, Foote's "serious" writing was limited to finishing and revising her autobiography. Her fictional stories, she realized, had become outdated. Literary tastes had changed; readers grown weary of Victorian restraint were drawn to writers who rebelled against the genteel tradition that Foote upheld. The quiet realism of *The Ground-Swell*, for example, no longer appealed to a society weaned on the robust realism of writers like F. Scott Fitzgerald, in *The Beautiful and*

Damned (1922), and Ernest Hemingway, in *The Sun Also Rises* (1926).

In her later years, Molly continued to live a literary life, devouring books and exchanging opinions about authors and their works with family and friends. Among the books she read in 1920, for example, were the published letters of Henry James and his brother William, and Henri Bergson's *Creative Evolution.* In 1927 she praised Willa Cather's *Death Comes to the Archbishop* and Thornton Wilder's *The Bridge of San Luis Rey.* But she did not care for some of the "queer things" the magazines were publishing or the novels that "morbid young women" were writing. "The latest over-sexed one," she avowed in 1927, "is *Dusty Answer*," the first novel of Rosamond Lehmann, a writer of great promise according to some critics. "And yet [these] young women can write!" she admitted. "They dont seem to have the least trouble breaking out at once in a first book with a full fledged competence in words that is amazing." As Molly and Arthur became older, they spent more time reading together; both particularly enjoyed biographies. "It's a great day for biography—or perhaps for the biographers!" Molly exclaimed in 1928. "They seem to have things pretty much their own way, in pawing over the past actions that one thought were stored in their niches as facts."

By the mid-1920s, however, Molly relied on the generosity of others for her supply of books. Jeannette's bachelor brother Albert Hooper frequently sent rather strange volumes, including the memoirs of Queen Hortense (mother of Napoleon III) and the works of Norwegian authors. Although Molly might not have chosen these for herself, still, she admitted to her sister-in-law, "it broadens one's reading to have books thrust upon you." Her great-nephew, James D. Hague, with whom she had forged a special bond, also sent books as he grew older. And he shared with his Uncle and "Aunt Arthur" (a whimsical name his grandfather had applied to Molly), books in the Hague library, often volumes purchased with their literary tastes in mind.

By the mid-twenties, or a little later, Molly and Arthur Foote were financially dependent upon their children. Once more Arthur was involved in what must have been a speculative mining venture. In January 1925 Elizabeth Jenkins wrote to her brother: "Your tale of mining operations quite breaks my heart . . . . I wish to Heaven your scheme could carry through." But that was not fated to be. Nearly two and a half years later, Molly declared in a letter to Elizabeth, whom she considered one of her closest woman friends: "We too often have been [wanderers and squanderers]. We ate our cake and had all sorts of good times doing it and now we are taken care of by our children. And if we dont like it we have only ourselves to thank. Dreams have their price." Without a particle of self-pity, Molly wrote of their near-penniless condition:

> Arthur (son) said to Betty when she was out here that money was the least of his worries. It has been one of my two supreme worries for fifty years—The supremest worry thank God is past. Arthur has command of himself (my husband) in that respect, and though he is fat he is not sodden nor in danger of drink apoplexy. Money cannot matter for the years that are left though it will hurt our pride. What is pride? . . . It is impossible for us to speak openly to anyone but our children about the scheme their father has now put his name to and is trying to raise money to finance. A lot must be left out of this letter, but I may say that I fear it, and can not share Arthur's confidence in its ever making returns to those who do put money into it.

Molly continued to find pleasure in her daily surroundings, however. Her Grass Valley grandchildren never failed to buoy her spirits. She took them on walks through the woods, read them stories, and made them poems and paper dolls. Many years later, Evelyn Foote Gardiner remembered that "Nana" (as she called her grandmother) fixed her dinner and sat with her when she was too young to eat at the dinner table. Gardiner also has written a vivid description of Mary Hallock Foote, as she appeared to the youngster during Molly's last years at the North Star House:

> [She] was a tiny woman, 4' 11", very quick and light on her feet, even in her seventies, when I remember her. She always dressed in long dresses, usually black, and made her own little caps [which she wore in the Quaker tradition]. Her hair was thin, and she curled the front, which gave her a youthful appearance, even when old. Her Eastern custom was to take a cold bath every day and she kept up her life-long habit of walks, with the dog in good weather, up and down the porch in bad. Sometimes she would have nothing but curds and whey for dinner, and worried about Grandad, who ate hugely, and didn't exercise much as he got older.

Molly took great joy also in Betty's weekly letters, filled with information about Agnes and Sally. Even better were the rare visits that Molly made to the Wharf-House. She had not seen Betty or her granddaughters in four years when, in 1923, Agnes Bourn generously paid for her trip to Massachusetts. Agnes repeated this gesture six years later, though on this occasion Molly cut short her visit when Arthur became ill.

Later, Molly wrote to her sister-in-law of Agnes Bourn's generosity: "It is a delicate matter the question of gifts between friends in such contrasted circumstances as Agnes Bourn's and ours. It is due to her imagination and really queenly attitude in these matters between us, of late years, that I dare to accept." Molly had remained good friends with Agnes over the years, as this letter reveals, but their meetings had become less frequent. William Bourn had suffered a series of strokes early in the decade and spent most of his time at Filoli, the Bourn country mansion near San Mateo. Molly's visit there in October 1925 to inspect the recently installed murals in the ballroom is captured in a letter that Agnes Bourn wrote to the artist, Ernest Peixotto:

> Yesterday afternoon Mary Hallock Foote came over. . . . And when she went in [to the ballroom] she shouted, "Oh, I could roll on the floor, it is so lovely"—rather a strange way to express it, but she was, as it were "carried off her feet" in the surprize [*sic*] and delight of it. And she . . . a little Quaker

> . . . replete with the vivacity of youth (though 77 years) and the joy in all that is aesthetic and beautiful.

In these later years, the Footes kept abreast of national politics, and in 1928 they came out solidly for Herbert Hoover. On election night the family "gathered as a household to hear the nation's votes roll in," Molly reported to her sister-in-law. "Splendid!—to have state after state pile up the odds for Hoover."

Still, Molly's world was about to undergo a major change. Even before the Great Depression rocked the nation, the North Star mine had experienced financial problems. Since 1918 it had made no profit, although it continued to produce substantial amounts of gold. When new shafts failed to uncover new bodies of ore, the mine was sold in 1929. Thereafter Molly's son practiced privately in Grass Valley as a consulting mining engineer. He and his wife purchased the North Star House and would continue living there for the rest of their lives. But as the Depression deepened, Betty convinced her mother and father to spend their last years with the Swifts in Hingham. Molly wrote about their forthcoming move in a letter to young James D. Hague dated May 4, [1932]:

> Betty had seen that the time had come for her and Tod to step into the place of our good son and his wife who have had the brunt of us so many years—all the lifetime and a little more, of Janet, that fair flower. We have seen those children one by one as they unfolded. There is a choke in one's breath with the thought we shall hardly see much more of them; but we shall see Agnes and Sally and they are another inheritance of the blood better than stocks and bonds. But, it is just now I fear a question of stocks and bonds with some of us.

Before Molly and Arthur left Grass Valley, the local newspaper carried a long farewell tribute, in which it chronicled Arthur's success at the North Star and his "Great Failure" in Idaho. It also stressed the accomplishments of Mary Hallock Foote, his artist-wife—"this exquisite gentlewoman of an era now closed, but with surprising understanding and toleration of the foibles of the present era."

And so after having lived more than fifty years in the West, Molly and Arthur Foote boarded a train in the summer of 1932 to spend their remaining years in Hingham. Anticipating their arrival, Betty told her Aunt Elizabeth Jenkins: "I want them and have wanted them these many years . . . . Thee can imagine how happy I am." When they reached the Wharf-House, Molly and Arthur moved into a large upstairs room with a stove in it. Shortly after Christmas, the eighty-four-year-old author penned this description in a letter to her sister-in-law: "We are settled now in our little snug harbor up-stairs; bed-room and sitting room in one, on the northwest corner of the house with a full view of the bay, of its shore lights at night when they seem to spring out of darkness and the void, and of its cold pink mornings and its deep-colored sunsets on the edge of darkness."

Sometime earlier, James D. Hague visited the Wharf-House and announced his plan "to settle $200 a month on Betty" for Molly and Arthur's benefit. He wanted to "spare Betty some of her household drudgery as well as secure us against illness and its extra expenses," Molly reported to a close family friend. His generosity, his youth and their old age, she said, made the offer "so piercingly sweet!" Betty felt she could not accept the money, however, but agreed to hold it in reserve—to draw on it in case of an emergency, the balance to return to James when it was no longer needed.

And there were the inevitable illnesses that came with age. Arthur suffered a stroke within six months of moving to Hingham, although it did not seem to impede his mental or writing abilities very much. In fact, he kept up a steady stream of correspondence to his son concerning a mining scheme, which Molly later confessed was a "sore subject between thy father and me." After suffering a second stroke, Arthur De Wint Foote died on August 24, 1933, at the age of eighty-four. According to his wishes, his body was returned to the family burial plot at Nutplains, near Guilford, Connecticut. Molly undoubtedly grieved for her husband. But she had worried "so constantly over Dad with the fear either of a [paralyzing] stroke that would leave him conscious or of his eyes giving out," her daughter reported shortly after the funeral, "that she is less tired by letter-writing—by living indeed, than she was before. One can see now that it is gone how great the strain has been."

In her last years, Molly was a little hard-of-hearing, which kept her from fully enjoying family conversations. And yet she found comfort in learning about the lives of her five granddaughters. "What a lovely group they are! So full of possibilities," she exclaimed to her son. And she continued to enjoy her walks and her books and magazines, including the *Saturday Review.* One of the last vivid images we have of Mary Hallock Foote is in a letter Betty wrote to her Aunt Elizabeth, tentatively dated October 13, 1934:

> Mamma and I are alone again—sitting this stormy afternoon in the kitchen! . . . It's a pleasant kitchen too with the waves going past the window at one side and the sun streaming in as well as shining on the backs of the waves. I have a shelf of books in it now and there are books and papers and magazines all over the table. When the two of us are alone more reading than cooking is done. When the girls are here there is also much talking and they sit on the table along with the books. But Mamma and I do not talk much. She grows deafer. When her eyes are tired of reading she sits and watches the waves a good deal or closes them but does not sleep.

In June of 1938 the Arthur B. Footes visited Hingham prior to their departure for Great Britain and the continent. Molly did not at first recognize her son, but it is presumed that his presence was a comfort to her. On the 25th of that month Mary Hallock Foote died at the age of ninety. The following day Betty sent a radiogram to her brother on board ship, informing him that "Mother died peacefully last night." Sometime earlier, Molly had told Betty that she disliked the idea of being buried at Nutplains but wished that a marker with her name might be placed there. She said she would like to be buried beside Agnes but felt it would be too costly. On another occasion, she spoke approvingly of her sister Bessie's request to be cremated. And so brother and sister settled on a plan just prior to Molly's death that they thought would please their mother. Her body was to be cremated and the ashes buried next to Agnes in the family plot at Grass Valley.

An obituary in the *Grass Valley Morning Union* identified Mary Hallock Foote as a "prominent American artist and novelist." Indeed, during her lifetime, this remarkable woman had excelled in two creative fields, this at a time when society counseled young ladies to value home and family over public careers. She initially gained fame illustrating the works of famous New England authors, and her talent was considered on a par with that of Thomas Moran and Joseph Pennell, both highly acclaimed nineteenth-century illustrators. Her mentor, William J. Linton, thought Foote was the very best that drew directly on wood. After her marriage and relocation in the West, Foote became equally well-known for her depiction of western scenes, mainly illustrating her own essays and fiction but also on occasion the works of other writers as well. Through her fine black and white drawings the public "saw" the West of Mary Hallock Foote, a domestic West that included mothers and babies, irrigation ditches, wives joining husbands in isolated locations, and children engaged in commonplace activities. It was also a West of striking natural beauty and a West that respected hard-toiling laborers and their work.

As a gifted writer, Foote received critical praise and wide popularity during the late nineteenth and early twentieth centuries. She became best known for her western stories and travel pieces, which appeared in the nation's elite journals and in books published by a prestigious Boston firm. Her early fiction often portrayed easterners as exiles in the West and revolved around conventional love plots. But even in her apprentice years, Foote excelled in creating vivid word-pictures of landscapes and personalities. As her writing matured, she relied less on idealized romantic situations and devised more complex stories that often illuminated parent-child relationships. Her later narratives also showed a greater acceptance and appreciation of the West as a place to live and raise families.

From the very beginning, however, as historian Richard W. Etulain has written, Mary Hallock Foote depicted in her stories "a much milder, more domestic West than dime novelists or local color writers" of her era. Even when she wrote about miners and engineers, as she often did, the woman's perspective is very much in evidence. Thus, by writing of real families and ordinary events, she provided readers, both young and old, with realistic glimpses of the American West, certainly more realistic than those found in the Wild West adventure stories of such contemporary male authors as Frederic Remington, Theodore Roosevelt, and Owen Wister.

Yet, Foote remained throughout her career a genteel realist. Much like William Dean Howells, sometimes called the father of American realism, she stressed the commonplace and avoided the sordid. And like Henry James, another great nineteenth-century realist, she wrote primarily of the educated and wellborn. Rarely did she illustrate the lives of homesteader or working-class women, for example. Although at the time of Foote's death her fiction was largely forgotten, academic interest in her work currently is growing. The legacy she bequeathed to the modern era, which is a sensitive visual and written portrayal of the West from a woman's point of view, is worthy of further study.

When Mary Hallock Foote first joined her husband in California, she never suspected that she would live half a century in the West. From the very first, she admired the region for its spectacular beauty and its opportunities for adventure, but she missed the refinements of eastern society and its supportive network of other artists. Her ambivalence about the West continued to grow the longer she lived there and is expressed most eloquently in a letter to Helena de Kay Gilder written at the end of Molly's stay in Boise Canyon:

> For us, a home here for a few years is inevitable, so there is nothing for it but to make the best of it. The best is not at all bad: it is only that there are people in the East I love, who draw my thoughts and longings away from what I should be wrapped up in, here. The only way to come west happily is to embrace the country, people, life, everything as colonists do, jealously maintaining its superiority and refusing to see a blemish. I love my West when I am in the East. But, practically, it is getting much more for our money than we could at home. We could not have horses and space and the freedom of our lives in a thousand ways.

Although Foote may have started out as a reluctant westerner, during the Idaho years she began to see the West as a permanent home. She had nurtured all three of her children through their formative years in the Boise area and, like Madeline Hendrie in "The Fate of a Voice," found that her art could endure, even thrive, in this new environment. Later, in Grass Valley, when the family's financial survival was assured, Foote completed the process of becoming a western woman. She enjoyed the coastal milieu, gained sustenance from a select circle of friends in San Francisco and Grass Valley, and came to embrace the West wholeheartedly. Foote, in fact, no longer considered herself as living in exile.

But Molly was never an ordinary westerner—never a pioneer woman who engaged in hard physical labor alongside a homesteader-husband. Instead, she used her skills as author and illustrator to support the family when the projects of her engineer-husband brought in little or no income. And even in the gloomiest days in Idaho, she had domestic help that freed time for her artistic pursuits. Still, she often found it difficult to balance her career as writer and artist with the demands of her home life. She attempted to abide by her often-expressed belief that wifehood and motherhood were a woman's highest calling. And she was, in fact, a dedicated wife and mother, remaining loyal to Arthur during the worst trials of their marriage and creating a warm and loving atmosphere for her growing children. She sought to instill in the younger Footes a respect for genteel standards while at the same time allowing them a good deal of freedom. It was only late in life, however, that she came to accept the idea that a modern woman might willingly choose a career over marriage.

Throughout her adult years, Molly remained sensitive to class boundaries, even though on occasion, as in *The Desert and the Sown* and in "Pilgrims to Mecca," she explored the superficialities of class biases. But she highly valued culture and education, proper manners and behavior. Conservative and traditional in outlook, she championed existing social arrangements in both fiction and private life. Although she voiced compassion for the hard-working poor, she criticized unions and had little understanding of the "common sort," people she believed to be crude or uncultivated. She was not conceited; she never boasted of her accomplishments, though she savored achievement. She was not a gregarious person; she achieved her greatest sense of well-being when immersed in drawing or writing, engaged in outdoor activity, or surrounded by her family. And she possessed the inner resources that allowed her to surmount with grace and courage the pain, failure, heartache, and disappointment that befell her life.

Although several women authors achieved public recognition during her time, Mary Hallock Foote was the only one among them to combine literary and artistic skills to depict the American West. A highly disciplined and dedicated worker, Molly also knew how to balance the various segments of her life—dealing with the household, rearing children, soldiering on with Arthur—all of which helps to account for her prodigious accomplishments. She was, in fact, a quiet pioneer, offering encouragement to younger authors through example and correspondence. Eventually with age her gait slowed and her hearing weakened, yet this extraordinary woman, who had "irretrievably married into the West," retained into her eighties the spirit of a younger Molly—still modest and charming and determined to write a story worthy of publication in the best journals.

The Works of Mary Hallock Foote

BOOKS

All published by Houghton, Mifflin and Company, Boston, unless indicated otherwise.

The Led-Horse Claim. Boston: James R. Osgood and Company, 1883.
John Bodewin's Testimony. Boston: Ticknor and Company, 1886.
The Last Assembly Ball. 1889.
The Chosen Valley. 1892.
Coeur d' Alene. 1894.
In Exile, and Other Stories. 1894.
The Cup of Trembling, and Other Stories. 1895.
The Little Fig-Tree Stories. 1899.
The Prodigal. 1900.
The Desert and the Sown. 1902.
A Touch of Sun, and Other Stories. 1903.
The Royal Americans. 1910.
A Picked Company. 1912.
The Valley Road. 1915.
Edith Bonham. 1917.
The Ground-Swell. 1919.
A Victorian Gentlewoman in the Far West: The Reminiscences of Mary Hallock Foote, ed. Rodman W. Paul. San Marino: The Huntington Library, 1972.

SHORT STORIES

"Friend Barton's 'Concern.'" *Scribner's Monthly* 18 (July 1879): 334–50.
"A Story of the Dry Season." *Scribner's Monthly* 18 (September 1879): 766–81.
"In Exile." *The Atlantic Monthly* 48 (August–September 1881): 184–92, 322–30.
"The Story of the Alcázar." *Century Magazine* 24 (June 1882): 185–89.
"A Cloud on the Mountain." *Century Magazine* 31 (November 1885): 28–38.
"The Fate of a Voice." *Century Magazine* 33 (November 1886): 61–73.

"The Rapture of Hetty." *Century Magazine* 43 (December 1891): 198–201.
"The Watchman." *Century Magazine* 47 (November 1893): 30–41.
"Maverick." *Century Magazine* 48 (August 1894): 544–50.
"The Trumpeter." *The Atlantic Monthly* 74 (November–December 1894): 577–97, 721–29.
"On a Side-Track." *Century Magazine* 50 (June 1895): 271–83.
"The Cup of Trembling." *Century Magazine* 50 (September 1895): 673–90.
"Pilgrim Station." *The Atlantic Monthly* 77 (May 1896): 596–613.
"The Harshaw Bride." *Century Magazine* 52 (May–June 1896): 90–104, 228-41.
"The Borrowed Shift." *Land of Sunshine* 10 (December 1898): 12–24.
"Pilgrims to Mecca." *Century Magazine* 57 (March 1899): 742–51.
"How the Pump Stopped at the Morning Watch." *Century Magazine* 58 (July 1899): 469–72.
"A Touch of Sun." *Century Magazine* 59 (January–February 1900): 339–50, 551–58.
"The Eleventh Hour." *Century Magazine* 71 (January 1906): 485–93.
"Gideon's Knock." *The Spinners' Book of Fiction* (San Francisco: Paul Elder and Company, 1907), 77–91.

SKETCHES

"A California Mining Camp." *Scribner's Monthly* 15 (February 1878): 480–93.
"A Sea-Port on the Pacific." *Scribner's Monthly* 16 (August 1878): 449–60.
"The Cascarone Ball." *Scribner's Monthly* 18 (August 1879): 614–17.
"A Diligence Journey in Mexico." *Century Magazine* 23 (November 1881): 1–14.
"A Provincial Capital of Mexico." *Century Magazine* 23 (January 1882): 321–33.
"From Morelia to Mexico City on Horseback." *Century Magazine* 23 (March 1882): 643–55.
"On an Old Plate." *The Atlantic Monthly* 80 (November 1897): 718–20.

CHILDREN'S STORIES

All published in St. Nicholas Magazine.
"The Picture in the Fire-place Bedroom." 2 (February 1875): 248–50.
"How Mandy Went Rowing with the 'Cap'n.'" 5 (May 1878): 449–53.
"A 'Muchacho' of the Mexican Camp." 6 (December 1878): 79-81.
"The Children's 'Claim.'" 7 (January 1880): 238–45.
"Cousin Charley's Story." 8 (February 1881): 271–76.
"Menhaden Sketches: Summer at Christmas-Time." 12 (December 1884): 116–24.

"An Idaho Picnic." 14 (August 1887): 729–39.
"Dream-Horses." 16 (November 1888): 3–7.
"The Lamb That Couldn't 'Keep Up.'" 16 (September 1889): 802–806.
"A Visit to John's Camp." 17 (April 1890): 479–83.
"The Gates on Grandfather's Farm." 18 (April 1891): 411–18.
"November in the Cañon." 19 (April 1892): 439–43.
"The Spare Bedroom at Grandfather's." 19 (July 1892): 656–60.
"The Garret at Grandfather's." 20 (March 1893): 338–44.
"A Four-Leaved Clover in the Desert." 21 (May–June 1894): 644–50, 694–99.
"Flower of the Almond and Fruit of the Fig." 24 (September 1897): 937–41.

MAJOR PUBLISHED ILLUSTRATIONS

Scribner's Monthly Magazine, 1872–1881.
Century Illustrated Monthly Magazine, 1881–1903.
St. Nicholas Magazine, 1875–1906.
Longfellow, Henry W. *The Hanging of the Crane*. Boston: James R. Osgood and Company, 1874.
___. *The Skeleton in Armor*. Boston: James R. Osgood and Company, 1876.
Whittier, John G. *Hazel-Blossoms*. Boston: James R. Osgood and Company, 1875.
___. *Mabel Martin*. Boston: James R. Osgood and Company, 1876.
Hawthorne, Nathaniel. *The Scarlet Letter*. Boston: James R. Osgood and Company, 1877.
Anonymous. *The Lovers of Provence, Aucassin and Nicolette*. New York: Fords, Howard, and Hulbert Publishers, 1880.
Harte, Bret. *The Writings of Bret Harte*. 19 vols. Boston: Houghton, Mifflin and Company, 1896–1903. Foote's drawings appear in vols. 1, 3, 10, and 12.

Bibliographical Essay

IN preparing this biography of Mary Hallock Foote, I have relied heavily on her letters to family, friends, and business associates. The major repository for Foote material is the Green Library at Stanford University. Located here are approximately six hundred letters that Foote wrote between 1868 and 1916 to her lifelong friend Helena de Kay Gilder. I have quoted extensively from this correspondence, which is also available on microfilm. Also in the Foote Collection at Stanford are approximately sixty-five letters that Foote wrote to Richard Gilder, her friend and literary mentor at *Scribner's* and the *Century*, nearly ninety letters from Betty Foote Swift to her mother, and approximately 137 letters from Foote, her family, friends, and business associates to each other. Also of importance for this study is an unpublished biographical fragment written by Foote, entitled "The People Called, in Scorn, Quakers." All published quotations from these materials are courtesy of the Department of Special Collections, Stanford University Libraries.

The letters of Helena de Kay Gilder to Mary Hallock Foote are located in the Lilly Library at Indiana University. This collection of approximately 130 letters primarily documents the affairs of the Gilder family in the East. Mary Hallock Foote's granddaughter, Evelyn Foote Gardiner—with the help of her daughters—is currently preparing the Foote-Gilder letters for publication.

The Huntington Library also holds extensive Mary Hallock Foote correspondence and memorabilia. I have made extensive use of Foote's letters in the James D. Hague Collection. This includes approximately twenty-four letters that Foote wrote to either James or his wife, Mary, between 1882 and 1903; fifty or more letters that she wrote to Bessie Hague (James D. Hague's daughter-in-law), Bessie's son James D. Hague, and Bessie's cousin Helen Boutecou between 1916 and 1933; and one letter from Betty Foote Swift to James D. Hague, Sept. 7, 1933, regarding the fund that James established for the senior Footes.

The Mary Hallock Foote Collection at the Huntington Library holds approximately forty of Foote's letters to the *Century Magazine*, which are helpful in documenting Foote's business relations with that firm. I also found useful the seven letters Foote wrote to Margaret Collier Graham between 1902 and 1907, located in the Graham Collection, and Foote's letter to Mary Austin, dated October 12, 1903, located in the Austin Collection at the Huntington Library. All published quotations from this institution are by permission of The Huntington Library, San Marino, California.

A rich collection of Mary Hallock Foote letters is housed in the Houghton Library at Harvard University. The correspondence is found under five different call numbers or locations. In the Rogers Room are seven letters that Foote wrote between 1876 and 1895 to A.V. S. Anthony, her long-time friend and mentor at the James R. Osgood company. Located under call number MS Am 801.4 are three of Foote's letters (1891–1896) to Horace Scudder, editor of the *Atlantic Monthly.* Located under call number bMS Am 1925.1 are six Foote letters (1896–1901) to the *Atlantic Monthly* and under call number bMS Am 1343 (166)–(173) are eight Foote letters (ca. 1900-1905) to Bliss Perry, editor of the *Atlantic Monthly.* The largest number of Foote letters are found under call number bMS Am 1925 (1611); this consists of sixty-three letters to the Houghton Mifflin company (1895-1923) and fourteen letters from Houghton Mifflin (1920–24). All published quotations from these letters is by permission of the Houghton Library, Harvard University. The Mary Hallock Foote Collection at the Houghton Library, plus the Foote letters to Richard Gilder at Stanford and Foote's letters to the *Century* at the Huntington Library, is the best place to find information on Foote's business arrangements.

A rich source for helping to document Foote's family life are the approximately sixty-three letters from or about Mary Hallock Foote located at the Harriet Beecher Stowe Center in Hartford, Conn. Many of the letters are to Arthur Foote's mother and to Arthur's sister Elizabeth Foote Jenkins. More than half the letters were written between 1920 and 1934 and help to document Molly's final years.

I have used other letters from or about Mary Hallock Foote (or Arthur D. Foote) located in the following repositories: Foote's letter to Edward S. Holden, March 28, 1894, in the Mary Lea Shane Archives of the Lick Observatory, University of California, Santa Cruz; three letters from Foote to Robert Underwood Johnson at the Harry Ransom Humanities Research Center, University of Texas at Austin; Foote's letter to Florence Bates (MSS 8243), Foote Collection, Clifton Waller Barrett Library of American Literature, Special Collections Department, University of Virginia Library, Charlottesville; the Joseph Hawley Papers (microfilm), Library of Congress (letters concerning Arthur Foote's family); New York City Public Library (letters in the Richard W. Gilder Letter-books, almost unreadable, and eight Foote letters to the *Century*). Also of importance are a small collection of letters and Foote's answers to queries from the Knickerbocker Publishing Co. at the State Historical Society of Wisconsin.

Foote's memoirs, *A Victorian Gentlewoman in the Far West: The Reminiscences of Mary Hallock Foote*, ed. Rodman W. Paul (San Marino: The

Huntington Library, 1972), are the starting point for any study of this author and illustrator. Paul's introduction gives a good biographical sketch of MHF, though I have not always agreed with his interpretations. I am indebted to Lee Ann Johnson for her ground-breaking *Mary Hallock Foote* (Boston: Twayne Publishers, 1980), until now the only book-length study of Foote. No complete list of Molly's published art work exists, but a good start is Doris Bickford-Swarthout's *Mary Hallock Foote: Pioneer Woman Illustrator* (Deansboro, N.Y.: Berry Hill Press, 1996).

Shorter works on Foote that I found most useful are Shelly Armitage, "The Illustrator as Writer: Mary Hallock Foote and the Myth of the West," in *Under the Sun: Myth and Realism in Western American Literature*, ed. Barbara Howard Meldrum (Troy, N.Y.: Whitston, 1985), pp. 150–174; Benay Blend, "A Victorian Gentlewoman in the Rocky Mountain West: Ambiguity in the Work of Mary Hallock Foote," in *Reading under the Sign of Nature: New Essays in Ecocriticism*, eds. John Tallmadge and Henry Harrington (Salt Lake City: University of Utah Press, 2000), pp. 85–100; Barbara Cragg, "Mary Hallock Foote's Images of the Old West," *Landscape* 24 (Winter 1980): 42–47; Barbara Cragg, Dennis M. Walsh, Mary Ellen Walsh, eds., "Introduction," *The Idaho Stories and Far West Illustrations of Mary Hallock Foote* (Pocatello: Idaho State University, 1988); Melody Graulich, "Legacy Profile: Mary Hallock Foote, (1847–1938)," *Legacy* 3 (Fall 1986): 43–52; James H. Maguire, *Mary Hallock Foote*, Boise State College Western Writers Series 2 (Boise: Boise State College, 1972); Rodman Paul, "When Culture Came to Boise: Mary Hallock Foote in Idaho," *Idaho Yesterdays* 20 (Summer 1976): 2–12; Christine Hill Smith, "Mary Hallock Foote," in *Nineteenth-Century American Western Writers*, ed. Robert L. Gale (Detroit: Gale Research, 1997), pp. 102–112.

Two brief pieces by Richard W. Etulain first led me to the sources: "Mary Hallock Foote (1847–1938)," *American Literary Realism 1870–1910* 5 (Spring 1972): 145–50; "Mary Hallock Foote: A Checklist," *Western American Literature* 10 (May 1975): 59–65. I have profited immensely from his more recent interpretations of MHF as writer and illustrator, found in his *Re-Imagining the Modern American West, A Century of Fiction, History, and Art* (Tucson: University of Arizona Press, 1996), pp. 10–15, 73–76, and in *Telling Western Stories, From Buffalo Bill to Larry McMurtry* (Albuquerque: University of New Mexico Press, 1999), pp. 32–41.

Recent dissertations that shed light on MHF's world include Lynn Cothern, "Becoming Western: Gender and Generation in Mary Hallock Foote's Dual Career" (George Washington University, 1997), Carol P. Milowski, "Revisioning the American Frontier: Mary Hallock Foote, Mary Austin, Willa Cather, and the Western Narrative" (Indiana University of Pennsylvania, 1996), and Christine Hill Smith, "'We lived on the crust of much that lay beneath': Social Class in the Writings of Mary Hallock Foote"

(University of Denver, 1999). Earlier scholarly work is also of interest: Barbara Cragg, "The Landscape Perception and Imagery of Mary Hallock Foote" (M.A. thesis, University of Montana, 1980), Nancy Evans Rushforth, "With Her Own Hand: The Correspondence of Mary Hallock Foote" (M.A. thesis, Brigham Young University, 1993), Jennifer M. Parra, "Altered Vision: Three Nineteenth-Century Western Authors: Caroline Kirkland, Mary Hallock Foote and Mary Austin" (M.A. thesis, Arizona State University, 1995), and Gwendolyn D. Ross, "Mary Hallock Foote: Literary Historian of the Mining Camps" (M.A. thesis, University of Texas at Arlington, 1970).

Important contemporary statements about MHF are found in Regina Armstrong, "Representative American Women Illustrators," *Critic* 37 (August 1900): 131–41; Alpheus Sherwin Cody, "Artist-Authors," *Outlook* 49 (May 26, 1894): 910–11; Thomas Donaldson, *Idaho of Yesterday* (reprint; Westport, Conn.: Greenwood Press, 1970), pp. 358–63; Helena de Kay Gilder, "Mary Hallock Foote," *Book Buyer* 11 (August 1894): 338–42; W. J. Linton, *The History of Wood-Engraving in America* (Boston: Estes and Lauriat, 1882), pp. 33–37; Charles F. Lummis, "The New League for Literature and the West," *Land of Sunshine* 8 (April 1898): 206–14; Harold Payne, "American Women Illustrators," *Munsey's Magazine* 11 (April 1894): 47–57; Joseph Pennell, *The Adventures of an Illustrator* (Boston: Little, Brown, and Co., 1925); Thomas Pinney, ed., *The Letters of Rudyard Kipling*, vol. 2 (Iowa City: University of Iowa Press, 1990), pp. 56–57; W. A. Rogers, *A World Worth While: A Record of "Auld Acquaintance"* (New York: Harper and Brothers, 1922), pp. 187–88; Basil de Sélincourt, ed., *Anne Douglas Sedgwick, A Portrait in Letters* (Boston: Houghton Mifflin Co., 1936), pp. 33–43; Heather Kirk Thomas, "'Development of the Literary West': An Undiscovered Kate Chopin Essay," *American Literary Realism* 22 (Winter 1990): 69–75; Owen Wister, *Members of the Family* (New York: MacMillan Co., 1911), p. 15.

Biographical information and other comments about those closest to MHF are found in the following: Cecilia Beaux, *Background with Figures* (Boston: Houghton Mifflin Co., 1930); Arthur B. Foote, "Memoir of Arthur De Wint Foote," *Transactions of the American Society of Civil Engineers* 99 (1934): 1449–52; Arthur D. Foote, "Memoir of William Hague," *Transactions of the American Society of Civil Engineers* 82 (1918): 1729–30; Rosamond Gilder, ed., *Letters of Richard Watson Gilder* (Boston: Houghton Mifflin Co., 1916); James Hart, *The Popular Book, A History of America's Literary Taste* (New York: Oxford University Press, 1950); Arthur John, *The Best Years of the Century, Richard Watson Gilder, Scribner's Monthly, and Century Magazine, 1870–1909* (Urbana: University of Illinois Press, 1981); Allan Nevins, *Grover Cleveland, A Study in Courage* (New York: Dodd, Mead and Co., 1932); Herbert F. Smith, *Richard Watson Gilder* (New York: Twayne Publishers, 1970); Thayer C. Tolles, "Helena De Kay Gilder: Her Role in the

New Movement" (M.A. thesis, University of Delaware, 1990). For the history of Agnes and William Bourn, see Ferol Egan, *Last Bonanza Kings, The Bourns of San Francisco* (Reno: University of Nevada Press, 1998), and for an overview of the life of Margaret Collier Graham, see Jane Apostol, "Margaret Collier Graham: First Lady of the Foothills," *Southern California Quarterly* 63 (Winter 1981): 348–73.

I have used several older works in describing the Milton, New York, countryside, including *Appletons' Illustrated Hand-Book of American Travel* (New York: D. Appleton and Co., 1857); *The Hudson River by Pen and Pencil* (New York: D. Appleton and Co., 1889); and John Burroughs, "Our River," *Scriber's Monthly Magazine* 20 (August 1880): 481–93. My description of the Hallock farm and farmhouse comes from Foote's *Reminiscences* and from three autobiographical stories found in Foote's *The Little Fig-Tree Stories* (Boston: Houghton Mifflin and Co., 1899), pp. 120–83.

For an understanding of the Society of Friends, I relied on Howard H. Brinton, *Quaker Education in Theory and Practice* (Wallingford, Penn.: Pendle Hill, 1949), and three books by Margaret H. Bacon, *Mothers of Feminism, The Story of Quaker Women in America* (San Francisco: Harper and Row, 1986); *Valiant Friend, The Life of Lucretia Mott* (New York: Walker and Co., 1980); and *The Quiet Rebels, The Story of the Quakers in America* (Philadelphia: New Society Publishers, 1985).

To understand female education in mid-nineteenth century America, I consulted Carl N. Degler, *At Odds: Women and the Family in America from the Revolution to the Present* (New York: Oxford University Press, 1980); Barbara Miller Solomon, *In the Company of Educated Women: A History of Women and Higher Education in America* (New Haven: Yale University Press, 1985); Nancy Woloch, *Women and the American Experience*, 2d ed. (New York: McGraw-Hill, 1994); and Thomas Woody, *A History of Women's Education in the United States*, 2 vols. (New York: Science Press, 1929). Information on the Poughkeepsie Female Collegiate Institute comes from the school's 1863–64 catalogue and the *Poughkeepsie Daily Eagle*. Good sources for Peter Cooper and Cooper Union are Allan Nevins, *Abram S. Hewitt, With Some Account of Peter Cooper* (reprint; New York: Octagon Books, Inc., 1967); Phyllis D. Krasnick, "Peter Cooper and the Cooper Union for the Advancement of Science and Art" (Ph.D. diss., New York University, 1985); and Cooper Union Annual Reports, 1864, 1866, 1868, housed in the Cooper Union Archives.

Most useful for understanding the Foote-Gilder friendship is Carroll Smith-Rosenberg's "The Female World of Love and Ritual: Relations between Women in Nineteenth-Century America," reprinted in her *Disorderly Conduct, Visions of Gender in Victorian America* (New York: Alfred A. Knopf, 1985), pp. 53–76. For insights into nineteenth-century romance and marriage I relied on Ellen K. Rothman, *Hands and Hearts: A History of*

Courtship in America (New York: Basic Books, Inc., 1984) and Karen Lystra, *Searching the Heart, Women, Men, and Romantic Love in Nineteenth Century America* (New York: Oxford University Press, 1989). Degler's *At Odds* also gives insight into concepts of wifehood and motherhood for that era.

The standard work on engineers in the West is Clark C. Spence, *Mining Engineers and the American West, The Lace-Boot Brigade, 1849–1933* (reprint; Moscow, Idaho: University of Idaho Press, 1993). Reliable works on mining in the West are Rodman W. Paul, *Mining Frontiers of the Far West, 1848-1880* (New York: Holt, Rinehart and Winston, 1963) and William S. Greever, *The Bonanza West, The Story of the Western Mining Rushes, 1848–1900* (Norman: University of Oklahoma Press, 1963). I also found valuable Thomas G. Manning, *Government in Science, The U.S. Geological Survey, 1867–1894* (Lexington: University of Kentucky Press, 1967). For background on New Almaden, I consulted Milton Lanyon and Laurence Bulmore, *Cinnabar Hills: The Quicksilver Days of New Almaden* (Los Gatos, Calif.: Village Printers, 1967); Kenneth M. Johnson, *The New Almaden Quicksilver Mine* (Georgetown, Calif.: Talisman Press, 1963); Arthur C. Todd, *The Cornish Miner in America* (Glendale, Calif.: Arthur H. Clark Co., 1967). For Leadville, I found helpful Don L. Griswold and Jean Harvey Griswold, *The Carbonate Camp Called Leadville* (Denver: University of Denver Press, 1951). Two letters MHF wrote in 1922 reflecting back on her Leadville days are found in Levette Jay Davidson, "Letters from Authors," *Colorado Magazine* 19 (July 1942): 122–26. See also Mary Lou Benn, "Mary Hallock Foote: Early Leadville Writer," *Colorado Magazine* 33 (April 1956): 93–108; this essay and another dealing with Foote's Idaho stories are taken from Benn's master's thesis, "Mary Hallock Foote: Pioneer Woman Novelist" (University of Wyoming, 1955), the first significant evaluation of Foote's life and work.

Background for the Boise irrigation project is found in "The Beginning of the New York Canal," no. 190, Idaho State Historical Society Reference Series, March 1972, and Paul L. Murphy, "Early Irrigation in the Boise Valley," *Pacific Northwest Quarterly* 44 (Oct. 1953): 177–84. For the Coeur d'Alene labor troubles, see Robert Wayne Smith, *The Coeur d'Alene Mining War of 1892* (Corvallis: Oregon State College, 1961). For Coxey's Army in Idaho, see Carlos A. Schwantes, *Coxey's Army, An American Odyssey* (reprint; Moscow, Idaho: University of Idaho Press, 1994). On western irrigation and William E. Smythe, see Richard White, *"It's Your Misfortune and None of My Own," A New History of the American West* (Norman: University of Oklahoma Press, 1991). For an early analysis of Foote's Idaho stories, see Mary Lou Benn, "Mary Hallock Foote in Idaho," *University of Wyoming Publications* 20 (July 15, 1956): 157–78.

The best sources for Grass Valley, California, and its mines are Marian F. Conway, *A History of the North Star Mines, Grass Valley, California, 1851–1929*

(Nevada County Historical Society, 1981); Ferol Egan, *Last Bonanza Kings, The Bourns of San Francisco*; Arthur B. Foote, "Men and Mines of Nevada County and Adjacent Territory for Forty Years" (manuscript in The Huntington Library); Roger Lescohier, *Gold Giants of Grass Valley, History of the Empire and North Star Mines, 1850-1956* (Grass Valley: Empire Mine Park Association, 1995); *Reproduction of Thompson and West's History of Nevada County California, with Illustrations, 1880* (Berkeley: Howell-North Books, 1970); Jack R. Wagner, *Gold Mines of California* (Berkeley: Howell-North Books, 1970); Robert M. Wyckoff, *Walking Tours and Twice-Told Tales of Grass Valley*, 3d ed. (Nevada City, Calif.: Robert M. Wyckoff, 1993).

For Arthur B. Foote's excursion to Lake Tahoe see Pat Jones, "Foote's Ford and the Silver Cup," *The American West* 15 (July–August 1978): 18–21. A good study of Julia Morgan is Sara Holmes Boutelle, *Julia Morgan, Architect*, revised ed. (New York: Abbeville Press, 1995). On the Spinners' Club, see the Introduction to Gertrude Atherton, et al., *The Spinners' Book of Fiction*, revised ed. (Boston: Gregg Press, 1979).

To understand the conservative stand on women's suffrage, I read Thomas J. Jablonsky, *The Home, Heaven, and Mother Party: Female Anti-Suffragists in the United States, 1868–1920* (Brooklyn: Carlson, 1994), and to understand women's involvement with temperance, I consulted Ruth Bordin, *Women and Temperance: The Quest for Power and Liberty, 1873–1900* (Philadelphia: Temple University Press, 1981). For women's involvement in the Columbian Exposition, see Maud Howe Elliott, ed., *Art and Handicraft in the Woman's Building of the World's Columbian Exposition, Chicago, 1893* (New York: Goupil and Co., 1893), and Jeanne Madeline Weimann, *The Fair Women* (Chicago: Academy Press, 1981).

A good discussion of illustration as art is found in Michele H. Bogart, *Artists, Advertising, and the Borders of Art* (Chicago: University of Chicago Press, 1995). For an overview of women in the graphic arts, with brief biographies, see Helena E. Wright, *With Pen and Graver: Women Graphic Artists Before 1900* (Washington, D.C.: Smithsonian Institution, 1995). See also Robert Taft, *Artists and Illustrators of the Old West, 1850-1900* (New York: Charles Scribner's Sons, 1953). The best account of the Armory Show is Milton W. Brown, *The Story of the Armory Show*, 2d ed. (New York: Abbeville Press, 1988).

The best study of nineteenth-century women writers as businesswomen is Susan Coultrap-McQuin, *Doing Literary Business, American Women Writers in the Nineteenth Century* (Chapel Hill: University of North Carolina Press, 1990). Works dealing with nineteenth- and early-twentieth-century women writers include Elizabeth Ammons, *Conflicting Stories, American Women Writers at the Turn into the Twentieth Century* (New York: Oxford University Press, 1991); Nina Baym, *Woman's Fiction: A Guide to Novels by and about Women in America, 1820–1870*, 2d ed. (Chicago: University of Illinois

Press, 1993); Mary Kelley, *Private Women, Public Stage, Literary Domesticity in Nineteenth-Century America* (New York: Oxford University Press, 1984); Barbara H. Solomon, ed., *Rediscoveries: American Short Stories by Women, 1812–1916* (New York: Mentor, 1994); Joyce W. Warren, ed., *The (Other) American Traditions, Nineteenth-Century Women Writers* (New Brunswick, N.J.: Rutgers University Press, 1993); Ann Douglas Wood, "The Literature of Impoverishment: The Women Local Colorists in America, 1865–1914," *Women's Studies* 1 (1972): 3–45.

For Wallace Stegner on Foote as a realist, see his *Selected American Prose, 1841–1900: The Realistic Movement* (New York: Holt, Rinehart and Winston, 1958). See also Stegner's *Angle of Repose* (reprint; New York: Penguin Books, 1992), originally published in 1971. For those wanting to explore Stegner's use of MHF as model for his fictional Susan Ward see Jackson J. Benson, *Wallace Stegner, His Life and Work* (New York: Viking Penguin, 1996), pp. 344–56; Wallace Stegner and Richard W. Etulain, *Conversations with Wallace Stegner about Western Literature and History* (Salt Lake City: University of Utah Press, 1983), pp. 83–100; Mary Ellen Walsh, "*Angle of Repose* and the Writings of Mary Hallock Foote: A Source Study," in *Critical Essays on Wallace Stegner*, ed. Anthony Arthur (Boston: G. K. Hall, 1982), pp. 184–209; and David Lavender, "The Tyranny of Facts," in *Old Southwest, New Southwest, Essays on a Region and its Literature*, ed. Judy Nolte Lensink (Tucson: Tucson Public Library, 1987), pp. 63–73.

Note: Because scholars and others may wish exact citations for quotations and information found in this biography, I have deposited copies of this manuscript with complete chapter endnotes in the Green Library at Stanford University, The Huntington Library in San Marino, the Idaho State Historical Society Library, and the Rio Grande Historical Collections at New Mexico State University.

Index